W9-BTZ-560

Glad You Asked

Intriguing Names, Facts, and Ideas for the Curious-Minded

From the Editors of *Encyclopædia Britannica*
Featuring Michael Feldman

TRIUMPH
B O O K S
CHICAGO

Library of Congress Cataloging-in-Publication Data

Glad you asked / from the editors of Encyclopædia Britannica; featuring Michael Feldman.
   p. cm.
 ISBN-13: 978-1-57243-820-0
 ISBN-10: 1-57243-820-7
1. Handbooks, vade-mecums, etc. 2. Curiosities and wonders. I. Feldman, Michael, 1949- II. Encyclopædia Britannica, Inc.
 AG106.G57 2006
 001.9–dc22

2006000836

This book is available in quantity at special discounts for your group or organization. For further information, contact:

Triumph Books
542 South Dearborn Street
Suite 750
Chicago, Illinois 60605
(312) 939-3330
Fax (312) 663-3557

Printed in U.S.A.
ISBN-13: 978-1-57243-820-0
ISBN-10: 1-57243-820-7
Design by Patricia Frey

Contents

Introduction

Which brilliant mathematician broke enemy codes during World War II, laid the foundation for artificial intelligence, underwent 12 months of "hormone therapy," and then was found dead in his bed, poisoned by cyanide? Which bank relies on peer pressure as collateral for loans? Which fitness champion walked barefoot to work carrying a 40-pound bag of sand and preached the virtues of nudity and sleeping on the floor? And the monks of which world religion cover their mouths with cloth to prevent them from ingesting insects and violating their belief in nonviolence? Stay tuned for the answers . . .

Encyclopædia Britannica is one of the most trusted sources of information around the globe. Its 44-million-word encyclopædia is often cited as the most authoritative reference work in the world, and its legendary print set, first published in three volumes beginning in 1768, is the oldest continuously published and revised work in the English language. And so it is with great pleasure that we offer today, in conjunction with Triumph Books and Michael Feldman, acclaimed radio host of *Whad'Ya Know?*, a fun and novel way to access Britannica's wealth of information.

The entries in *Glad You Asked* are a select few of the more than 28,000 articles found in the one-volume *Britannica Concise Encyclopedia*. Many of the entries are on subjects that we all *should* know; other entries are on subjects we might just *want* to know because they're simply too intriguing and entertaining to pass up. The entries are divided into six categories—art, culture, and pastimes; history; religion, philosophy, and ideas; science, technology, and life; the world and its wonders; and trailblazers—and each section contains a wide range of topics and article types, from biographies to specific subject-based entries.

Also, introducing each section is a short essay by Michael Feldman, who's also contributed the sidebars and quizzes sprinkled throughout this volume. His "riffs" on the various subjects covered in this book are all written in Michael's inimitable style, which has made his comedy-quiz show one of the most popular programs on American radio.

So we hope you enjoy this novel addition to Britannica's family of reference works. And for those of you curious about the answers to the questions posed earlier, we suggest you turn to pages 147, 161, 198, and 100. More information is also available, on these particular subjects and thousands of others, at www.britannica.com, where authoritative answers are always just a click away.

—Theodore Pappas
Executive Editor
Encyclopædia Britannica, Inc.

Introduction

Silly Putty, dynamite, polyethylene, and Post-It notes are but a few of the things discovered serendipitously; I discovered that fact while looking for something else entirely. *Serendipity* comes from Horace Walpole's telling of the Persian fairy tale "The Three Princes of Serendip" (Sri Lanka, really, but try saying "Sri-lankaty"). The princes found a lame, blind-in-one-eye, toothless camel with a pregnant maiden atop that no one else, somehow, noticed, and received great *unexpected* riches. My experience is that while looking for answers to certain questions, I always discover other answers:

> —The first bath was probably taken around 2500 BC at Mohenjo-Daro in the Indus Valley, the cradle of bathing, but it was the Romans who made the world safe for bathing by conquering it and making it take a bath—first in the *tepidarium* (lukewarm), next in the *calidarium* (hot), and finishing off in the *frigidarium* (cold).

> —There apparently are two types of people in the world, although some debate as to which two: Hippocrates saw the phthisic (tall, thin, tubercular) and the apoplectic (short, fat, stroke-prone); Coleridge believed you were born either an Aristotelian or a Platonist, depending on whether you were an "insie" or an "outsie"; and Nietzsche considered men either Apollonian conservatives or Nietzschean rebels. Not much doubt where he fell.

—If there are no panaceas, it's not because people haven't tried: bezoars, fossilized stones of animal dung, were once widely praised and prized as magical cure-alls, or as Samuel Johnson noted, the bezoar stones of the wild "pazan" goat were especially "good for gout, rickets, hysteria, diabetes, varicose veins, smallpox, dilated stomach, afflictions of the spleen, and malposition of the pelvic organs."

Thanks to the wonderful resources of Encyclopædia Britannica, there's plenty more where this information came from.

—Michael Feldman

Art, Culture, and Pastimes

A rt is something you know when you see it, but culture tells you which reproduction to hang over the couch. Does the house cry out for a piece from the Ashcan school, the talented if somewhat morose city-life realists who worked after the turn of the last century and whose ranks included Edward Hopper? In the master bedroom, with its Mediterranean bedstead, wouldn't Diego Velázquez be in order, perhaps Los Borrachos (The Feast of Bacchus), or The Supper at Emmaus by Caravaggio if you want to tone things down a bit? I'd avoid the royal portraits unless you have an unusually large foyer. Kandinsky pretty much goes with any décor, but Picasso's Blue Period in the powder room has been done to death. And don't even think about a Calder unless you own the air space.

Although culture started as an opportunity for the wealthy to prove that money can't buy taste, the franchise has been extended now that pop culture has its own department; maybe Keith Haring and Michelangelo had more in common than meets the eye (Haring did not design siege weapons on the side). I think that we all can agree that manga (Japanese for comics and/or cartoons) and illustrated manuscripts were cut from the same cloth. The good thing about popular culture is that there's little to read. The bad thing about it is that it's popular and, therefore, inescapable.

Aesthetics. There, I've said it, and I'm glad. Keats wrote, "Beauty is truth, truth beauty," so we'll find little guidance there, but taste is something you can work at. Start with the curtains and don't stop there. Take an adult education course—maybe they'll have nude models. Visit a museum other than one that preserves Indiana high school basketball jerseys or Studebakers (although the one in South Bend is not to be missed the next time you're there to cheer on the Irish—hey, it's all culture). Find a gallery, pick a period you feel comfortable with—for me it would have to be the Expressionists, Otto Müller in particular because I feel like his subjects look—and immerse yourself. Start to dress like a character in early Nabokov (maybe not Humbert Humbert) after first reading all of Nabokov, including his essays, and get back to me. You might want to follow the example of my parents-in-law and join a Great Books sect in Sterling, Illinois, although if it's just a lot of Michener you could be wasting your time. Vow to learn Greek so that you can read the original Euripides, all the while remembering Chico's "You-rip-a-dese, you pay!" Make your next movie one with subtitles, but don't read them aloud. Opera is not out of the question, although probably not the Ring Cycle right off of the bat. But don't go to the opera if you're going to sit there the whole time wondering, "All right already, where's the fat lady?" Try *The Merry Widow*—it might be as instructive as the following entries on Art, Culture, and Pastimes.

Achebe, Chinua

Achebe, (Albert) Chinua (Iumogu) (born Nov. 16, 1930, Ogidi, Nigeria) Nigerian Igbo novelist. Concerned with emergent Africa at its moments of crisis, he is acclaimed for depictions of the disorientation accompanying the imposition of Western customs and values on traditional African society. *Things Fall Apart* (1958) and *Arrow of God* (1964) portray traditional Igbo life as it clashes with colonialism. *No Longer at Ease* (1960), *A Man of the People* (1966), and *Anthills of the Savannah* (1988) deal with corruption and other aspects of postcolonial African life. *Home and Exile* (2000) is in part autobiographical, in part a defense of Africa against Western distortions.

Aesop

Supposed author of a collection of Greek fables, almost certainly a legendary figure. Though Herodotus, in the 5th century BC, said that he was an actual personage, "Aesop" was probably no more than a name invented to provide an author for fables centering on beasts. Aesopian fables emphasize the social interactions of human beings, and the morals they draw tend to embody advice on how to deal with the competitive realities of life. The Western fable tradition effectively begins with these tales. Modern editions list some 200 Aesopian fables.

Aesop, with a fox, from the central medallion of a kylix, c. 470 BC; in the Gregorian Etruscan Museum, the Vatican

Armstrong, Louis

(Born Aug. 4, 1901, New Orleans, La., U.S.—died July 6, 1971, New York, N.Y.) U.S. jazz trumpeter and singer. As a youth in New Orleans, he participated in marching, riverboat, and cabaret bands. A childhood nickname, Satchelmouth, was shortened to Satchmo and used throughout his life. In 1922 he moved to Chicago to join King

Louis Armstrong

Oliver's Creole Jazz Band. In 1924 he joined the Fletcher Henderson Orchestra in New York City; the following year he switched from cornet to trumpet and began recording under his own name with his Hot Five and Hot Seven ensembles. In these recordings the prevailing emphasis on collective improvisation gives way to his developing strength as a soloist and vocalist. By the time of his "West End Blues" (1928), Armstrong had established the preeminence of the virtuoso soloist in jazz. His vibrant melodic phrasing, inventive harmonic improvisation, and swinging rhythmic conception established the vernacular of jazz music. His powerful tone, great range, and dazzling velocity set a new technical standard. He also was one of the first scat singers, improvising nonsense syllables in the manner of a horn. He became something more than a jazz musician: solo attraction, bandleader, film actor, and international star.

Austen, Jane

(Born Dec. 16, 1775, Steventon, Hampshire, Eng.—died July 18, 1817, Winchester, Hampshire) English novelist. The daughter of a rector, she lived in the circumscribed world of minor landed gentry and country clergy that she was to use in her writing; her closest companion was her sister, Cassandra. Her earliest known writings are mainly parodies, notably of sentimental fiction. In her six full-length novels—*Sense and Sensibility* (1811), *Pride and Prejudice* (1813), *Mansfield Park* (1814), *Emma* (1815), *Persuasion* (1817), and *Northanger Abbey* (published 1817 but written before the others)—she created the comedy of manners of middle-class English life in her time. Her writing is noted for its wit, realism, shrewd sympathy, and brilliant prose style. Through her treatment of ordinary people in everyday life, she was the first to give the novel its distinctly modern character. She published her novels anonymously; two appeared only after her death, which probably resulted from Addison's disease.

Jane Austen, pencil and watercolor by Cassandra Austen, c. 1810; in the National Portrait Gallery, London

Baker, Josephine

Josephine Baker

Orig. Freda Josephine McDonald (born June 3, 1906, St. Louis, Mo., U.S.—died April 12, 1975, Paris, France) U.S.-born French entertainer. She joined a dance troupe at age 16 and soon moved to New York City, where she performed in Harlem nightclubs and on Broadway in *Chocolate Dandies* (1924). She went to Paris in 1925 to dance in *La Revue nègre*. To French audiences she personified the exoticism and vitality of African American culture, and she became Paris's most popular music-hall entertainer, receiving star billing at the Folies Bergère. In World War II she worked with the Red Cross and entertained Free French troops. From 1950 she adopted numerous orphans of all nationalities as "an experiment in brotherhood." She returned periodically to the U.S. to advance the cause of civil rights.

baseball

Game played with a bat and ball between two teams of nine players (or 10, if a designated hitter bats and runs for the pitcher). Baseball is played on a large field that has four bases laid out in a square, positioned like a diamond, whose outlines mark the course a runner must take to score. Teams alternate positions as batters and fielders, exchanging places when three members of the batting team are put out. Batters try to hit a pitched ball out of reach of the fielding team and complete a circuit around the bases in order to score a "run." The team that scores the most runs in nine innings (times at bat) wins the game. If a game is tied, extra innings are played until the tie is broken. Baseball is traditionally considered the national pastime of the United States. It was once thought to have been

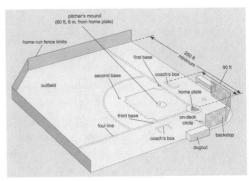

A typical college or professional baseball field

invented in 1839 by Abner Doubleday in Cooperstown, N.Y., but it is more likely that baseball developed from an 18th-century English game called rounders that was modified by Alexander Cartwright. The first professional association was formed in 1871; in 1876 it became the National League. Its rival, the American League, was founded in 1900, and since 1903 (except in 1904 and 1994) the winning teams of each league have played a postseason championship known as the World Series. The Baseball Hall of Fame is located in Cooperstown, N.Y. Professional baseball leagues also exist in several Latin American countries. The champions of leagues in the Dominican Republic, Mexico, Puerto Rico, and Venezuela compete in the Caribbean Series each February. In Asia there are professional baseball leagues in Japan, South Korea, and Taiwan. Japan has two major leagues, the Central and the Pacific, which face off in the Japan Series every October.

Basho

Or Matsuo Basho. Orig. Matsuo Munefusa (born 1644, Ueno, Iga province, Japan—died Nov. 28, 1694, Osaka) Japanese haiku poet, the greatest practitioner of the form. Following the Zen philosophy he studied, he attempted to compress the meaning of the world into the simple pattern of his poetry, disclosing hidden hopes in small things and showing the interdependence of all objects. His *The Narrow Road to the Deep North* (1694), a poetic prose travelogue, is one of the loveliest works of Japanese literature.

basketball

Court game between two teams of five players. They score by tossing, or "shooting," an inflated ball through a raised hoop, or "basket," located in their opponent's end of the court. A goal is worth two points, three if shot from outside a specified limit. A player who is fouled (through unwarranted physical contact) by another is awarded one to three free-throw attempts (depending on the circumstances of the foul). A successful free throw is worth one point. Invented in 1891 by James A. Naismith at the YMCA Training School in Springfield, Mass., basketball quickly became popular throughout the U.S., with games organized at the high school and collegiate level for both sexes. (For the first game, Naismith used two half-bushel peach baskets as goals, which gave the sport its name.) Women first played the game under a markedly different set of rules. The game developed internationally at a slower pace. The first Olympic basketball

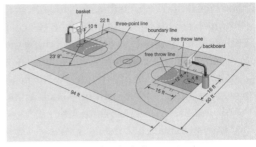

The U.S. professional basketball court is shown

contest was held in 1936, and the Fédération Internationale de Basketball Amateur (FIBA) introduced world championships for men and women in 1950 and 1953, respectively. In the U.S., high school and collegiate championship tournaments are traditionally held in March and generate considerable excitement. A men's professional league was organized in 1898 but did not gain much of a following until 1949, when it was reconstituted as the National Basketball Association (NBA). The first women's professional leagues in the U.S. emerged during the 1970s but failed after a year or two. The current Women's National Basketball Association (WNBA), owned by the NBA, was organized in 1997. Club and professional basketball outside the U.S. developed rapidly in the latter part of the 20th century. The Basketball Hall of Fame is located in Springfield, Mass.

Beatles

British rock group that came to personify the counterculture of the 1960s. Its principal members, all born in Liverpool, Eng., were Paul McCartney, John Lennon, George Harrison, and Ringo Starr. The group began with the pairing of McCartney and Lennon in 1956; Harrison joined in 1957, and Stu Sutcliffe and Pete Best later. In 1960 they adopted the name the Beatles. In 1962 they signed a recording contract and replaced Best with Starr (Sutcliffe had left the group in 1961). The release in 1962–63 of such songs as "Please Please Me" and "I Want to Hold Your Hand" made them England's most popular rock group, and in 1964 "Beatlemania" struck the U.S. Originally inspired by Chuck Berry, Elvis Presley, Little Richard, and Buddy Holly, among others, their direct, energetic songs kept them at the top of the pop charts. Their long hair and tastes in dress were influential throughout the world, as were their experimentation with hallucinogenic drugs and Indian mysticism and their involvement with the politics of peace. From 1965 to 1967 the Beatles's music rapidly evolved, becoming increasingly subtle, sophisticated, and varied—ranging from ballads such as "Yesterday" to the psychedelic hard rock of "Tomorrow Never Knows." Their public performances ended in 1966. Albums such as *Rubber Soul* (1965), *Revolver* (1966), and *The Beatles* ("White Album," 1968) set new trends in rock. In 1967 they produced *Sgt. Pepper's Lonely Hearts Club Band*, an album novel for its conception as a dramatic whole, use of electronic music, and character as a studio work not reproducible onstage. They appeared in the films *A Hard Day's Night* (1964) and *Help!* (1965). The group dissolved in 1970. In 1988 the Beatles were inducted into the Rock and Roll Hall of Fame, and Lennon (1994), McCartney (1999), and Harrison (2004) were also inducted as solo performers.

Bollywood

Indian moviemaking industry that began in Bombay (now Mumbai) in the 1930s and developed into an enormous film empire. Bombay Talkies, launched in 1934 by Himansu Rai, spearheaded the growth of Indian cinema. Throughout the years, several classic genres emerged from Bollywood: the historical epic, notably *Mughal-e-azam* (1960; "The Great Mughal"); the curry western, such as *Sholay* (1975; "The Embers"); the courtesan film, such as *Pakeezah* (1972; "Pure Heart"), which highlights stunning cinematography and sensual dance choreography; and the mythological movie, represented by *Jai Santoshi Maa* (1975; "Hail Santoshi Maa"). Star actors, rather than the films themselves, have accounted for most box-office success. Standard features of Bollywood films include formulaic story lines, expertly choreographed fight scenes, spectacular song-and-dance routines, emotion-charged melodrama, and larger-than-life heroes. At the beginning of the 21st century, Bollywood produced as many as 1,000 feature films annually, and international audiences began to develop among Asians in the U.K. and the U.S.

buzkashi

(Persian; "goat dragging") An equestrian game in which riders compete to gain control of a goat or calf carcass that has been decapitated and

Buzkashi, or goat dragging, is a sport American troops found challenging to master while serving in Afghanistan. Persian in origin, the sport's object is to seize and maintain possession of a headless, eviscerated goat carcass from horseback—not quite goat polo. The feat must be accomplished, according to tudabaray rules, without grabbing hair or reins or using weapons, although there is no referee. Teams and boundaries are ad hoc, as they often are in the region, and expert players, chapandazan, are celebrities. The game is won once a player has maintained possession of the carcass while riding "free and clear" of the other riders, although "free and clear" is a judgment call without judges. During the Buzkashi Open in Kabul, the Kentucky Derby of goat dragging, khans back individual riders, making the event as much political as sporting, with status hanging in the balance for tribal leaders. The passing of power from the central authority in Kabul to the mujahideen commanders paralleled the central authority's buzkashi tournament losses to the commanders.—M.F.

dehoofed. Buzkashi likely originated as an entertaining variant of ordinary herding or raiding. It is popular predominantly among Turkic peoples in Afghanistan but can be found in the Muslim republics of Central Asia and in parts of northwestern China. Buzkashi has two main forms. The traditional version, *tudabaray*, has no formal teams and is not played within clearly defined boundaries. Games often involve hundreds of riders, and the objective is to gain sole possession of the carcass and ride it free and clear of all other riders. The modern government-sponsored *qarajay* style involves two teams of 10–12 riders that contend on a defined field with goals. Beginning in the early 1950s, the Kabul-based Afghan government hosted national tournaments.

camel racing

Sport of running camels at speed, with a rider astride, over a predetermined course. The sport is generally limited to running the dromedary—whose name is derived from the Greek verb *dramein*, "to run"—rather than the Bactrian camel. Camel racing on the Arabian Peninsula can be traced to at least the 7th century. Although traditionally overshadowed by horse racing in that region, the racing of camels was long a folk sport practiced at social gatherings and festivals. In the late 20th century it was organized into a formal sport, similar to Thoroughbred horse racing. The sport is popular in India, Australia, parts of East Africa, and especially the Arab countries of the Middle East. A race typically has 25 to 30 entries and covers distances ranging from 2.5 to 6 mi (4 to 10 km).

Chanel, Gabrielle

Known as Coco Chanel (born Aug. 19, 1883, Saumur, France—died Jan. 10, 1971, Paris) French fashion designer. Little is known of her early life. In 1913 she opened a millinery shop in Deauville, and within five years her innovative use of jersey fabric and accessories was attracting wealthy patrons. Her nonconformist designs, stressing simplicity and comfort, revolutionized the fashion industry for the next 30 years. She popularized turtleneck sweaters, the "little black dress," and the much-copied "Chanel suit." Chanel industries included a Parisian fashion house, a textile business, perfume laboratories, and a workshop for costume jewelry. The financial basis of her empire was Chanel No. 5 perfume, introduced in 1922, which is still popular.

Chaplin, Charlie

In full Sir Charles Spencer Chaplin (born April 16, 1889, London, Eng.—died Dec. 25, 1977, Corsier-sur-Vevey, Switz.) British-U.S. actor and director. The son of poverty-stricken music-hall entertainers, he became a vaudeville performer at age eight. On tour in New York (1913), he caught the eye of Mack Sennett, who signed him to a film contract. While making his second film, *Kid Auto Races at Venice* (1914), Chaplin developed the costume—baggy pants, derby hat, oversized shoes, and cane—that was to become the hallmark of his famous "little tramp" character. He was soon directing his own films, and he became an instant star in *The Tramp* (1915). After cofounding United Artists in 1919, he produced, directed, and starred in such classics as *The Gold Rush* (1925), *City Lights* (1931), *Modern Times* (1936), *The Great Dictator* (1940), *Monsieur Verdoux* (1947), and *Limelight* (1952). Harassed for his leftist political views, he moved to Switzerland in 1952. In 1972 he returned to the U.S. to accept a special Academy Award.

Chaucer, Geoffrey

(Born *c.* 1342/43, London?, Eng.—died Oct. 25, 1400, London) English poet. Of middle-class birth, he was a courtier, diplomat, and civil servant, trusted by three kings in his active and varied career, and a poet only by avocation. His first important poem, *Book of the Duchesse* (1369/70), was a dream vision elegy for the duchess of Lancaster. In the 1380s he produced mature works, including *The Parliament of Fowls*, a dream vision for St. Valentine's Day about a conference of birds choosing their mates; the fine tragic verse romance *Troilus and Criseyde*; and the unfinished dream vision *Legend of Good Women*. His best-known work, the unfinished *Canterbury Tales* (written 1387–1400), is an intricate dramatic narrative that employs a pilgrimage to the shrine of St. Thomas Becket in Canterbury as a framing device for a highly varied collection of stories; not only the most famous literary work in Middle English, it is one of the finest works of English literature. In this and other works Chaucer established the southern English dialect as England's literary language, and he is regarded as the first great English poet.

chess

Checkerboard game for two players, each of whom moves 16 pieces according to fixed rules across the board and tries to capture or immobilize (checkmate) the opponent's king. The game may have originated in Asia around the 6th century, though it continued to evolve as it spread into Europe in Byzantine times; its now-standard rules first became generally accepted in Europe in the 16th century. The players, designated white or black, start with their pieces arranged on opposite ends of the board. Kings move one square in any direction—but not into attack (check). Bishops move diagonally and rooks horizontally or

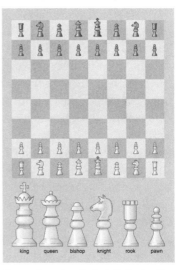

Chess pieces located at their starting positions on the chessboard

vertically, any number of unobstructed squares. Queens move like either bishops or rooks. Knights move to the nearest nonadjacent square of the opposite color (an "L" shape) and ignore intervening chessmen. Pieces capture by moving to an enemy-occupied square. Pawns move forward one square (except one or two on their first move) and are promoted to any non-king piece if they eventually reach the last row. Pawns capture only one diagonal square forward of them. For one turn only, a pawn has the option, known as en passant, of capturing an enemy pawn that has just made a first move of two squares to avoid being captured by moving only one; the capture occurs as though the pawn had moved only one square. When the first row between a king and either rook is clear, and as long as the king and that rook have not moved, a maneuver known as castling can be done in which the king is shifted two squares toward that rook and the rook is placed directly on the other side of the king. Kings cannot castle when in check or through any square in which they would be in check. A draw, known as a stalemate, occurs if a player is not in check but any move he could make would place him in check. A draw also occurs if the same position occurs three times (such as through "perpetual check").

Dante (Alighieri)

(Born *c.* May 21–June 20, 1265, Florence, Italy—died Sept. 13/14, 1321, Ravenna) Italian poet. Dante was of noble ancestry, and his life was shaped by the conflict between papal and imperial partisans (the Guelphs and Ghibellines). When an opposing political faction within the Guelphs (Dante's party) gained ascendancy, he was exiled (1302) from Florence, to which he never returned. His life was given direction by his spiritual love for Beatrice Portinari (d. 1290), to whom he dedicated most of his poetry. His great friendship with Guido Cavalcanti shaped his later career as well. *La Vita Nuova* (1293?) celebrates Beatrice in verse. In his difficult years of exile, he wrote the verse collection *The Banquet* (*c.* 1304–07); *De vulgari eloquentia* (1304–07; "Concerning Vernacular Eloquence"), the first theoretical discussion of the Italian literary language; and *On Monarchy* (1313?), a major Latin treatise on medieval political philosophy. He is best known for the monumental epic poem *The Divine Comedy* (written *c.* 1310–14; originally titled simply *Commedia*), a profoundly Christian vision of human temporal and eternal destiny. It is an allegory of universal human destiny in the form of a pilgrim's journey through hell and purgatory, guided by the Roman poet Virgil, then to Paradise, guided by Beatrice. By writing it in Italian rather than Latin, Dante almost singlehandedly made Italian a literary language, and he stands as one of the towering figures of European literature.

Dickens, Charles

In full Charles John Huffam Dickens (born Feb. 7, 1812, Portsmouth, Hampshire, Eng.—died June 9, 1870, Gad's Hill, near Chatham, Kent) British novelist, generally considered the greatest of the Victorian period. The defining moment of Dickens's life occurred when he was 12 years old. With his father in debtors' prison, he was withdrawn from school and forced to work in a factory. This deeply affected the sensitive boy. Though he returned to school at 13, his formal education ended at 15. As a young man, he worked as a reporter. His fiction career began with short pieces reprinted as *Sketches by "Boz"* (1836). He exhibited a great ability to spin a story in an entertaining manner and this quality, combined with the serialization of his comic novel *The Pickwick Papers* (1837), made him the most popular English author of his time. The serialization of such works as *Oliver Twist* (1838) and *The Old Curiosity Shop* (1841) followed. After a trip to America, he wrote *A Christmas Carol* (1843) in a few weeks. With *Dombey and Son* (1848), his novels began to express a heightened uneasiness about the evils of Victorian industrial society, which intensified in the semiautobiographical *David Copperfield* (1850), as well as in *Bleak House* (1853), *Little Dorrit* (1857), *Great Expectations* (1861), and others. *A Tale of Two Cities* (1859) appeared in the period when he achieved great popularity for his public readings. Dickens's works are characterized by an encyclopaedic knowledge of London, pathos, a vein of the macabre, a pervasive spirit of benevolence and geniality, inexhaustible powers of character creation, an acute ear for characteristic speech, and a highly individual and inventive prose style.

Euripides

(Born *c.* 484 BC, Athens—died 406 BC, Macedonia) Greek playwright. With Aeschylus and Sophocles, he is recognized as one of Athens's three great tragic dramatists. An associate of the philosopher Anaxagoras, he expressed his questions about Greek religion in his plays. Beginning in

455, he was repeatedly chosen to compete in the dramatic festival of Dionysus; he won his first victory in 441. He competed 22 times, writing four plays for each occasion. Of his 92 plays, about 19 survive, including *Medea* (431), *Hippolytus* (428), *Electra* (418), *The Trojan Women* (415), *Ion* (413), *Iphigenia at Aulis* (406), and *The Bacchae* (406). Many of his plays include prologues and rely on a deus ex machina. Unlike Aeschylus and Sophocles, Euripides made his characters' tragic fates stem almost entirely from their own flawed natures and uncontrolled passions. In his plays, chance, disorder, and human irrationality and immorality frequently result in apparently meaningless suffering that is looked on with indifference by the gods.

falconry

Sport of employing falcons or other hawks in hunting game. Falconry has been practiced in the Middle East at least since the 8th century BC. It flourished among the privileged classes in Europe in the Middle Ages. It began to die out after the advent of the shotgun and the enclosure of open lands in the 17th century, but there was a revival of interest in the sport beginning in the 1970s; there are many hawking clubs and associations. The bird most commonly used is the peregrine falcon, though the goshawk and sparrow hawk have also been used. Birds are caught wild or raised from birth. Training involves selective use of a leather hood (called a rufter) and leg thongs (jesses) to keep the animal under control while familiarizing it with its new environment. During the hunt the trained bird is released to bring down its prey; it then returns to the hawker or is collected at the kill site.

film noir

(French; "dark film") Film genre that offers dark or fatalistic interpretations of reality. The term is applied to U.S. films of the late 1940s and early 1950s that often portrayed a seamy or criminal underworld and cynical characters. The films were noted for their use of stark, expressionistic lighting and stylized camera work, often employed in urban settings. The genre includes films such as John Huston's *The Maltese Falcon* (1941), Jacques Tourneur's *Out of the Past* (1947), Alfred Hitchcock's *Spellbound* (1945), and Billy Wilder's *Double Indemnity* (1944) and *Sunset*

Boulevard (1950). The trend was on the wane by the mid-1950s, but the influence of these films is evident in many subsequent ones, including classics such as Roman Polanski's *Chinatown* (1974) and Ridley Scott's *Blade Runner* (1982). More recent examples include *L.A. Confidential* (1997) and *The Man Who Wasn't There* (2001).

football

Or association football or soccer. Game in which two 11-member teams try to propel a ball into the opposing team's goal, using any part of the body except the hands and arms. Only the goalkeeper, when positioned within the penalty area in front of the goal, may use hands and arms. The game's first uniform set of rules was put in place in 1863, when England's Football Association was created. Professional leagues began

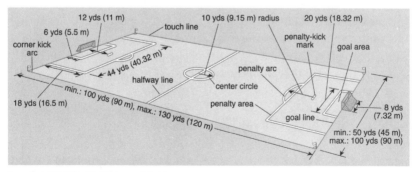

A professional football (soccer) field

appearing in the late 1880s, first in England and then in other countries. The Fédération Internationale de Football Association (FIFA) was founded in 1904 and has hosted the World Cup every four years since 1930. Football has been included in the Olympic Games since 1908. Now played on all continents in more than 150 nations, with more than 40 million registered players, it is the world's most popular ball game.

Goethe, Johann Wolfgang von

(Born Aug. 28, 1749, Frankfurt am Main—died March 22, 1832, Weimar, Saxe-Weimar) German poet, novelist, playwright, and natural philosopher. In 1773 Goethe provided the Sturm und Drang movement with its first major drama, *Götz von Berlichingen*, and in 1774 with its first novel, *The Sorrows of Young Werther*, an extraordinarily popular work in its time, in which he created the prototype of the Romantic hero. In 1775 he accepted an appointment at the ducal court at Weimar, where he would remain the rest of his life; his presence would establish Weimar as a literary and intellectual center. His poetry includes lyrics in praise of natural beauty and ballads such as "The Elf King" (1782) that echo folk themes. Many early works were inspired by a series of passionate loves. Contact with classical Greek and Romantic culture during an Italian sojourn helped shape his plays, including *Iphigenie auf Tauris* (1787), *Egmont* (1788), and *Torquato Tasso* (1790), and the poems in *Roman Elegies* (1795). From 1794, Friedrich Schiller became his most important and influential friend. *Wilhelm Meister's Apprenticeship* (1795–96) is often called the first bildungsroman; it was followed many years later by *Wilhelm Meister's Travels* (1821–29). His chief masterpiece, the philosophical drama *Faust* (Part I, 1808; Part II, 1832), concerns the struggle of the soul for knowledge, power, happiness, and salvation. Goethe also wrote extensively, if idiosyncratically, on botany, optics, and other scientific topics. In his late years he was celebrated as a sage and visited by world luminaries. The greatest figure of German Romanticism, he is regarded as a giant of world literature.

Gogh, Vincent (Willem) van

(Born March 30, 1853, Zundert, Neth.—died July 29, 1890, Auvers-sur-Oise, near Paris, France) Dutch painter. At 16 he was apprenticed to art dealers in The Hague, and he worked in their London and Paris branches (1873–76). After brief attempts at missionary work and theology, he studied drawing at the Brussels Academy; late in 1881 he settled at The Hague to work with a Dutch landscape painter, Anton Mauve. During his early years he painted three types of subjects—still life, landscape, and figure—all interrelated by their reference to the daily life of peasants (e.g., *The Potato Eaters*, 1885). After briefly studying at the Antwerp Academy, he left in 1886 to join his brother Theo, an art dealer, in Paris. There he met Henri de Toulouse-Lautrec, Paul Gauguin, and others involved in Impressionism and Post-Impressionism. By the summer of 1887 he was painting in pure colors and using broken brushwork that was at times pointillistic, and by the beginning of 1888 his Post-Impressionist style had crystallized. He left Paris in February 1888 for Arles, in southeastern France. The pictures he created over the following 12 months—depicting blossoming fruit trees, views of the town and surroundings, self-portraits, portraits of Roulin the postman and other friends, interiors and exteriors of the house, sunflowers, and landscapes—marked his first great period. Gauguin arrived in October 1888, and for two months he and van Gogh worked together; but, while each influenced the other to some extent, their relations rapidly deteriorated. On Christmas Eve 1888, physically and emotionally exhausted, van Gogh snapped under the strain; after arguing with Gauguin, he cut off the lower half of his own left ear. At the end of April 1889, van Gogh entered an asylum but continued to paint; during his 12-month stay he completed 150 paintings and drawings. A move to Auvers-sur-Oise in 1890 was followed by another burst of activity, but he soon suffered a relapse and died that July of a self-inflicted gunshot wound. His 10-year artistic career produced more than 800 paintings and 700 drawings, of which he sold only one in his lifetime. His work had a powerful influence on the development of modern painting, and he is considered the greatest Dutch painter since Rembrandt.

Harlem Renaissance

Or New Negro Movement. Period of outstanding vigor and creativity centered in New York's black ghetto of Harlem in the 1920s. Its leading literary figures included Alain Locke, James Weldon Johnson, Claude McKay, Countee Cullen, Langston Hughes, Zora Neale Hurston, Jessie Redmon Fauset, Jean Toomer, Wallace Thurman, and Arna Bontemps. The literary movement, which both fed and took inspiration from the great creative and commercial growth of jazz and a concurrent burgeoning of the visual arts—in Harlem as well as in Paris, Chicago, Washington, D.C., London, and the Caribbean—altered the character of much African American literature. Increasingly, this literature reflected a newfound confidence in self-expression and examined the African American experience in all its variety.

Hemingway, Ernest (Miller)

Ernest Hemingway; photograph by Yousuf Karsh, 1959

(Born July 21, 1899, Cicero [now in Oak Park], Ill., U.S.—died July 2, 1961, Ketchum, Idaho) U.S. writer. He began work as a journalist after high school. He was wounded while serving as an ambulance driver in World War I. One of a well-known group of expatriate writers in Paris, he soon embarked on a life of travel, skiing, fishing, and hunting that would be reflected in his work. His story collection *In Our Time* (1925) was followed by the novel *The Sun Also Rises* (1926). Later novels include *A Farewell to Arms* (1929) and *To Have and Have Not* (1937). His lifelong love for Spain (including a fascination with bullfighting) led to his working as a correspondent during the Spanish Civil War, which resulted in the novel *For Whom the Bell Tolls* (1940). Other short-story collections include *Men Without Women* (1927), *Winner Take Nothing* (1933), and *The Fifth Column* (1938). He lived primarily in Cuba from *c.* 1940, the locale of his novella *The Old Man and the Sea* (1952, Pulitzer Prize). He was awarded the Nobel Prize for Literature in 1954. He left Cuba shortly after its 1959 revolution; a year later, depressed and ill, he shot himself. The succinct and concentrated prose style of his early works strongly influenced many British and American writers for decades.

Henson, Jim

In full James Maury Henson (born Sept. 24, 1936, Greenville, Miss., U.S.—died May 16, 1990, New York, N.Y.) U.S. puppeteer and producer. He created a puppet show for a television station while in college and developed the first Muppets (melding *marionettes* and *puppets*). In the 1960s he made TV commercials. When PBS featured the Muppets on *Sesame Street* (from 1969), Henson achieved nationwide notice. He premiered *The Muppet Show* on television in 1976 and gained audiences in more than 100 countries. He also produced and directed *The Muppet Movie* (1979) and its sequels.

Hollywood

District of the city of Los Angeles, Calif., U.S. Its name is synonymous with the American movie industry. In 1887 it was laid out as a subdivision by Horace Wilcox, a prohibitionist who envisioned a community based on his religious principles. It was consolidated with Los Angeles in 1910 and became the center of the movie industry by 1915. By the 1960s it also was the source of much American network television programming.

Homer

(Flourished 9th or 8th century BC, Ionia?) Greek poet, one of the greatest and most influential writers of all time. Though almost nothing is known of his life, tradition holds that he was blind. The ancient Greeks attributed to him the great epic poems *The Iliad* and *The Odyssey*. Modern scholars generally agree that he composed (but probably did not literally write) *The Iliad*, most likely relying on oral traditions, and at least inspired the composition of *The Odyssey*. *The Iliad*, set during the Trojan War, tells the story of the wrath of Achilles; *The Odyssey* tells the story of Odysseus as he travels home from the war. The two epics provided the basis of Greek education and culture in the Classical age, and they have remained among the most significant poems of the European tradition.

Joplin, Scott

(Born Nov. 24, 1868, Bowie county, Texas, U.S.—died April 1, 1917, New York, N.Y.) U.S. pianist and composer, the outstanding exponent of ragtime music. Joplin was a classically trained pianist and composer. His compositions, including "Maple Leaf Rag" (1899), ragtime's first hit, and "The Entertainer" (1902), show an acute logic that transcends the sometimes mechanical dimension of the genre. He also wrote a ballet and two operas, including *Treemonisha* (1911), as well as several didactic works. He suffered a nervous collapse in 1911 and was institutionalized in 1916.

Kahlo, Frida

"Diego and I," oil on masonite, self-portrait (with forehead portrait of Diego Rivera); by Frida Kahlo, 1949; in the gallery of Mary-Anne Martin/Fine Art, New York City

In full Frida Kahlo de Rivera, original name Magdalena Carmen Frida Kahlo y Calderón (born July 6, 1907, Coyoacán, Mex.—died July 13, 1954) Mexican painter. The daughter of a German Jewish photographer, she had polio as a child and at 18 was in a serious bus accident. She subsequently underwent some 35 operations; during her recovery, she taught herself to paint. She is noted for her intense self-portraits, many reflecting her physical ordeal. Like many artists working in post-revolutionary Mexico, Kahlo was influenced by Mexican folk art; this is apparent in her use of both fantastical elements and bold color and in her depictions of herself wearing traditional Mexican, rather than European-style, dress. Her marriage to painter Diego Rivera (from 1929) was tumultuous but artistically rewarding. The Surrealists André Breton and Marcel Duchamp helped arrange exhibits of her work in the U.S. and Europe, and though she denied the connection, the dreamlike quality of her work has often led historians to identify her as a Surrealist. She died at 47. Her house in Coyoacán is now the Frida Kahlo Museum.

kite

Light frame covered with paper or cloth, often provided with a balancing tail, and designed to be flown in the air at the end of a long string; it is held aloft by wind. Its name comes from the kite, a member of the hawk family. Kites have been in use in Asia from time immemorial, and religious significance is still connected to some ceremonial kite-flying there.

In a famous experiment in 1752, Benjamin Franklin hung a metal key from a kite line during a storm to attract electricity. Kites were used to carry weather-recording devices aloft before the advent of balloons and airplanes. Types of kite commonly in use today include the hexagonal (or three-sticker), the malay (modified diamond), and the box kite, invented in the 1890s. Newer wing-like kites, with pairs of controlling strings for superior maneuverability, are also flown.

Kurosawa, Akira

(Born March 23, 1910, Tokyo, Japan—died Sept. 6, 1998) Japanese film director. He studied painting before becoming an assistant director and scenarist at PCL (later Toho) movie studio (1936–43). He wrote and directed his first feature film, *Sanshiro Sugata,* in 1943, won notice with *Drunken Angel* (1948), starring Mifune Toshiro, and was internationally acclaimed for *Rashomon* (1950). His later classic films include *Ikiru* (1952), *Seven Samurai* (1954), *Throne of Blood* (1957), *Yojimbo* (1961), *Kagemusha* (1980), and *Ran* (1985). His ability to combine Japanese aesthetic and cultural elements with a Western sense of action and drama made him, in Western eyes, the foremost Japanese filmmaker.

Leonardo da Vinci

(Born April 15, 1452, Anchiano, Republic of Florence—died May 2, 1519, Cloux, France) Italian Renaissance painter, sculptor, draftsman, architect, engineer, and scientist. The son of a landowner and a peasant, he received training in painting, sculpture, and mechanical arts as an apprentice to Andrea del Verrocchio. In 1482, having made a name for himself in Florence, he entered the service of the duke of Milan as "painter and engineer." In Milan his artistic and creative genius unfolded. About 1490 he began his project of writing treatises on the "science of painting," architecture, mechanics, and anatomy. His theories were based on the belief that the painter, with his powers of perception and ability to pictorialize his observations, was uniquely qualified to probe nature's secrets. His numerous surviving manuscripts are noted for being written in a backward script that requires a mirror to be read. In 1502–03, as military architect and engineer for Cesare Borgia, he helped lay the groundwork for modern cartography. After five years of painting and scientific study back in Florence (1503–08), he returned to Milan, where his scientific work flourished. In 1516, after an interlude under Medici patronage in Rome, he entered the service of Francis I of France; he never returned to Italy. Though only some 17 completed paintings survive, they are universally seen as masterpieces. The power of *The Last Supper* (1495–97) comes in part from its masterly composition. In the *Mona Lisa* (*c.* 1503–06) the features and symbolic overtones of the subject achieve a complete synthesis. The unique fame that Leonardo enjoyed in his lifetime and that, filtered by historical criticism, he has remained undimmed to the present day is due largely to his unlimited desire for knowledge, a trait that guided all his thinking and behavior.

Madonna

(Italian; "My lady") In Christian art, a depiction of the Virgin Mary. Though often shown with the infant Jesus, the Madonna may also be represented alone. Byzantine art was the first to develop a set of Madonna types—the Madonna and child enthroned, the Madonna as intercessor, the

The Grand-Duke's Madonna, oil painting by Raphael, 1505; in the Pitti Palace, Florence

Madonna nursing the child, and so on. Western art adapted and added to the Byzantine types during the Middle Ages, producing images of the Virgin that sought to inspire piety through beauty and tenderness. In the Renaissance and Baroque periods, the most popular image of the Madonna foreshadowed the crucifixion, showing the Virgin looking gravely away from the playful child.

Marley, Bob

Orig. Robert Nesta Marley (born Feb. 6, 1945, Nine Miles, St. Ann, Jamaica— died May 11, 1981, Miami, Fla., U.S.) Jamaican singer and songwriter. Born in the hill country of Jamaica to a white father and a black mother, Marley was living in the Kingston slum known as Trench Town in the early 1960s when he formed the Wailers with Peter Tosh and Bunny Livingston (Bunny Wailer). Mixing the Jamaican musical forms of ska and rock steady with rock, they helped to pioneer reggae and became its first international stars with releases such as *Catch a Fire* (1973), *Exodus* (1977), and *Uprising* (1980). Marley's political lyrics, grounded in his belief in the Jamaican religious movement Rastafari and calling for social and economic justice, made him a voice for the poor and dispossessed. His reputation grew after his death from cancer at age 36.

Michelangelo

In full Michelangelo di Lodovico Buonarroti Simoni (born March 6, 1475, Caprese, Republic of Florence—died Feb. 18, 1564, Rome, Papal States) Italian sculptor, painter, architect, and poet. He served a brief apprenticeship with Domenico Ghirlandaio in Florence before beginning the first of several sculptures for Lorenzo de'Medici. After Lorenzo's death in 1492, he left for Bologna and then for Rome. There his *Bacchus* (1496–97) established his fame and led to a commission for the *Pietà* (now in St. Peter's Basilica), the masterpiece of his early years, in which he demonstrated his unique ability to extract two distinct figures

Pietà, marble sculpture by Michelangelo, 1499; in St. Peter's Basilica, Rome

from one marble block. His *David* (1501–04), commissioned for the cathedral of Florence, is still considered the prime example of the Renaissance ideal of perfect humanity. On the side, he produced several Madonnas for private patrons and his only universally accepted easel painting, *The Holy Family* (known as the *Doni Tondo*). Attracted to ambitious sculptural projects, which he did not always complete, he reluctantly agreed to paint the ceiling of the Sistine Chapel (1508–12). The first scenes, depicting the story of Noah, are relatively stable and on a small scale, but his confidence grew as he proceeded, and the later scenes evince boldness and complexity. His figures for the tombs in Florence's Medici Chapel (1519–33), which he designed, are among his most accomplished creations. He devoted his last 30 years largely to the *Last Judgment* fresco in the Sistine Chapel, to writing poetry (he left more than 300 sonnets and madrigals), and to architecture. He was commissioned to complete St. Peter's Basilica, begun in 1506 and little advanced since 1514. Though it was not quite finished at Michelangelo's death, its exterior owes more to him than to any other architect. He is regarded today as among the most exalted of artists.

Mishima, Yukio

Orig. Hiraoka Kimitake (born Jan. 14, 1925, Tokyo, Japan—died Nov. 25, 1970) Japanese writer. Having failed to qualify physically for military service in World War II, Mishima worked in a Tokyo factory and after the war studied law. He won acclaim with his first novel, *Confessions of a Mask* (1949). Many of his characters are obsessed with unattainable ideals and erotic desires, as in *The Temple of the Golden Pavilion* (1956). His epic *The Sea of Fertility*, 4 vol. (1965–70), is perhaps his most lasting achievement. He strongly opposed Japan's close ties to the West in the postwar era (notably the new constitution that forbade rearmament) and yearned to preserve Japan's martial spirit and reverence for the emperor. In a symbolic gesture of these beliefs, he died by committing seppuku (ritual disembowelment) after seizing a military headquarters. He is often considered one of Japan's most important 20th-century novelists.

Monet, Claude

(Born Nov. 14, 1840, Paris, France—died Dec. 5, 1926, Giverny) French landscape painter. Monet spent his early years in Le Havre, where his first teacher, Eugène Boudin, taught him to paint in the open air. Moving to Paris, he formed lifelong friendships with other young painters, including Pierre-Auguste Renoir, Alfred Sisley, and Paul Cézanne. Beginning in the mid-1860s, Monet pursued a new style; rather than trying to reproduce faithfully the scene before him in detail, he recorded on the spot the impression that relaxed, momentary vision might receive. In 1874 he helped organize an independent exhibition, apart from the official Salon, of work he and his friends produced in this style. One of Monet's works at the exhibition, *Impression: Sunrise* (1872), inspired the journalist Louis Leroy to give the group its name. Throughout the 1870s, Monet and the other Impressionists explored this style and exhibited together. By 1881 the original group had begun to disintegrate; only Monet continued with the same fervor to carry on the scrutiny of nature. In his mature works Monet developed his method of producing a series of several studies of the same motif (e.g., haystacks, 1891, and Rouen Cathedral, 1894), changing canvases as the light or his interest shifted. In 1893, in the garden at his home in Giverny, Monet created the water-lily pond that inspired his most famous works, the lyrical *Nymphéas* (water-lilies) paintings. Wildly popular retrospective exhibitions of his work toured the world during the last decades of the 20th century and established his unparalleled public appeal, sustaining his reputation as one of the most significant and popular figures in the modern Western painting tradition.

Mozart, Wolfgang Amadeus

Orig. Johannes Chrysostomus Wolfgangus Theophilus Mozart (born Jan. 27, 1756, Salzburg, Archbishopric of Salzburg—died Dec. 5, 1791, Vienna) Austrian composer. Son of the violinist and composer Leopold Mozart (1719–87), he was born the year of the publication of Leopold's best-selling treatise on violin playing. He and his older sister, Maria Anna (1751–1829), were prodigies; at age five he began to compose and gave his first public performance. From 1762 Leopold toured throughout Europe with his children, showing off the "miracle that God allowed to be born in Salzburg." The first round of touring (1762–69) took them as far as France and England, where Wolfgang met Johann Christian Bach and wrote his first symphonies (1764). Tours of Italy followed (1769–74); there he first saw the string quartets of Joseph Haydn and wrote his own first Italian opera. In 1775–77 he composed his violin concertos and his first piano sonatas. His mother died in 1779. He returned to Salzburg as a cathedral organist and in 1781 wrote his opera seria *Idomeneo*. Chafing under the archbishop's rule, he was released from his position in 1781; he moved in with his friends the Weber family and began his independent career in Vienna. He married Constanze Weber, gave piano lessons, and wrote *The Abduction from the Seraglio* (1782) and many of his great piano concertos. The later 1780s were the height of his success, with the string quartets dedicated to Haydn (who called Mozart the greatest living composer), the three great operas on Lorenzo Da Ponte's librettos—*The Marriage of Figaro* (1786), *Don Giovanni* (1787), and *Così fan tutte* (1790)—and his superb late symphonies. In his last year he composed the opera *The Magic Flute* and his great *Requiem* (left unfinished). Despite his success, he always lacked money (possibly because of gambling debts and a fondness for fine clothes) and had to borrow heavily from friends. His death at age 35 may have resulted from a kidney infection. No other composer left such an extraordinary legacy in so short a lifetime.

Murasaki Shikibu

(Born *c.* 978, Kyoto, Japan) Japanese writer. Her real name is unknown, and the primary source of knowledge about her life is a diary she kept (1007–10). Her *Tale of Genji* (completed *c.* 1010) is a long and complex tale, concerned mostly with the loves of Prince Genji and the women in his life. Supremely sensitive to human emotions and the beauties of nature, it provides delightful glimpses of life at the court of the empress

Joto mon'in, whom Murasaki served. It is generally considered the greatest work of Japanese literature and perhaps the world's first novel.

Olivier, Laurence (Kerr)

Baron Olivier (of Brighton) (born May 22, 1907, Dorking, Surrey, Eng.—died July 11, 1989, near London) British actor, director, and producer. He began his professional career in 1926 and joined the Old Vic company in 1937, playing many major Shakespearean roles. With Ralph Richardson he codirected the Old Vic (1944–50), and he acted in some of its greatest productions, including *Richard III, Henry IV*, and *Oedipus Rex*. He was knighted in 1947. From 1950 he directed and acted under his own management; his notable productions included *Antony and Cleopatra* and *The Entertainer*. He was the founding director of the National Theatre (1962–73), one of whose theaters is now named for him. In 1970 he was created a life peer, the first actor ever to be so honored. His many films include *Wuthering Heights* (1939), *Rebecca* (1940), *Hamlet* (1948, Academy Award), *The Entertainer* (1960), and *Othello* (1965). He was married to the actresses Vivien Leigh and (from 1961) Joan Plowright.

Olympic Games

Sports festival. In ancient Greece it was a Panhellenic festival held every fourth year and made up of contests of sports, music, and literature. Since 1896 the name has been used for a modified revival of the ancient Games, consisting of international athletic contests held at four-year intervals. The original Games included footraces, the discus and javelin throws, the long jump, boxing, wrestling, the pentathlon, and chariot races. After the subjugation of Greece by Rome, the Games declined; they were finally abolished about AD 400. They were revived in the late 19th century through efforts led in part by Pierre, baron de Coubertin; the first modern Games were held in Athens. The first Winter Games were held in 1924. The direction of the modern Olympic movement and the regulation of the Games are vested in the International Olympic Committee, headquartered at Lausanne, Switz. Until the 1970s the Games adhered to a strict code of amateurism, but since that time professional players have also been allowed to participate. Programs for the Summer Games include competition in archery, baseball, basketball, boxing, canoeing, cycling, diving, equestrian sports, fencing, field hockey, football (soccer), gymnastics, handball, judo, the modern pentathlon, rowing, sailing, shooting, softball, swimming, table tennis, tennis, track and field (athletics), the triathlon, volleyball, water polo, weightlifting, and wrestling. The program for the Winter Games includes the biathlon, bobsledding, ice hockey, lugeing, skeleton sledding, snowboarding, and numerous ice skating and skiing events. Events are periodically added and dropped.

Paz, Octavio

(Born March 31, 1914, Mexico City, Mex.—died April 19, 1998) Mexican poet, writer, and diplomat. Educated at the University of Mexico, Paz published his first book of poetry, *Savage Moon*, in 1933. He later founded and edited several important literary reviews. Influenced in turn by Marxism, Surrealism, existentialism, Buddhism, and Hinduism, his poetry uses rich imagery in dealing with metaphysical questions, and his most prominent theme is the human ability to overcome existential solitude through erotic love and artistic creativity. His prose works include *The Labyrinth of Solitude* (1950), an influential essay on Mexican history and culture. He was Mexico's ambassador to India (1962–68). He was awarded the Nobel Prize for Literature in 1990.

Picasso, Pablo

In full Pablo Ruiz y Picasso (born Oct. 25, 1881, Málaga, Spain—died April 8, 1973, Mougins, France) Spanish-born French painter, sculptor, printmaker, ceramicist, and stage designer. Trained by his father, a professor of drawing, he exhibited his first works at 13. After moving permanently to Paris in 1904, he replaced the predominantly blue tones of his so-called Blue Period (1901–04) with those of pottery and flesh in his Rose Period (1904–06). His first masterpiece, *Les Demoiselles d'Avignon* (1907), was controversial for its violent treatment of the female body and the masklike faces derived from his study of African art. From 1909 to 1912 Picasso worked closely with Georges Braque—the only time Picasso ever worked with another painter in this way—and they developed what came to be known as Cubism. The artists presented a new kind of reality that broke away from Renaissance tradition, especially from the use of perspective and illusion. Neither Braque nor Picasso desired to move into the realm of total abstraction in their Cubist works, although they implicitly accepted inconsistencies such as different points of view, different axes, and different light sources in the same picture. By 1912 they had taken Cubism further by gluing paper and other materials onto their canvases. Between 1917 and 1924 Picasso designed stage sets for five ballets for Sergey Diaghilev's Ballets Russes. In the 1920s and 1930s, the Surrealists spurred him to explore new subject matter, particularly the image of the Minotaur. The Spanish Civil War inspired perhaps his greatest work, the enormous *Guernica* (1937), whose violent imagery condemned the useless destruction of life. After World War II he joined the Communist Party and devoted his time to sculpture, ceramics, and lithography as well as painting. In his late years he created variations on the works of earlier artists, the most famous being a series of 58 pictures based on *Las Meninas* of Diego Velázquez. For nearly 80 of his 91 years Picasso devoted himself to an artistic production that contributed significantly to and paralleled the whole development of modern art in the 20th century.

poker

Any of several card games—played in homes, poker clubs, casinos, and over the Internet—in which a player bets that the value of his or her hand is greater than that of the hands held by others. Each subsequent player must either equal or raise the bet or drop out. The pot is eventually won by either the player showing the best hand when it comes to a showdown or the only player left when everyone else has dropped out, or "folded." In this case the winner need not show his hand and could conceivably have won the pot with a lower hand than any other at the table. It is for this reason that poker is described as a game of bluff. Three principal forms of the game have developed: straight poker, in which all cards of the standard five-card hand are dealt facedown; stud poker, in which some but not all of a player's cards are dealt faceup; and community-card poker, in which some cards are exposed and used by all the players to form their best hand. In draw poker, the main variant of straight poker, cards may be discarded and additional cards drawn. The traditional ranking of hands is (1) straight flush (five cards of the same suit in sequence, the highest sequence—ace, king, queen, jack, ten—being called a royal flush), (2) four of a kind, (3) full house (three of a kind, plus a pair), (4) flush (five of a single suit), (5) straight (five in sequence), (6) three of a kind, (7) two pair, (8) one pair. Poker has been called the national card game of the United

States, and its play and jargon permeate American culture. Early forms of the game appear in literature as early as 1526.

Presley, Elvis (Aaron)

(Born Jan. 8, 1935, Tupelo, Miss., U.S.—died Aug. 16, 1977, Memphis, Tenn.) U.S. popular singer, the "King of Rock and Roll." Presley was raised in Memphis, where he sang Pentecostal church music and listened to black bluesmen and Grand Ole Opry broadcasts. In 1954 he began to record for the producer Sam Phillips, who had been searching for a white singer who sounded like a black man. In 1956, under his new manager, "Colonel" Tom Parker, he released "Heartbreak Hotel," the first of numerous million-selling hits that included "Hound Dog" and "All Shook Up." In the same year, he appeared in *Love Me Tender*, the first of 33 mediocre films, and on several TV shows, notably the *Ed Sullivan Show*. Presley's intensely charismatic style—including his sexy hip shaking, ducktail haircut, and characteristic sneer—excited young fans, especially females, to wild adulation. After a stint in the army (1958–60) he resumed recording and acting, but his earlier raucous style was moderated. In 1968 he introduced a Las Vegas–based touring act with orchestra and gospel-type choir. Battling public pressures, weight gain, and drug dependence, he underwent a personal decline. His death at age 42, attributed to natural causes, was mourned by hundreds of thousands of fans at Graceland, his Memphis estate, which remains a place of international pilgrimage.

Renaissance

(French; "Rebirth") Late medieval cultural movement in Europe. The Renaissance brought renewed interest in Classical learning and values to Italy and subsequently the rest of western and central Europe from the late 13th to the early 17th century. Attracted by the values and rhetorical eloquence of ancient writers, figures such as Petrarch, Giovanni Boccaccio, and Lorenzo Valla rejected medieval Scholasticism in favor of human-centered forms of philosophy and literature. In northern Europe, Desiderius Erasmus cultivated Christian humanism, and writers such as François Rabelais and William Shakespeare produced works that emphasized the intricacies of human character. Inspired by ancient Greece and Rome, Renaissance painters and sculptors took the visible world for their subject and practiced according to mathematical principles of balance, harmony, and perspective. The new aesthetic found expression in the works of Italian artists such as Leonardo da Vinci, Sandro Botticelli, Raphael, Titian, and Michelangelo, and the Italian city of Florence became the center of Renaissance art. The term has also been applied to cultural revivals in England in the 8th century, the Frankish kingdoms in the 9th century, and Europe in the 12th century.

Sappho

(Flourished 610–*c.* 570 BC, Lesbos, Asia Minor) Greek lyric poet. Although legends about her abound, little is known of her life. She was born on the island of Lesbos and became the leader of a *thiasos*, an informal female community, whose purpose was the education of young women, especially for marriage. The principal themes of her poetry are personal and reflect the activities and atmosphere of the *thiasos*. Her writing, mostly vernacular and not formally literary, is concise, direct, picturesque, and various. It includes nuptial songs and an expression of her love for other women, which produced the word *lesbian* (from the island's name). Though she was much admired in antiquity, most of her work was lost by the early Middle Ages; only an ode to Aphrodite—28 lines long—is complete.

Shakespeare, William

(Baptized April 26, 1564, Stratford-upon-Avon, Warwickshire, Eng.— died April 23, 1616) British poet and playwright, often considered the greatest writer in world literature. He spent his early life in Stratford-upon-Avon, receiving at most a grammar-school education, and at age 18 he married a local woman, Anne Hathaway. By 1594 he was apparently a rising playwright in London and an actor in a leading theater company, the Lord Chamberlain's Men (later King's Men); the company performed at the Globe Theatre from 1599. The order in which his plays were written and performed is highly uncertain. His earliest plays seem to date from the late 1580s to the mid-1590s and include the comedies *Love's Labour's Lost*, *The Comedy of Errors*, *The Taming of the Shrew*, and *A Midsummer Night's Dream*; plays based on the lives of the English kings, including *Henry VI* (parts 1, 2, and 3), *Richard III*, and *Richard II*; and the tragedy *Romeo and Juliet*. The plays written between

1596 and 1600 are mostly comedies, including *The Merchant of Venice*, *The Merry Wives of Windsor*, *Much Ado about Nothing*, and *As You Like It*, and histories, including *Henry IV* (parts 1 and 2), *Henry V*, and *Julius Caesar*. Approximately between 1600 and 1607 he wrote the comedies *Twelfth Night*, *All's Well That Ends Well*, and *Measure for Measure*, as well as the great tragedies *Hamlet* (probably begun in 1599), *Othello*, *Macbeth*, and *King Lear*, which mark the summit of his art. Among his later works (*c.* 1607 to 1614) are the tragedies *Antony and Cleopatra*, *Coriolanus*, and *Timon of Athens*, as well as the fantastical romances *The Winter's Tale* and *The Tempest*. He probably also is responsible for some sections of the plays *Edward III* and *The Two Noble Kinsmen*.

Shakespeare's plays, all of them written largely in iambic pentameter verse, are marked by extraordinary poetry; vivid, subtle, and complex characterizations; and a highly inventive use of English. His 154 sonnets, published in 1609 but apparently written mostly in the 1590s, often express strong feeling within an exquisitely controlled form. Shakespeare retired to Stratford before 1610 and lived as a country gentleman until his death. The first collected edition of his plays, or First Folio, was published in 1623. As with most writers of the time, little is known about his life and work, and other writers, particularly the 17th earl of Oxford, have frequently been proposed as the actual authors of his plays and poems.

Soyinka, Wole

In full Akinwande Oluwole Soyinka (born July 13, 1934, Abeokuta, Nigeria) Nigerian playwright. After studying in Leeds, Eng., he returned to Nigeria to edit literary journals, teach drama and literature at the uni-

versity level, and found two theater companies. His plays, written in English and drawing on West African folk traditions, often focus on the tensions between tradition and progress. Symbolism, flashback, and ingenious plotting contribute to a rich dramatic structure. His serious plays reveal his disillusionment with African authoritarian leadership and with Nigerian society as a whole. His works include *A Dance of the Forests* (1960), *The Lion and the Jewel* (1963), *Death and the King's Horseman* (1975), and *From Zia, with Love* (1992). He has

Wole Soyinka

written several volumes of poetry; his best-known novel is *The Interpreters* (1965). A champion of Nigerian democracy, he was repeatedly jailed and exiled. In 1986 he became the first black African to be awarded the Nobel Prize for Literature.

Stieglitz, Alfred

Alfred Stieglitz at his gallery "291" in 1934; behind him is a painting by his wife, Georgia O'Keeffe

(Born Jan. 1, 1864, Hoboken, N.J., U.S.—died July 13, 1946, New York, N.Y.) U.S. photographer and exhibitor of modern art. He was taken to Europe by his wealthy family to further his education in 1881. In 1883 he abandoned engineering studies in Berlin for a photographic career. Returning to the U.S. in 1890, he made the first successful photographs in snow, in rain, and at night. In 1902 he founded the Photo-Secession group to establish photography as an art. His own best photographs are perhaps two series (1917–27), one of portraits of his wife, painter Georgia O'Keeffe, and the other of cloud shapes corresponding to emotional experiences. His photographs were the first to be exhibited in major U.S. museums. He also was the first to exhibit, at his "291" gallery in New York City, works of modern European and U.S. painters, five years before the famed Armory Show.

SUMO

Japanese form of wrestling. A contestant loses if he is forced out of the ring (a 15-ft circle) or if any part of his body except the soles of his feet touches the ground. In sumo, a wrestler's weight, size, and strength are of the greatest importance, though speed and suddenness of attack are also useful. The wrestlers, who are fed a special protein diet and may weigh more than 300 lbs (136 kg), wear only loincloths and grip each other by the belt. Sumo wrestling is an ancient sport with a complex system of ranking; at the top of the hierarchy is the *yokozuna* ("grand champion"). Lengthy rituals and elaborate posturings accompany the bouts, which are extremely brief, often lasting only a few seconds.

Feldman-ISM

Tolstoy, Leo

(Russian; Lev Nikolayevich, Count Tolstoy) (born Sept. 9, 1828, Yasnaya
Polyana, Tula province, Russian Empire—died Nov. 20, 1910, Astapovo,
Ryazan province) Russian writer, one of the world's greatest novelists.
The scion of prominent aristocrats, Tolstoy spent much of his life at his
family estate of Yasnaya Polyana. After a somewhat dissolute youth, he
served in the army and traveled in Europe before returning home and
starting a school for peasant children. He was already known as a brilliant writer for the short stories in *Sevastopol Sketches* (1855–56) and the
novel *The Cossacks* (1863) when *War and Peace* (1865–69) established
him as Russia's preeminent novelist. Set during the Napoleonic Wars, the
novel examines the lives of a large group of characters, centering on the
partly autobiographical figure of the spiritually questing Pierre. Its structure, with its flawless placement of complex characters in a turbulent
historical setting, is regarded as one of the great technical achievements
in the history of the Western novel. His other great novel, *Anna Karenina*
(1875–77), concerns an aristocratic woman who deserts her husband for
a lover and the search for meaning by another autobiographical character, Levin. After its publication Tolstoy underwent a spiritual crisis and
turned to a form of Christian anarchism. Advocating simplicity and nonviolence, he devoted himself to social reform. His later works include

The Death of Ivan Ilich (1886), often considered the greatest novella in Russian literature, and *What Is Art?* (1898), which condemns fashionable aestheticism and celebrates art's moral and religious functions. He lived humbly on his great estate, practicing a radical asceticism and in constant conflict with his wife. In November 1910, unable to bear his situation any longer, he left his estate incognito. During his flight he contracted pneumonia, and he was dead within a few days.

Twain, Mark

Orig. Samuel Langhorne Clemens (born Nov. 30, 1835, Florida, Mo., U.S.—died April 21, 1910, Redding, Conn.) U.S. humorist, writer, and lecturer. He grew up in Hannibal, Mo., on the Mississippi River. At age 13 he was apprenticed to a local printer. In 1856 he signed on as an apprentice to a steamboat pilot. He plied the Mississippi for almost four years before going to Nevada and California. In 1863 he took his pseudonym, the riverman's term for water "two fathoms deep." In a California mining camp he heard the story that he would make famous as "The Celebrated Jumping Frog of Calaveras County" (1865). He traveled widely, using his travels as subject matter for lectures and books, including the humorous narratives *The Innocents Abroad* (1869) and *Roughing It* (1872). He won a worldwide audience for his stories of youthful adventures, especially *Tom Sawyer* (1876), *The Prince and the Pauper* (1881), *Life on the Mississippi* (1883), and *Huckleberry Finn* (1884), one of the masterpieces of American fiction. The satirical *A Connecticut Yankee in King Arthur's Court* (1889) and increasingly grim works including *Pudd'nhead Wilson* (1894) and *The Man Who Corrupted Hadleyburg* (1900) followed. In the 1890s financial speculations bankrupted him, and his eldest daughter died. After his wife's death (1904), he expressed his pessimism about human character in such late works as the posthumously published *Letters from the Earth* (1962).

vampire

In popular legend, a bloodsucking creature that rises from its burial place at night, sometimes in the form of a bat, to drink the blood of humans. By daybreak it must return to its grave or to a coffin filled with its native earth. Tales of vampires are part of the world's folklore, most

In Mark Twain's *Extracts from Eve's Diary*, Eve is perplexed as to the nature of the beast she thinks of as "the other experiment":

> I followed the other experiment around yesterday afternoon, at a distance, to see what it might be for, if I could. But I was not able to make out. I think it is a man. I had never seen a man, but it looked like one, and I feel sure that that is what it is. I realize I feel more curiosity about it than about any of the other reptiles. If it is a reptile, and I suppose it is. . . . I was afraid of it at first, and started to run every time it came around, for I thought it was going to chase me. But by-and-by I found it was only trying to get away, so after that I was not timid anymore, but tracked it along, several hours, about 20 yards behind, which made it nervous and unhappy. At last it was a good deal worried, and climbed a tree. . . . Today the same thing over. I've got it up the tree again.

For his part, Adam, no less puzzled by the creature Eve says she found in the woods and has named Cain, sets off for the forests of the north hoping to find another one, reasoning "this one will be less dangerous when it has company of its own species." Three months later he writes in his diary:

> It has been a weary, weary hunt, yet I have no success. In the meantime, without stirring from the home estate, she has caught another one! I never saw such luck. I might have hunted these woods a hundred years, I never should have run across that thing.

The Diaries were but two examples of Twain's wry take on religious topics, many of which were suppressed by his daughter Clara, who thought they conflicted with her father's public persona; one volume, *Letters from the Earth*, Satan's reports to God after having been exiled to earth, was not published until 1965.—M.F.

---

notably in Hungary and the Balkan Peninsula. The disinterment in Serbia in 1725 and 1732 of several fluid-filled corpses that villagers claimed were behind a plague of vampirism led to widespread interest and imaginative treatment of vampirism throughout western Europe. Vampires are supposedly dead humans (originally suicides, heretics, or criminals) who maintain a kind of life by biting the necks of living humans and sucking their blood; their victims also become vampires after death. These "undead" creatures cast no shadow and are not reflected in mirrors. They can be warded off by crucifixes or wreaths of garlic and can be killed by exposure to the sun or by an oak stake driven through the heart. The most famous vampire is Count Dracula from Bram Stoker's novel *Dracula* (1897).

Virgil

Or Vergil. Orig. Publius Vergilius Maro (born Oct. 15, 70 BC, Andes, near Mantua—died Sept. 21, 19 BC, Brundisium) Greatest of Roman poets. The well-educated son of a prosperous provincial farmer, Virgil led a quiet life, though he eventually became a member of the circle around Octavian (later Caesar Augustus) and was patronized by Maecenas. His first major work, the 10 pastoral *Eclogues* (42–37), may be read as a prophecy of tranquility, and one has even been read as a prophecy of Christianity. The *Georgics* (37–30) point toward a Golden Age in the form of practical goals: the repopulation of rural lands and the rehabilitation of agriculture. His great epic, the *Aeneid* (begun *c.* 29, but unfinished at his death), is one of the masterpieces of world literature. A celebration of the founding of Rome by the legendary Aeneas at the request of Augustus, whose consolidation of power in 31–30 unified the Roman world, it also explores the themes of war and the pathos of unrequited love. In later centuries his works were regarded in the Roman Empire as virtually sacred. He was taken up reverently by Christians as well, including Dante, who, in his poem *The Divine Comedy*, made Virgil his guide through hell and purgatory.

Wagner, (Wilhelm) Richard

(Born May 22, 1813, Leipzig, Ger.—died Feb. 13, 1883, Venice, Italy) German composer. His childhood was divided between Dresden and Leipzig, where he had his first composition lessons; his teacher refused payment because of his talent. His first opera, *The Fairies* (1834), was followed by *The Ban on Love* (1836); the premiere performance was so unprepared that the event was a fiasco, and he henceforth determined not to settle for modest productions. The success of *Rienzi* (1840) led him to be more adventurous in *The Flying Dutchman* (1843) and even more so in *Tannhäuser* (1845). Caught up in the political turmoil of 1848, he was forced to flee Dresden for Zürich. During this enforced vacation, he wrote influential essays, asserting (following G.W.F. Hegel) that music had reached a limit after Ludwig van Beethoven and that the "artwork of the future" would unite music and theater in a *Gesamtkunstwerk* ("total artwork"). In 1850 he saw *Lohengrin* produced. He had begun his most ambitious work, *The Ring of the Nibelung*, a four-opera cycle. The need for large-scale unity brought him to the concept of the leitmotiv. He ceased work on the *Ring*'s third opera, *Siegfried*, in the throes of an adulterous love with Mathilde Wesendonk and wrote an opera of forbidden love, *Tristan und Isolde* (1859), which also seemed to break the bonds of tonality. He published the *Ring* librettos in 1863, with a plea for financial support, and Louis II of Bavaria responded, inviting Wagner to complete the work in Munich. From the late 1860s to the early 1880s, Wagner completed work on *Die Meistersinger*, *Siegfried*, *Götterdämmerung*, and the long-deferred *Parsifal*, as he also oversaw the building of the great festival theater at Bayreuth (1872–76) that would be dedicated to his operas. His astonishing works made Wagner one of the most influential and consequential figures in the history of Western music and, indeed, of Western culture. In the late 20th century his undoubted musical stature was challenged somewhat by the strongly racist and anti-Semitic views expressed in his writings, and evidence of anti-Semitism in his operas was increasingly documented.

Woolf, (Adeline) Virginia

Orig. Adeline Virginia Stephen (born Jan. 25, 1882, London, Eng.—died March 28, 1941, near Rodmell, Sussex) British novelist and critic. Daughter of Leslie Stephen, she and her sister became the early nucleus of the Bloomsbury group. She married Leonard Woolf in 1912; in 1917 they founded the Hogarth Press. Her best novels—including *Mrs. Dalloway* (1925) and *To the Lighthouse* (1927)—are experimental; in them she examines the human experience of time, the indefinability of character, and external circumstances as they impinge on consciousness. *Orlando* (1928) is a historical fantasy about a single character who experiences England from the Elizabethan era to the early 20th century, and *The Waves* (1931), perhaps her most radically experimental work, uses interior monologue and recurring images to trace the inner lives of six characters. Such works confirmed her place among the major figures of literary modernism. Her best critical studies are collected in *The Common Reader* (1925, 1932). Her long essay *A Room of One's Own* (1929) addressed the status of women, and women artists in particular. Her other novels include *Jacob's Room* (1922), *The Years* (1937), and *Between the Acts* (1941). She also wrote a biography of Roger Fry. Her health and mental stability were delicate throughout her life; in a recurrence of mental illness, she drowned herself. Her diaries and correspondence have been published in several editions.

Feldman's Art, Culture, and Pastimes

Quiz

1. While camels have been raced for thousands of years in the Middle East and North Africa, what new innovation in the sport has been announced in the United Arab Emirates?
   (a) one hump instead of two
   (b) robotic camels
   (c) robotic jockeys

(c) Incredible as it may seem, robotic jockeys are now being tested to replace the young boys who have traditionally ridden astride the animals, a practice that has come under fire in recent years as being harmful to the child's physical and social welfare.

2. The Bollywood sign stands in the hills overlooking:
   (a) Brooklyn
   (b) Bombay
   (c) Calcutta
   (d) none of the above

(d) Bollywood, the Indian film industry, was born with Himansu Rai's Bombay Talkies; by the late 1930s it was cranking out epics, curry westerns, courtesan films with elaborate dance sequences, and mythological movies—as many as 1,000 per year at its height. But no sign exists.

Wright, Frank Lloyd

(Born June 8, 1867, Richland Center, Wis., U.S.—died April 9, 1959, Phoenix, Ariz.) U.S. architect. After studying engineering briefly at the University of Wisconsin, he worked for the firm of Dankmar Adler (1844–1900) and Louis Sullivan in Chicago before opening his own practice there in 1893. Wright became the chief practitioner of the Prairie school, building about 50 Prairie houses from 1900 to 1910. Early nonresidential buildings include the forward-looking Larkin Building in Buffalo, N.Y. (1904; destroyed 1950) and Unity Temple in Oak Park, Ill. (1906). In 1911 he began work on his own house, Taliesin, near Spring Green, Wis. The lavish Imperial Hotel in Tokyo (1915–22; dismantled 1967) was significant for its revolutionary floating cantilever construction, which made it one of the only large buildings to withstand the earthquake of 1923. In the 1930s he designed his low-cost Usonian houses, but his most admired house, Fallingwater, in Bear Run, Pa. (1936), is an extravagant country retreat cantilevered over a waterfall. His Johnson Wax Building (1936–39), an example of humane workplace design, touched off an avalanche of major commissions. Of particular note is the Guggenheim Museum (1956–59), which has no separate floor levels but instead uses a spiral ramp, realizing Wright's ideal of a continuous space. Throughout his career he retained the use of ornamental detail, earthy colors, and rich textural effects. His sensitive use of materials helped to control and perfect his dynamic expression of space, which opened a new era in American architecture. Often considered the greatest U.S. architect of all time, his greatest legacy is "organic architecture," or the idea that buildings harmonize both with their inhabitants and with their environment.

zydeco

Form of dance music from southwestern Louisiana, U.S., with roots in French, African American, and Afro-Caribbean styles. Similar to the music of the Cajuns (displaced French Canadians who settled in Louisiana), zydeco was created by the Creoles (those of African heritage in Louisianan French culture). Its name is thought to come from a modified pronunciation of the French phrase *les haricots* ("the beans") heard in a popular song. The music usually features guitar, accordion, fiddle (violin), and washboard played to a driving beat, but it may also include electric guitar, electric bass, saxophone, and keyboards. It became widely popular in the 1980s through the performances of Clifton Chenier, Queen Ida, Buckwheat Zydeco, Boozoo Chavis, and others.

History

T hey say Voltaire invented history. They? All right, not *they*, but rather it was Marie de Vichy-Chamrond, marquise du Deffand, who said Voltaire "has invented" history— something she had, apparently, been waiting for. She may have meant Voltaire was making it all up. He penned the histories of Charles XII, Louis XIV, Louis XV, and Peter the Great of Russia, among others, spurring Thomas Carlyle's wry quip, "History is the essence of innumerable biographies." The marquise was perhaps unaware of the *Historia Augusta*, a 4th-century collection of biographies of the Roman emperors Hadrian through Numerian, or she might have declared, "Unknown, and perhaps several authors have invented history." Even so, this would slight Herodotus of Halicarnassus (484–430 BC), the Greek who documented the Persian War, and Thucydides, the general who lost the battle Athens vs. Sparta but won the war of words with his *History of the Peloponnesian War*, the first moral analysis of warfare—if that is possible.

The first written histories were actually those of the Sumerians, incised between 2500 and 2000 BC. The Old Testament is basically a history with implications, being a long story starting around 1200 BC and not ending until 100 BC. Moses is credited with being the author of the first five books, and he did have the advantage of taking dictation from God.

Alexander the Great

Or Alexander III (born 356 BC, Pella, Macedonia—died June 13, 323 BC,
Babylon) King of Macedonia (336–323) and the greatest military leader of
antiquity. The son of Philip II of Macedonia, he was taught by Aristotle.
He soon showed military brilliance, helping win the Battle of Chaeronea
at age 18. He succeeded his assassinated father in 336 and promptly took
Thessaly and Thrace; he brutally razed Thebes except for its temples and
the house of Pindar. Such destruction was to be his standard method, and
other Greek states submitted meekly. In 334 he crossed to Persia and
defeated a Persian army at the Granicus River. He is said to have cut the
Gordian knot in Phrygia (333), by which act, according to legend, he was
destined to rule all Asia. At the Battle of Issus in 333, he defeated another

Feldman-ISM

Alexander picked up where his father left off when the
latter was assassinated and left the weak Greek coalition
incapable of taking on King Darius and the legions of his
number-one-and-rising-higher Persian Empire. At the Thrilla in
Gaugamela (the battle site's name in present-day Iraq), Alexander routed
Darius's troops, although Darius once again eluded capture. (Alexander
never did get him; Darius died, unexpectedly, of natural causes.) Darius's
much-feared weapons of mass destruction, 15 long-range elephants,
seemed to have had little effect on the outcome, other than crushing
Alexander's dog, Peritas the Greyhound.

It's hard to conquer the world, even if it's only the known world, and not
get grandiose. Alexander had his handsome (at least that was the official
rendition), beardless visage painted, stamped, or chiseled on the appropriate medium wherever he went and even became a god after conquering
Egypt, where it took little convincing that he was not Philip's son, after all,
but Amon's. He never did much of anything with the world after winning it,
unless you count the symbolic marriage of Europe and Asia, when 1,000 of
his closest field commanders took Asian women in troth, Alexander characteristically adding insult to injury by choosing one of Darius's daughters
(the thin one). After enjoying the fruits of his labors on the banks of the
Euphrates in 323 BC, Alexander fell asleep drunk and woke up dead, the
cue for all his extended families to murder one another, for the coins to go
out of circulation, and for the known world to relax for a while before the
next great white, yellow, or black hope came along.—M.F.

army, this one led by the Persian king Darius III, who managed to escape. He then took Syria and Phoenicia, cutting off the Persian fleet from its ports. In 332 he completed a seven-month siege of Tyre, considered his greatest military achievement, and then took Egypt. There he received the pharaohs' double crown, founded Alexandria, and visited the oracle of the god Amon, the basis of his claim to divinity. In control of the eastern Mediterranean coast, in 331 he defeated Darius in a decisive battle at Gaugamela, though Darius again escaped. He next took the province of Babylon. He burnt Xerxes's palace at Persepolis, Persia, in 330, and he envisioned an empire ruled jointly by Macedonians and Persians. He continued eastward, quashing real or imagined conspiracies among his men and taking control to the Oxus and Jaxartes rivers, founding cities (most named Alexandria) to hold the territory. Conquering what is now Tajikistan, he married the princess Roxana and embraced Persian absolutism, adopting Persian dress and enforcing Persian court customs. By 326 he reached the Hyphasis in India, where his weary men mutinied; he turned back, marching and pillaging down the Indus, and reached Susa with much loss of life. He continued to promote his unpopular policy of racial fusion, a seeming attempt to form a Persian-Macedonian master race. When his favorite, Hephaestion (324), died, Alexander gave him a hero's funeral and demanded that divine honors be given at his own funeral. He fell ill at Babylon after long feasting and drinking and died at age 33. He was buried in Alexandria, Egypt. His empire, the greatest that had existed to that time, extended from Thrace to Egypt and from Greece to the Indus valley.

American Civil War

Or Civil War or War Between the States (1861–65) Conflict between the U.S. federal government and 11 Southern states that fought to secede from the Union. It arose out of disputes over the issues of slavery, trade and tariffs, and the doctrine of states' rights. In the 1840s and 1850s, Northern opposition to slavery in the Western territories caused the Southern states to fear that existing slaveholdings, which formed the economic base of the South, were also in danger. By the 1850s abolitionism was growing in the North, and when the antislavery Republican candidate Abraham Lincoln was elected president in 1860, the Southern states seceded to protect what they saw as their right to keep slaves. They were organized as the

Confederate States of America under Jefferson Davis. The Northern states of the federal Union, under Lincoln, commanded more than twice the population of the Confederacy and held greater advantages in manufacturing and transportation capacity. The war began in Charleston, S.C., when Confederate artillery fired on Fort Sumter on April 12, 1861. Both sides quickly raised armies. In July 1861, 30,000 Union troops marched toward the Confederate capital at Richmond, Va., but were stopped by Confederate forces in the Battle of Bull Run and forced to retreat to Washington, D.C. The defeat shocked the Union, which called for 500,000 more recruits. The war's first major campaign began in February 1862, when Union troops under Ulysses S. Grant captured Confederate forts in western Tennessee. Union victories at the battles of Shiloh and New Orleans followed. In the East, Robert E. Lee won several Confederate victories in the Seven Days' Battles and, after defeat at the Battle of Antietam, in the Battle of Fredericksburg (December 1862). After the Confederate victory at the Battle of Chancellorsville, Lee invaded the North and engaged Union forces under George Meade at the momentous Battle of Gettysburg. The war's turning point in the West occurred in July 1863 with Grant's success in the Vicksburg Campaign, which brought the entire Mississippi River under Union control. Grant's command was expanded after the Union defeat at the Battle of Chickamauga, and in March 1864 Lincoln gave him supreme command of the Union armies. He began a strategy of attrition and, despite heavy Union casualties at the battles of the Wilderness and Spotsylvania, began to surround Lee's troops in Petersburg, Va. Meanwhile William T. Sherman captured Atlanta in September, set out on a destructive march through Georgia, and soon captured Savannah. Grant captured Richmond on April 3, 1865, and accepted Lee's surrender on April 9 at Appomattox Court House. On April 26 Sherman received the surrender of Joseph Johnston, thereby ending the war. The mortality rates of the war were staggering—there were about 620,000 deaths out of a total of 2.4 million soldiers. The South was devastated. But the Union was preserved, and slavery was abolished.

American Revolution

Or United States War of Independence (1775–83) War that won political independence for 13 of Britain's North American colonies, which formed the United States of America. After the end of the costly French and Indian War (1763), Britain imposed new taxes and trade restrictions on the colonies, fueling growing resentment and strengthening the colonists' objection to their lack of representation in the British Parliament. Determined to achieve independence, the colonies formed the Continental Army, composed chiefly of minutemen, to challenge Britain's large, organized militia. The war began when Britain sent a force to destroy rebel military stores at Concord, Mass. After fighting broke out on April 19, 1775, rebel forces began a siege of Boston that ended when American forces under Henry Knox forced out the British troops under William Howe on March 17, 1776. Britain's offer of pardon in exchange for surrender was refused by the Americans, who declared themselves independent on July 4, 1776. British forces retaliated by driving the army of George Washington from New York to New Jersey. On December 25, Washington crossed the Delaware River and won the battles of Trenton and Princeton. The British army split to cover more territory, a fatal error. In engaging the Americans in Pennsylvania, notably in the Battle of the Brandywine, they left the troops in the north vulnerable. Despite a victory in the Battle of Ticonderoga, British troops under John Burgoyne were defeated by Horatio Gates and Benedict Arnold in the Battle of Saratoga (Oct. 17, 1777). Washington quartered his 11,000 troops through a bleak winter at Valley Forge, where they received training from Frederick Steuben that gave them victory in Monmouth, N.J., on June 28, 1778. British forces in the north thenceforth chiefly concentrated near New York. France, which had been secretly furnishing aid to the Americans since 1776, finally declared war on Britain in June 1778. French troops assisted American troops in the south, culminating in the successful Siege of Yorktown, where Charles Cornwallis surrendered his forces on Oct. 19, 1781, bringing an end to the war on land. War continued at sea, fought chiefly between Britain and the U.S.'s European allies. The navies of Spain and the Netherlands contained most of Britain's navy near Europe and away from the fighting in America. The last battle of the war was won by the American navy under John Barry in March 1783 in the Straits of Florida. With the Treaty of Paris (Sept. 3, 1783), Britain recognized the independence of the U.S. east of the Mississippi River and ceded Florida to Spain.

Arab-Israeli wars

Series of military conflicts fought between various Arab countries and Israel (1948–49, 1956, 1967, 1969–70, 1973, and 1982). The first war (1948–49) began when Israel declared itself an independent state following the United Nations' partition of Palestine. Protesting this move, five Arab countries—Egypt, Iraq, Jordan, Lebanon, and Syria—attacked Israel. The conflict ended with Israel gaining considerable territory. The 1956 Suez Crisis began after Egypt nationalized the Suez Canal. A French, British, and Israeli coalition attacked Egypt and occupied the canal zone but soon withdrew under international pressure. In the Six-Day War of 1967, Israel attacked Egypt, Jordan, and Syria. The war ended with Israel occupying substantial amounts of Arab territory. An undeclared war of attrition (1969–70) was fought between Egypt and Israel along the Suez Canal and ended with the help of international diplomacy. Egypt and Syria attacked Israel in 1973 (the Yom Kippur War), but, despite early Arab success, the conflict ended inconclusively. In 1979 Egypt made peace with Israel. In 1982 Israel invaded Lebanon in order to expel Palestinian guerrillas based there. Israel withdrew from most of Lebanon by 1985 but maintained a narrow buffer zone inside that country until 2000.

Aztec

Nahuatl-speaking people who in the 15th and early 16th centuries ruled a large empire in what is now central and southern Mexico. They may have originated on the northern Mexican plateau before migrating to their later location. Their migration may have been linked to the collapse of the Toltec civilization. The Aztec empire, which at its height comprised roughly five to six million people spread over some 80,000 sq mi (200,000 sq km), was made possible by their successful agricultural methods, including intensive cultivation, irrigation, and reclamation of wetlands. The Aztec state was despotic, militaristic, and sharply stratified according to class and caste. Aztec religion was syncretic, drawing especially on the beliefs of the Maya. The Aztec practiced human sacrifice, an activity that sometimes reached mass proportions. The empire came to an end when the Spanish conquistador Hernán Cortés took the emperor Montezuma II prisoner and conquered the great city Tenochtitlán (modern Mexico City).

Black Death

Fierce and widespread outbreak of plague, probably bubonic and pneumonic, that ravaged Europe during the 14th century. The epidemic originated in Asia and was transmitted to Europeans in 1347 when a Turkic army besieging a Genoese trading post in the Crimea catapulted plague-infested corpses into the town. It spread from the Mediterranean ports and ravaged all of Europe between 1347 and 1351. Renewed outbreaks occurred in 1361–63, 1369–71, 1374–75, 1390, and 1400. Towns and cities were more heavily hit than the countryside, and whole communities were sometimes destroyed. Much of Europe's economy was devastated. About one-third of the European population, or a total of 25 million people, died in the Black Death.

Caesar, (Gaius) Julius

(Born July 12/13, 100 BC, Rome—died March 15, 44 BC) Celebrated Roman general, statesman, and dictator. A patrician by birth, he held the prominent posts of quaestor and praetor before becoming governor of Farther Spain in 61–60. He formed the First Triumvirate with Pompey and Marcus Licinius Crassus in 60 and was elected consul in 59 and proconsul in Gaul and Illyria in 58. After conducting the Gallic Wars, during which he invaded Britain (55, 54) and crossed the Rhine (55, 53), he was instructed by the Senate to lay down his command. Senate conservatives had grown wary of his increasing power, as had a suspicious Pompey. When the Senate would not command Pompey to give up his command simultaneously, Caesar, against regulations, led his forces across the Rubicon River (49) between Gaul and Italy, precipitating the Roman Civil War. Pompey fled from Italy but was pursued and defeated by Caesar in 48; he then fled to Egypt, where he was murdered. Having followed Pompey to Egypt, Caesar became lover to Cleopatra and supported her militarily. He defeated Pompey's last supporters in 46–45. He was named dictator for life by the Romans. He was offered the crown (44) but refused it, knowing the Romans' dislike for kings. He was in the midst of launching a series of political and social reforms when he was assassinated in the Senate House on the ides of March by conspirators led by Cassius and Brutus. His writings on the Gallic and Civil wars are considered models of classical historiography.

Capone, Al(phonse)

(Born Jan. 17, 1899, Brooklyn, N.Y., U.S.—died Jan. 25, 1947, Palm Island, Fla.) U.S. gangster. Quitting school after the sixth grade, he joined the

James Street Boys gang, led by Johnny Torrio. In a youthful fight in a brothel-saloon he was slashed across the left cheek, prompting the later nickname "Scarface." In 1919 he joined Torrio in Chicago to help run prostitution there. When Torrio retired (1925), Capone became the city's crime czar, running gambling, prostitution, and bootlegging rackets. He expanded his territory by killing his rivals, most famously in the St. Valentine's Day Massacre, in which members of the Bugs Moran gang were machine-gunned in a garage on Feb. 14, 1929. In 1931 Capone was convicted for income-tax evasion and sentenced to 11 years in prison; eventually he served time in the new Alcatraz prison. Granted an early release from prison in 1939, in part because he suffered from an advanced stage of syphilis, he died a powerless recluse at his Florida estate.

Charlemagne

Or Carolus Magnus ("Charles the Great") (born April 2, *c.* 742—died Jan. 28, 814, Aachen, Austrasia) King of the Franks (768–814) and emperor (800–14). The elder son of the Frankish king Pippin III (the Short), he ruled the Frankish kingdom jointly with his brother Carloman until the latter's death in 771. He then became sole king of the Franks and began a series of campaigns to conquer and Christianize neighboring kingdoms. He defeated and became king of the Lombards in northern Italy (774). His expedition against the Muslims in Spain failed (778), but he successfully annexed Bavaria (788). Charlemagne fought against the Saxons for many years, finally defeating and Christianizing them in 804. He subdued the Avars of the Danube and gained control of many of the Slav states. With the exception of the British Isles, southern Italy, and part of Spain, he united in one vast state almost all the Christian lands of Western Europe. His coronation as emperor at Rome on Christmas Day, 800, after restoring Leo III to the papacy, marks the revival of the empire in Latin Europe and was the forerunner of the Holy Roman Empire. Charlemagne established his capital at Aachen (Aix-la-Chapelle), where he built a magnificent palace. He invited many scholars and poets to assist him in the promotion of the religious and cultural revival known as the Carolingian renaissance. He also codified the laws and increased the use of writing in government and society. He was succeeded on his death by his son Louis the Pious, whom Charlemagne had crowned coemperor in 813.

Cleopatra

In full Cleopatra VII Thea Philopator (born 69 BC—died Aug. 30, 30 BC, Alexandria) Egyptian queen (of Macedonian descent), last ruler of the Ptolemaic dynasty in Egypt. Daughter of Ptolemy XII (b. 112?—d. 51 BC), she ruled with her two brother-husbands, Ptolemy XIII (r. 51–47) and Ptolemy XIV (r. 47–44), both of whom she had killed, and with her son, Ptolemy XV, or Caesarion (r. 44–30). She claimed the latter was fathered by Julius Caesar, who had become her lover after entering Egypt in 48 BC in pursuit of Pompey. She

Cleopatra, detail of a bas relief, c. 69–30 BC; in the Temple of Hathor, Dandarah, Egypt

was with Caesar in Rome when he was assassinated (44), after which she returned to Egypt to install her son on the throne. She lured Mark Antony, Caesar's heir apparent, into marriage (36), inviting the wrath of Octavian (later Augustus), whose sister Antony had earlier wed. She schemed against and antagonized Antony's friend Herod the Great, thereby losing his support. At a magnificent celebration in Alexandria after Antony's Parthian campaign (36–34), he bestowed Roman lands on his foreign wife and family. Octavian declared war on Cleopatra and Antony and defeated their joint forces at the Battle of Actium (31). Antony committed suicide, and, after a failed attempt to beguile Octavian, so did Cleopatra, possibly by means of an asp.

Cold War

Open yet restricted rivalry and hostility that developed after World War II between the U.S. and the Soviet Union and their respective allies. The U.S. and Britain, alarmed by the Soviet domination of Eastern Europe, feared the expansion of Soviet power and communism in Western Europe and elsewhere. The Soviets were determined to maintain control of Eastern Europe, in part to safeguard against a possible renewed threat from Germany. The Cold War (the term was first used by Bernard Baruch during a congressional debate in 1947) was waged mainly on political, economic, and propaganda fronts and had only limited recourse to weapons. It was at its peak in 1948–53 with the Berlin blockade and airlift, the formation of NATO, the victory of the communists in the

Chinese civil war, and the Korean War. Another intense stage occurred in 1958–62 with the Cuban missile crisis, which resulted in a weapons buildup by both sides. A period of détente in the 1970s was followed by renewed hostility. The Cold War ended with the collapse of the Soviet Union in 1991.

Columbus, Christopher

(Italian, Cristoforo Colombo; Spanish, Cristóbal Colón) (born Aug. 26–Oct. 31?, 1451, Genoa—died May 20, 1506, Valladolid, Spain) Genoese navigator and explorer whose transatlantic voyages opened the way for European exploration, exploitation, and colonization of the Americas. He began his career as a young seaman in the Portuguese merchant marines. In 1492 he obtained the sponsorship of the Spanish monarchs Ferdinand II and Isabella I for an attempt to reach Asia by sailing westward over what was presumed to be open sea. On his first voyage he set sail in August 1492 with three ships—the *Santa María*, the *Niña*, and the *Pinta*—and land was sighted in the Bahamas on October 12. He sailed along the northern coast of Hispaniola and returned to Spain in 1493. He made a second voyage (1493–96) with at least 17 ships and founded La Isabela (in what is now the Dominican Republic), the first European town in the New World. This voyage also began Spain's effort to promote Christian evangelization. On his third voyage (1498–1500) he reached South America and the Orinoco River delta. Allegations of his poor administration led to his being returned to Spain in chains. On his fourth voyage (1502–04) he returned to South America and sailed along the coasts of present-day Honduras and Panama. He was unable to attain his goals of nobility and great wealth. His character and achievements have long been debated, but scholars generally agree that he was an intrepid and brilliant navigator.

Crusades

Military expeditions, beginning in the late 11th century, that were organized by Western Christians in response to centuries of Muslim wars of expansion. Their objectives were to check the spread of Islam, to retake control of the Holy Land, to conquer pagan areas, and to recapture formerly Christian territories. The Crusades were seen by many of their participants as a means of redemption and expiation for sins. Between 1095, when the First Crusade was launched by Pope Urban II at the Council of Clermont, and 1291, when the Latin Christians were finally expelled from their kingdom in Syria, there were numerous expeditions to the Holy Land, to Spain, and even to the Baltic; the Crusades continued for several centuries after 1291, usually as military campaigns intended to halt or slow the advance of Muslim power or to conquer pagan areas. The Crusaders initially enjoyed success, founding a Christian state in Palestine and Syria, but the continued growth of Islamic states ultimately reversed those gains. By the 14th century the Ottoman Turks had established themselves in the Balkans and would penetrate deeper into Europe despite repeated efforts to repulse them. Crusades were also called against heretics (the Albigensian Crusade, 1209–29) and various rivals of the popes, and the Fourth Crusade (1202–04) was diverted against the Byzantine Empire. Crusading declined rapidly during the 16th century with the advent of the Protestant Reformation and the decline of papal authority. The Crusades constitute a controversial chapter in the history of Christianity, and their excesses have been the subject of centuries of historiography. Historians have also concentrated on the role the Crusades played in the expansion of medieval Europe and its institutions, and the notion of "crusading" has been transformed from a religio-military campaign into a modern metaphor for zealous and demanding struggles to advance the good ("crusades for") and to oppose perceived evil ("crusades against").

Cuban missile crisis

(1962) Major confrontation between the U.S. and the Soviet Union over the presence of Soviet nuclear missiles in Cuba. In October 1962 a U.S. spy plane detected a ballistic missile on a launching site in Cuba. Pres. John F. Kennedy placed a naval blockade around the island, and for several days the U.S. and the Soviet Union hovered on the brink of war. Soviet premier Nikita Khrushchev finally agreed to remove the missiles in return for a secret commitment from the U.S. to withdraw its own missiles from Turkey and to never invade Cuba. The incident increased tensions during the Cold War and fueled the nuclear arms race between the two countries.

Dracula

Epithet of a cruel 15th-century ruler and the name of the character created by Bram Stoker in his 1897 novel of the same name. A mesmerizing, ruthless vampire, the fictional Dracula captured the public imagination, especially following Bela Lugosi's elegant and chilling portrayal of Count Dracula in Tod Browning's 1931 horror film version. Stoker had named the character after Vlad III Tepes

Bela Lugosi with Frances Dade in *Dracula*

(1431–76), a ruler of Walachia, whose epithet was Dracula, meaning "Son of the Dragon" (his father was a military commander and a member of a chivalric order called "Order of the Dragon"). Vlad was said to have put to death 20,000 men, women, and children by impaling them upright on stakes. The Dracula character became a stock figure in the horror repertoire, portrayed with varying degrees of sympathy and repulsion.

French Revolution

Movement that shook France between 1787 and 1799, reaching its first climax in 1789, and ending the ancien régime. Causes included the loss of peasant support for the feudal system, broad acceptance of the reformist writings of the philosophes, an expanding bourgeoisie that was excluded from political power, a fiscal crisis worsened by participation in the American Revolution, and crop failures in 1788. The efforts of the regime in 1787 to increase taxes levied on the privileged classes initiated a crisis. In response, Louis XVI convened the Estates-General, made up of clergy, nobility, and the Third Estate (commoners), in 1789. Trying to pass reforms, it swore the Tennis Court Oath not to disperse until France had a new constitution. The king grudgingly concurred in the formation of the National Assembly, but rumors of an "aristocratic conspiracy" led to the Great Fear of July 1789, and Parisians seized the Bastille on July 14. The assembly drafted a new constitution that introduced the Declaration of the Rights of Man and of the Citizen, proclaiming liberty, equality, and fraternity. The Constitution of 1791 also established a short-lived constitutional monarchy. The assembly nationalized church lands to pay off the public debt and reorganized the church. The king tried to flee the country but was apprehended at Varennes. France, newly nationalistic, declared war on Austria and Prussia in 1792, beginning the French Revolutionary Wars. Revolutionaries imprisoned the royal family and massacred nobles and clergy at the Tuileries in 1792. A new assembly, the National Convention—divided between Girondins and the extremist Montagnards—abolished the monarchy and established the First Republic in September 1792. Louis XVI was judged by the National Convention and executed for treason on Jan. 21, 1793. The Montagnards seized power and adopted radical economic and social policies that provoked violent reactions, including the Wars of the Vendée and citizen revolts. Opposition was broken by the Reign of Terror. Military victories in 1794 brought a change in the public mood, and Maximilien Robespierre was overthrown in the Convention on 9 Thermidor, year II (in 1794 in the French republican calendar), and executed the next day. Royalists tried to seize power in Paris but were crushed by Napoleon on 13 Vendémaire, year IV (in 1795). A new constitution placed executive power in a Directory of five members. The war and schisms in the Directory led to disputes that were settled by coups d'état, chiefly those of 18 Fructidor, Year V (in 1797), and 18–19 Brumaire, Year VIII (in 1799), in which Napoleon abolished the Directory and declared himself leader of France.

Genghis Khan

Or Chinggis Khan. Orig. Temüjin (born 1162, near Lake Baikal, Mongolia—died Aug. 18, 1227) Mongolian warrior-ruler who consolidated nomadic tribes into a unified Mongolia and whose troops fought from China's Pacific coast to Europe's Adriatic Sea, creating the basis for one of the greatest continental empires of all time. The leader of a destitute clan, Temüjin fought various rival clans and formed a Mongol confederacy, which in 1206 acknowledged him as Genghis Khan ("Universal Ruler"). By that year the united Mongols were ready to move out beyond the steppe. He adapted his method of warfare, moving from depending solely on cavalry to using sieges, catapults, ladders, and other equipment and techniques suitable for the capture and destruction of cities. In less than 10 years he took over most of Juchen-controlled China; he then destroyed the Muslim Khwārezm-Shah dynasty while his generals raided Iran and Russia. He is infamous for slaughtering the entire populations of cities and destroying fields and irrigation systems but admired for his military brilliance and ability to learn. He died on a military campaign, and the empire was divided among his sons and grandsons.

Eight percent of the men in Asia and Europe today have the genetic calling cards of Genghis Khan (my mother was a Kahn—k-a-h-n—so I wonder how far his lineage might have gone); he may have just been trying to make up for depopulating large swaths of Asia, 20 million in China alone. By the time the dust settled, the Mongol empire dominated 100 million people over 14 million square miles, from Peking to Poland. So what kind of guy was he? A man capable of experiencing great joy:

> The greatest joy a man can know is to conquer his enemies and drive them before him. To ride their horses and take away their possessions. To see the faces of those who were dear to them bedewed with tears, and to clasp their wives and daughters in his arms.

Bedewed shows a poetic touch. Anybody who says he was not the greatest conqueror in the world can take it up with him. And, generally, if you didn't resist, you were okay with Genghis Khan. If you resisted—even if only sometimes—he pretty much evened the score. I'm talking ethnic groups being removed from the human record type of even. Genghis Khan, the administrator, did allow a certain amount of autonomy in the provinces, but if the Persians hadn't really ticked him off, Iran would be a lot bigger now. They even say that in his later years he was fiddling with a form of governance that would allow for some human rights in his Great Yassa, or code, but before he could implement it, he fell off his horse in Outer Tangut in 1227. They brought him back to Mongolia for secret burial, diverting a river over his grave because this was one guy you didn't want to disturb.—M.F.

Geronimo

(Born June 1829, No-Doyohn Canyon, Mex.—died Feb. 17, 1909, Fort Sill, Okla., U.S.) Chiricahua Apache leader. In the 1870s Geronimo led a revolt of 4,000 Apaches who had been forcibly removed by U.S. authorities to a barren reservation in east-central Arizona. Years of turmoil and bloodshed followed; Geronimo finally surrendered in 1884, only to escape with a band of followers. On a false promise of safe return to Arizona, Geronimo was arrested (1886) and put to hard labor. He was later placed on a reservation at Fort Sill, Okla.; there he dictated his autobiography, *Geronimo: His Own Story.*

gold rush

Rapid influx of fortune seekers to the site of newly discovered gold deposits. In North America, the first major gold strike occurred in

California in 1848, when John Marshall, a carpenter building a sawmill for John Sutter, found gold. Within a year about 80,000 "forty-niners" (as the fortune seekers of 1849 were called) had flocked to the California gold fields, and 250,000 had arrived by 1853. Some mining camps grew into permanent settlements, and the demand for food, housing, and supplies propelled the new state's economy. As gold became more difficult to extract, companies and mechanical mining methods replaced individual prospectors. Smaller gold rushes occurred throughout the second half of the 19th century in Colorado, Nevada, Idaho, Montana, South Dakota, Arizona, and Alaska, resulting in the rapid settlement of many areas; where gold veins proved small, the settlements later became ghost towns. Major gold rushes also occurred in Australia (1851), South Africa (1886), and Canada (1896).

Great Depression

Longest and most severe economic depression ever experienced by the Western world. It began in the U.S. soon after the New York Stock Market Crash of 1929 and lasted until about 1939. By late 1932 stock values had dropped to about 20 percent of their previous value, and by 1933, 11,000 of the U.S.'s 25,000 banks had failed. These and other conditions, worsened by monetary policy mistakes and adherence to the gold standard, led to much-reduced levels of demand and hence of production, resulting in high unemployment (by 1932, 25–30 percent). Because the U.S. was the major creditor and financier of postwar Europe, the U.S. financial breakdown precipitated economic failures around the world, especially in Germany and Britain. Isolationism spread as nations sought to protect domestic production by imposing tariffs and quotas, ultimately reducing the value of international trade by more than half by 1932. The Great Depression contributed to political upheaval. It led to the election of U.S. Pres. Franklin Roosevelt, who introduced major changes in the structure of the U.S. economy through his New Deal. The Depression also advanced Adolf Hitler's rise to power in Germany in 1933 and fomented political extremism in other countries. Before the Great Depression, governments relied on impersonal market forces to achieve economic correction; afterward, government action came to assume a principal role in ensuring economic stability.

Hammurabi

(Flourished 18th century BC) Sixth and best-known ruler of the 1st (Amorite) dynasty of Babylon. His kingdom was one of several prominent realms in Babylonia. His desire to control the Euphrates River led him to conquer the cities of Uruk (Erech) and Isin in 1787 BC, but he gave up on further military campaigns in that area, turning instead to the northwest and the east in 1784. Twenty

Hammurabi, limestone relief; in the British Museum

years of peace followed, and then 14 years of almost continuous warfare that resulted in a unified Mesopotamia. He used control of waterways (damming them to deny his enemies water or to create a flood by releasing them) to defeat his enemies. He also engaged in building and restoring temples, city walls, public buildings, and canals. His laws, collected in the Code of Hammurabi, demonstrated his desire to be a just ruler.

Hannibal

(Born 247 BC, North Africa—died c.183–181 BC, Libyssa, Bithynia) Carthaginian general, one of the great military leaders of antiquity. Taken to Spain by his father, the Carthaginian general Hamilcar Barca (d. 229/228 BC), he was sworn to eternal enmity with Rome. After the death of his father and brother-in-law, he took charge of Carthage's army in Spain (221). He secured Spain, then crossed the Ebro River into Roman territory and entered Gaul. He marched over the Alps into Italy; encumbered by elephants and horses, he was beset by Gallic tribes, harsh winter weather, and defection of his Spanish troops. He defeated Gaius Flaminius but was severely harassed by Quintus Fabius Maximus Cunctator. In 216 he won the Battle of Cannae. In 203 he left for northern Africa to help Carthage fend off Scipio Africanus the Elder's forces. He lost decisively to Scipio's ally, Masinissa, at the Battle of Zama but escaped. He headed the Carthaginian government (c. 202–195); forced to flee, he sought refuge with Antiochus III, whose fleet he commanded against Rome, with disastrous results. After the Battle of Magnesia (190) the Romans demanded he be handed over; he eluded them until, seeing no escape, he took poison.

Hammurabi had a code, which is more than you can say for a lot of Mesopotamian despots. The basis for what later came to be known as an-eye-for-an-eye jurisprudence, some of the ordinances today seem a bit harsh. Anyone stealing the property of the court or temple, even so much as a stylus, would be put to death, as would he who bought it off him. Anyone buying a slave, ox, sheep, ass, or anything from the son of another man without doing the paper (actually clay-tablet) work, would be put to death. Finders keepers? No, a death sentence for any finder foolish enough to try to pawn the item. The building code was stiff, too: if a builder cut corners on a house and it caved in on the client, he would be put to death. A barber caught changing brands on a slave (barbers were full service in those days)—death. Physicians were shown some mercy suitable to their place in society; if a doctor operated on and killed a free man he merely had his hands cut off, although if it were a slave he was liable for replacement value only. A man who knocked the teeth out of his equal got his teeth knocked out, although poking somebody upscale was, well, to be avoided.—M.F.

Hatshepsut

Queen of Egypt (*c.* 1472–58 BC). Daughter of Thutmose I and wife of Thutmose II, she first acted as regent for her stepson, Thutmose III, but soon ordered herself crowned as pharaoh. She attained unprecedented power, adopting the titles and regalia of a pharaoh, complete with a false beard. She devoted much of the profit from expanded trade and tribute to an extensive building program, most notably to a splendid temple at Dayr al-Bahri. Thutmose III, who had become head of the army, succeeded her; whether she died naturally or was deposed and killed is uncertain.

Hatshepsut, limestone sculpture, c. 1485 BC; in the Metropolitan Museum of Art, New York City

Hiroshima

City (pop., 2002 est.: 1,113,786), southwestern
Honshu, Japan. Founded as a castle town in the
16th century, it was from 1868 a military center. In
1945 it became the first city ever to be struck by an
atomic bomb, dropped by the U.S. in the last days
of World War II. Rebuilding began in 1950, and
Hiroshima is now the largest industrial city in the
region. It has become a spiritual center of the
peace movement to ban nuclear weapons; Peace
Memorial Park is dedicated to those killed by the
bomb, and Atomic Bomb Dome is the ruin of the
only building to survive the blast.

Cenotaph in Peace
Memorial Park,
Hiroshima, Japan;
Atomic Bomb Dome is
visible through the arch

Hitler, Adolf

(Born April 20, 1889, Braunau am Inn, Austria—died April 30, 1945, Berlin,
Ger.) Dictator of Nazi Germany (1933–45). As a soldier in the German
army in World War I, he was wounded and gassed. In 1920 he became
head of propaganda for the renamed National Socialists (Nazi Party) and
in 1921 party leader. He set out to create a mass movement, using unre-
lenting propaganda. The party's rapid growth climaxed in the Beer Hall
Putsch (1923), for which he served nine months in prison; there he started
to write his virulent autobiography, *Mein Kampf.* Believing that "races"
were unequal and that this was part of the natural order, he exalted the
"Aryan race" while propounding anti-Semitism, anticommunism, and
extreme German nationalism. The economic slump of 1929 facilitated
Hitler's rise to power. In the Reichstag elections of 1930 the Nazis became
the country's second largest party and in 1932 the largest. Hitler ran for
president in 1932 and lost but entered into intrigues to gain power, and in
1933 Paul von Hindenburg invited him to be chancellor. Adopting the title
of Führer ("Leader"), Hitler gained dictatorial powers through the
Enabling Act and suppressed opposition with assistance from Heinrich
Himmler and Joseph Goebbels. Hitler also began to enact anti-Jewish
measures, which culminated in the Holocaust. His aggressive foreign
policy led to the signing of the Munich Agreement with France, Britain,
and Italy, which permitted German annexation of Czechoslovakia's
Sudetenland. He became allied with Benito Mussolini in the Rome-Berlin

Axis. The German-Soviet Nonaggression Pact (1939) enabled him to invade Poland, precipitating World War II. As defeat grew imminent in 1945, he married Eva Braun in an underground bunker in Berlin, and the next day they committed suicide.

Holocaust

(Hebrew; Sho'ah) Systematic state-sponsored killing of Jews and others by Nazi Germany and its collaborators during World War II. Fueled by anti-Semitism, the Nazi persecution of Jews began soon after Adolf Hitler became chancellor of Germany in 1933 with a boycott of Jewish businesses and the dismissal of Jewish civil servants. Under the Nürnberg Laws (1935), Jews lost their citizenship. About 7,500 Jewish businesses were gutted and some 1,000 synagogues burned or damaged in the Kristallnacht pogrom in 1938, and thereafter Jews were imprisoned in concentration camps or forced into ghettos. German victories early in World War II (1939–45) brought most European Jews under the control of the Nazis and their satellites. As German armies moved into Poland, the Balkans, and the Soviet Union, special mobile killing units, the *Einsatzgruppen*, rounded up and killed Jews, Roma (Gypsies), communists, political leaders, and intellectuals. Other groups targeted by the Nazis included homosexuals and the mentally retarded, physically disabled, and emotionally disturbed. At the Wannsee Conference (1942), a "final solution" was formulated for the extermination of European Jewry, and thereafter Jews from all over Nazi-occupied Europe were systematically evacuated to concentration and extermination camps, where they were either killed or forced into slave labor. Underground resistance movements arose in several countries, and Jewish uprisings took place against overwhelming odds in the ghettos of Poland. Individuals such as Raoul Wallenberg saved thousands by their efforts; whether the Allied governments and the Vatican could have done more to aid Jews has long been a matter of controversy. By the end of the war, an estimated six million Jews and millions of others had been killed by Nazi Germany and its collaborators.

Industrial Revolution

Process of change from an agrarian, handicraft economy to one dominated by industry and machine manufacture. It began in England in the 18th century. Technological changes included the use of iron and steel, new energy sources, the invention of new machines that increased production (including the steam engine and the spinning jenny), the development of the factory system, and important developments in transportation and communication (including the railroad and the telegraph). The Industrial Revolution was largely confined to Britain from 1760 to 1830 and then spread to Belgium and France. Other nations lagged behind, but, once Germany, the U.S., and Japan achieved industrial power, they outstripped Britain's initial successes. Eastern European countries lagged into the 20th century, and not until the mid-20th century did the Industrial Revolution spread to such countries as China and India. Industrialization effected changes in economic, political, and social organization. These included a wider distribution of wealth and increased international trade; political changes resulting from the shift in economic power; sweeping social changes that included the rise of working-class movements, the development of managerial hierarchies to oversee the division of labor, and the emergence of new patterns of authority; and struggles against externalities such as industrial pollution and urban crowding.

Jamestown Colony

First permanent English settlement in North America. It was founded in May 1607 on a peninsula in the James River of Virginia. Named after King James I, Jamestown began cultivating tobacco and established the continent's first representative government (1619); the colony, its leader John Smith, and the Indian Pocahontas—who, according to lore, saved Smith's life—have been the subject of numerous novels, dramas, and films, many of them highly fanciful. When nearby Williamsburg replaced it as the capital of colonial Virginia in 1699, it fell into decline. By the mid-19th century, erosion had transformed the peninsula into Jamestown Island. In 1936 the site was incorporated into the Colonial National Historical Park.

Jefferson, Thomas

(Born April 13, 1743, Shadwell, Va., U.S.—died July 4, 1826, Monticello) Third president of the U.S. (1801–09). He was a planter and became a lawyer in 1767. While a member of the House of Burgesses (1769–75), he initiated the Virginia Committee of Correspondence (1773) with Richard Henry Lee and Patrick Henry. In 1774 he wrote the influential *A Summary View of the Rights of British America*, stating that the British Parliament had no authority to legislate for the colonies. A delegate to the Second Continental Congress, he was appointed to the committee to draft the Declaration of Independence and became its primary author. He was elected governor of Virginia (1779–81) but was unable to organize effective opposition when British forces invaded the colony (1780–81). Criticized for his conduct, he retired, vowing to remain a private citizen. Again a member of the Continental Congress (1783–85), he drafted the first of the Northwest Ordinances for dividing and settling the Northwest Territory. In 1785 he succeeded Benjamin Franklin as U.S. minister to France. Appointed the first secretary of state (1790–93) by George Washington, he soon became embroiled in a bitter conflict with Alexander Hamilton over the country's foreign policy and their opposing interpretations of the Constitution. Their divisions gave rise to political factions and eventually to political parties. Jefferson served as vice president (1797–1801) under John Adams but opposed Adams's signing of the Alien and Sedition Acts (1798); the Virginia and Kentucky Resolutions, adopted by the legislatures of those states in 1798 and 1799 as a protest against the Acts, were written by Jefferson and James Madison. In the presidential election of 1800 Jefferson and Aaron Burr received the same number of votes in the electoral college; the decision was thrown to the U.S. House of Representatives, which chose Jefferson on the 36th ballot. As president, Jefferson attempted to reduce the powers of the embryonic federal government and to eliminate the national debt; he also dispensed with a great deal of the ceremony and formality that had attended the office of president to that time. In 1803 he oversaw the Louisiana Purchase, which doubled the land area of the country, and he authorized the Lewis and Clark Expedition. In an effort to force Britain and France to cease their molestation of U.S. merchant ships during the Napoleonic Wars, he signed the Embargo Act. In 1809 he retired to his plantation, Monticello, where he pursued his interests in science, philosophy, and architecture. He served as president of the American Philosophical Society (1797–1815), and in 1819 he founded and designed the University of Virginia. In 1812, after a long estrangement, he and Adams were reconciled and began a lengthy correspondence that illuminated their opposing political philosophies. They died within hours of each other on July 4, 1826, the 50th anniversary of the signing of the

Declaration of Independence. Though a lifelong slaveholder, Jefferson was an anomaly among the Virginia planter class for his support of gradual emancipation. In January 2000 the Thomas Jefferson Memorial Foundation accepted the conclusion, supported by DNA evidence, that Jefferson had fathered at least one child with Sally Hemings, one of his house slaves.

Joan of Arc, Saint

(French; Jeanne d'Arc) (born c. 1412, Domrémy, Bar, France—died May 30, 1431, Rouen; canonized May 16, 1920; feast day May 30) French military heroine. She was a peasant girl who from an early age believed she heard the voices of Sts. Michael, Catherine, and Margaret. When she was about 16, her voices began urging her to aid France's Dauphin (crown prince) and save France from the English attempt at conquest in the Hundred Years' War. Dressed in men's clothes, she visited the Dauphin and convinced him, his advisers, and the church authorities to support her. With her inspiring conviction, she rallied the French troops and raised the English siege of Orléans in 1429. She soon defeated the English again at Patay. The Dauphin was crowned king at Reims as Charles VII, with Joan beside him. Her siege of Paris was unsuccessful, and in 1430 she was captured by the Burgundians and sold to the English. Abandoned by Charles, she was turned over to the ecclesiastical court at Rouen, controlled by French clerics who supported the English, and tried for witchcraft and heresy (1431). She fiercely defended herself but finally recanted and was sentenced to life imprisonment; when she again asserted that she had been divinely inspired, she was burned at the stake. She was not canonized until 1920.

Jurassic Period

Interval of geologic time, 206–144 million years ago, that is one of the three major divisions of the Mesozoic Era, preceded by the Triassic Period and followed by the Cretaceous. During the Jurassic, Pangea began to break up into the present-day continents. Marine invertebrates flourished, and large reptiles dominated many marine habitats. On land, ferns, mosses, cycads, and conifers thrived, some developing flowerlike structures in place of cones. The dinosaurs rose to supremacy on land, and by the end of the Jurassic the largest species had evolved. Archaeopteryx, the first primitive bird, appeared before the end of the period. Early mammals, tiny shrewlike creatures that appeared near the close of the preceding Triassic, managed to survive and evolve.

Kennedy, John F(itzgerald)

(Born May 29, 1917, Brookline, Mass., U.S.— died Nov. 22, 1963, Dallas, Texas) 35th president of the U.S. (1961–63). The son of Joseph P. Kennedy, he graduated from Harvard University in 1940 and joined the navy the following year. He commanded a patrol torpedo (PT) boat in World War II and was gravely injured in an attack by a Japanese destroyer; he was later decorated for heroism. Elected to the U.S. House of Representatives in 1946 and the U.S. Senate in 1952, he supported social-welfare legislation and became increasingly committed to civil rights; in foreign affairs, he supported the Cold War policies of the Truman administration. In 1960 he won the Democratic nomination for president, beating out Lyndon B. Johnson, who became his running mate. In his acceptance speech Kennedy declared, "We stand on the edge of a New Frontier"; thereafter the phrase "New Frontier" was associated with his programs. After a vigorous campaign managed by his brother Robert F. Kennedy and aided financially by his father, he narrowly defeated the Republican candidate, Richard Nixon. He was the youngest person and the first Roman Catholic elected president. In his inaugural address he called on Americans to "ask not what your country can do for you, ask what you can do for your country." His legislative program, including massive income-tax cuts and a sweeping civil-rights measure, received little support in the Congress, though he did win approval of the Peace Corps and the Alliance for Progress. In 1961 he committed the U.S. to land a man on the Moon by the end of the decade. In foreign affairs he approved a plan drawn up during the Eisenhower administration to land an invasion force of Cuban exiles on their homeland, but the Bay of Pigs invasion (1961) was a fiasco. Determined to combat the spread of communism in Asia, he sent military advisers and other assistance to

John F. Kennedy, 1961

South Vietnam. During the Cuban missile crisis (1962) he imposed a naval blockade on Cuba and demanded that the Soviet Union remove its nuclear missiles from the island. In 1963 he successfully concluded the Nuclear Test-Ban Treaty with Britain and the Soviet Union. In November 1963, while riding in a motorcade in Dallas, he was assassinated by a sniper, allegedly Lee Harvey Oswald. The killing is considered the most notorious political murder of the 20th century. Kennedy's youth, energy, and charming family brought him world adulation and sparked the idealism of a generation, for whom the Kennedy White House became known as "Camelot." Revelations about his powerful family and his personal life, especially concerning his extramarital affairs, tainted his image in later years.

Korean War

(1950–53) Conflict arising after the post–World War II division of Korea, at latitude 38° N, into North Korea and South Korea. At the end of World War II, Soviet forces accepted the surrender of Japanese forces north of that line, as U.S. forces accepted Japanese surrender south of it. Negotiations failed to reunify the two halves, the northern half being a Soviet client state and the southern half being backed by the U.S. In 1950 North Korea invaded South Korea, and U.S. Pres. Harry Truman ordered troops to assist South Korea. The UN Security Council, minus the absent Soviet delegate, passed a resolution calling for the assistance of all UN members in halting the invasion. At first North Korean troops drove the South Korean and U.S. forces down to the southern tip of the Korean peninsula, but a brilliant amphibious landing at Inch'on, conceived by Gen. Douglas MacArthur, turned the tide in favor of the UN troops, who advanced near the border of North Korea and China. The Chinese then entered the war and drove the UN forces back south; the front line stabilized at the 38th parallel. MacArthur insisted on voicing his objections to U.S. war aims in a public manner and was relieved of his command by Truman. U.S. Pres. Dwight D. Eisenhower participated in the conclusion of an armistice that accepted the front line as the de facto boundary between the two Koreas. The war resulted in the deaths of approximately two million Koreans, 600,000 Chinese, 37,000 Americans, and 3,000 Turks, Britons, and other nationals in the UN forces.

Lincoln, Abraham

(Born Feb. 12, 1809, near Hodgenville, Ky.,
U.S.—died April 15, 1865, Washington, D.C.)
16th president of the U.S. (1861–65). Born in a
Kentucky log cabin, he moved to Indiana in
1816 and to Illinois in 1830. After working as a
storekeeper, a rail-splitter, a postmaster, and a
surveyor, he enlisted as a volunteer in the
Black Hawk War (1832) and was elected
captain of his company. He taught himself law
and, having passed the bar examination,
began practicing in Springfield, Ill., in 1836.
As a successful circuit-riding lawyer from

Log cabin, Abraham Lincoln's
boyhood home, Knob Creek,
Kentucky, originally built early
19th century

1837, he was noted for his shrewdness, common sense, and honesty
(earning the nickname "Honest Abe"). From 1834 to 1840 he served in
the Illinois state legislature, and in 1847 he was elected as a Whig to the
U.S. House of Representatives. In 1856 he joined the Republican Party,
which nominated him as its candidate in the 1858 Senate election. In a
series of seven debates with Stephen A. Douglas (the Lincoln-Douglas
Debates), he argued against the extension of slavery into the territories.
Though morally opposed to slavery, he was not an abolitionist; indeed,
he attempted to rebut Douglas's charge that he was a dangerous radical
by reassuring audiences that he did not favor political equality for
blacks. Despite his loss in the election, the debates brought him national
attention. In the 1860 presidential election, he ran against Douglas again
and won by a large margin in the electoral college, though he received
only two-fifths of the popular vote. The South opposed his position on
slavery in the territories, and before his inauguration seven Southern
states had seceded from the Union. The ensuing American Civil War
completely consumed Lincoln's administration. He excelled as a wartime
leader, creating a high command for directing all the country's energies
and resources toward the war effort and combining statecraft and
overall command of the armies with what some have called military
genius. However, his abrogation of some civil liberties, especially the writ
of habeas corpus, and the closing of several newspapers by his generals
disturbed both Democrats and Republicans, including some members of
his own cabinet. To unite the North and influence foreign opinion, he
issued the Emancipation Proclamation (1863); his Gettysburg Address

(1863) further ennobled the war's purpose. The continuing war affected some Northerners' resolve and his reelection was not assured, but strategic battle victories turned the tide, and he easily defeated George B. McClellan in 1864. His platform included passage of the 13th Amendment outlawing slavery (ratified 1865). At his second inaugural, with victory in sight, he spoke of moderation in reconstructing the South and building a harmonious Union. On April 14, five days after the war ended, he was shot and mortally wounded by John Wilkes Booth.

Louisiana Purchase

Territory purchased by the U.S. from France in 1803 for $15 million. It extended from the Mississippi River to the Rocky Mountains and from the Gulf of Mexico to British America (Canada). In 1762 France had ceded Louisiana west of the Mississippi River to Spain, but Spain returned it to French control in 1800. Alarmed by this potential increase in French power, Pres. Thomas Jefferson threatened to form an alliance with Britain. Napoleon then sold the U.S. the entire Louisiana Territory, although its boundaries remained unclear; its northwestern and southwestern limits were not established until 1818–19. The purchase doubled the area of the U.S.

Magellan, Ferdinand

(Portuguese, Fernão de Magalhães; Spanish, Fernando de Magallanes) (born c. 1480, Sabrosa, or Porto?, Port.—died April 27, 1521, Mactan, Phil.) Portuguese navigator and explorer. Born to the nobility, Magellan from 1505 served in expeditions to the East Indies and Africa. Having twice asked King Manuel I for a higher rank and been refused, he went to Spain in 1517 and offered his services to King Charles I (later Emperor Charles V), proposing to sail west to the Moluccas (Spice Islands) to prove that they lay in Spanish rather than Portuguese territory. In 1519 he left Sevilla with five ships and 270 men. He sailed around South America, quelling a mutiny on the way, and discovered the Strait of Magellan. With three ships left, Magellan crossed the "Sea of the South," which he later called the Pacific Ocean because of their calm crossing. He was killed by natives in the Philippines, but two of his ships reached the Moluccas, and one, the *Victoria*, commanded by Juan de Elcano

Ferdinand Magellan was first to circumnavigate the world—although with an asterisk after his record since he was dead for the last third of the trip—foolishly visiting the Philippines in the off-season. There were hard feelings about the whole trip; Magellan, who rubbed people the wrong way, added to those feelings by switching flags, Portuguese for Spanish, and thriving afterward. It certainly didn't hurt his career that he became a naturalized Spaniard and confidante of Charles I, a.k.a. the fledgling Holy Roman Emperor Charles V. In Seville he fell in with the anti-Columbus crowd, only too happy to put up the money to make the darling of Isabella look bad. Magellan's selling point was his proclamation that a funnel from the Spice Islands to Spain—and, by extension, to Magellan—existed in South America. The five ships under Magellan's command leaving Seville on August 10, 1519, were pursued by a Portuguese fleet hoping to find the funnel; Portugal's King Manuel couldn't take a joke. Eluding the naval detachment, Magellan reached the Cape Verde Islands and set sail for Brazil, having to gaze at Rio from the harbor through spyglasses, as their arch enemies had already landed on that property. Sailing down the South American coast, the fleet probed for a way through, finally finding one at Rio de la Plata in January 1520, after mutiny, one execution, several maroonings, and one wreck. Another ship's crew balked and decided to repatriate; on November 28 the three remaining ships wended their 373-mile way through the fledgling Strait of Magellan to a rather large body of water that was calm that day or never would have been called *La Mar Pacifico*, the Pacific Ocean.—M.F.

(1476?–1526), continued west to Spain, accomplishing the first circumnavigation of the world in 1522.

Magna Carta

(Latin; "Great Charter") Document guaranteeing English political liberties, drafted at Runnymede, a meadow by the Thames, and signed by King John in 1215 under pressure from his rebellious barons. Resentful of the king's high taxes and aware of his waning power, the barons were encouraged by the archbishop of Canterbury, Stephen Langton, to demand a solemn grant of their rights. Among the charter's provisions were clauses providing for a free church, reforming law and justice, and controlling the behavior of royal officials. It was reissued with alterations in 1216, 1217, and 1225. Though it reflects the feudal order rather than democracy, the Magna Carta is traditionally regarded as the foundation of British constitutionalism.

Manhattan Project

(1942–45) U.S. government research project that produced the first atomic bomb. In 1939 U.S. scientists urged Pres. Franklin D. Roosevelt to establish a program to study the potential military use of fission, and $6,000 was appropriated. By 1942 the project was code-named Manhattan, after the site of Columbia University, where much of the early research was done. Research also was carried out at the University of California and the University of Chicago. In 1943 a laboratory to construct the bomb was established at Los Alamos, N.M., and staffed by scientists headed by J. Robert Oppenheimer. Production

First atomic bomb test, near Alamogordo, New Mexico, July 16, 1945

also was carried out at Oak Ridge, Tenn., and Hanford, Wash. The first bomb was exploded in a test at Alamogordo air base in southern New Mexico. By its end the project had cost some $2 billion and had involved 125,000 people.

Mao Zedong

Or Mao Tse-tung (born Dec. 26, 1893, Shaoshan, Hunan province, China—died Sept. 9, 1976, Beijing) Chinese Marxist theorist, soldier, and statesman who led China's communist revolution and served as chairman of the People's Republic of China (1949–59) and chairman of the Chinese Communist Party (CCP; 1931–76). The son of a peasant, Mao joined the revolutionary army that overthrew the Qing dynasty but, after six months as a soldier, left to acquire more education. At Beijing University he met Li Dazhao and Chen Duxiu, founders of the CCP, and in 1921 he committed himself to Marxism. At that time, Marxist thought held that revolution lay in the hands of urban workers, but in 1925 Mao concluded that in China it was the peasantry, not the urban proletariat, that had to be mobilized. He became chairman of a Chinese Soviet Republic formed in rural Jiangxi province; its Red Army withstood repeated attacks from Chiang Kai-shek's Nationalist army but at last undertook the Long March to a more secure position in northwestern China. There Mao became the undisputed head of the CCP. Guerrilla warfare tactics, appeals to the local population's nationalist sentiments, and Mao's agrarian policies gained the party military advantages against their Nationalist and Japanese enemies and broad support among the peasantry. Mao's agrarian Marxism differed from the Soviet model, but, when the communists succeeded in taking power in China in 1949, the Soviet Union agreed to provide the new state with technical assistance. However, Mao's Great Leap Forward and his criticism of "new bourgeois elements" in the Soviet Union and China alienated the Soviet Union irrevocably; Soviet aid was withdrawn in 1960. Mao followed the failed Great Leap Forward with the Cultural Revolution, also considered to have been a disastrous mistake. After Mao's death, Deng Xiaoping introduced social and economic reforms that began reversing the policies put in place by Mao.

Mau Mau

Militant Kikuyu-led Nationalist movement of the 1950s in Kenya. The Mau Mau (the name's origin is uncertain) advocated violent resistance to British domination in Kenya. In response to actions by Mau Mau rebels, the British Kenya government banned the movement in 1950 and launched a series of military operations between 1952 and 1956. Some 11,000 Kikuyu, 100 Europeans, and 2,000 African loyalists were killed in the fighting; another 20,000 Kikuyu were put into detention camps. Despite their losses, Kikuyu resistance spearheaded the independence movement, and Jomo Kenyatta, jailed as a Mau Mau leader in 1953, became prime minister of independent Kenya in 1963. In 2003 the ban on the Mau Mau was lifted.

Maya

Group of Mesoamerican Indians who between AD 250 and 900 developed one of the Western Hemisphere's greatest civilizations. By AD 200 they had developed cities containing palaces, temples, plazas, and ball courts. They used stone tools to quarry the immense quantities of stone needed for those structures; their sculpture and relief carving were also highly developed. Mayan hieroglyphic writing survives in books and inscriptions. Mayan mathematics featured positional notation and the use of the zero; Mayan astronomy used an accurately determined solar year and precise tables of the positions of Venus and the Moon. Calendrical accuracy was important for the elaborate rituals and ceremonies of the Mayan religion, which was based on a pantheon of gods. Ritual bloodletting, torture, and human sacrifice were employed in an attempt to propitiate the gods, ensure fertility, and stave off cosmic chaos. At the height of its Classic period, Mayan civilization included more than 40 cities of 5,000–50,000 people. After 900 the civilization declined rapidly for unknown reasons. Descendants of the Maya are now subsistence farmers in southern Mexico and Guatemala.

Mesopotamia

Region between the Tigris and Euphrates rivers in the Middle East, constituting the greater part of modern Iraq. The region's location and fertility gave rise to settlements from *c.* 10,000 BC, and it became the cradle of some of the world's earliest civilizations and the birthplace of writing. It was first settled by the Sumerians, who were succeeded by the Akkadians and later by the Babylonians. Successive peoples came to dominate the region until the rise of the Persian Achaemenian dynasty in the 6th century BC. The Achaemenids were overthrown by Alexander the Great in the early 4th century BC, and Mesopotamia was ruled by the Seleucid dynasty from *c.* 312 BC until the mid-2nd century BC, when it became part of the Parthian empire. In the 7th century AD the region was conquered by Muslim Arabs. The region's importance declined after the Mongol invasion in 1258. Rule by the Ottoman Empire over most of the region began in the 16th century. The area became a British mandate in 1920; the following year Iraq was established there.

Napoleon

(French; Napoléon Bonaparte). Orig. (Italian; Napoleone Buonaparte) (born Aug. 15, 1769, Ajaccio, Corsica—died May 5, 1821, St. Helena Island) French general and emperor (1804–15). Born to parents of Italian ancestry, he was educated in France and became an army officer in 1785. He fought in the French Revolutionary Wars and was promoted to brigadier general in 1793. After victories against the Austrians in northern Italy, he negotiated the Treaty of Campo Formio (1797). He attempted to conquer Egypt (1798–99) but was defeated by the British under Horatio Nelson in the Battle of the Nile. The Coup of 18–19 Brumaire brought him to power in 1799, and he installed a military dictatorship, with himself as First Consul. He introduced numerous reforms in government, including the Napoleonic Code, and reconstructed the French education system. He negotiated the Concordat of 1801 with the pope. After victory against the Austrians at the Battle of Marengo (1800), he embarked on the Napoleonic Wars. The formation of coalitions of European countries against him led Napoleon to declare France a hereditary empire and to crown himself emperor in 1804. He won his greatest military victory at the Battle of Austerlitz against Austria and Russia in 1805. He defeated Prussia at the Battles of Jena and Auerstedt (1806) and Russia at the Battle of Friedland (1807). He then imposed the Treaty of Tilsit on Russia, ending the fourth coalition of countries against France. Despite his loss to Britain at the Battle of Trafalgar, he sought to weaken British commerce and established the Continental System of port blockades. He consolidated his European empire until 1810 but became embroiled in the Peninsular War (1808–14). He led the French army into Austria and defeated the Austrians at the Battle of Wagram (1809), signing the Treaty of Vienna. To enforce the Treaty of Tilsit, he led an army of about 600,000 into Russia in 1812, winning the Battle of Borodino, but was forced to retreat from Moscow with disastrous losses. His army greatly weakened, he was met by a strong coalition of allied powers, who defeated him at the Battle of Leipzig (1813). After Paris was taken by the allied coalition, Napoleon was forced to abdicate in 1814 and was exiled to the island of Elba. In 1815 he mustered a force and returned to France to reestablish himself as emperor for the Hundred Days, but he was decisively defeated at the Battle of Waterloo. He was sent into exile on the remote island of St. Helena, where he died six years later. One of the most celebrated figures in history, Napoleon revolutionized military organization and training and brought about reforms that permanently influenced civil institutions in France and throughout Europe.

Normandy Campaign

Allied invasion of northern Europe in World War II that began on June 6, 1944, with the largest amphibious landing in history in Normandy, France. Also called Operation Overlord, the landing transported 156,000 U.S., British, and Canadian troops across the English Channel in more than 5,000 ships and 10,000 planes. Commanded by Gen. Dwight D. Eisenhower, the Allied forces landed at five beaches on the Normandy coast and soon established lodgement areas, despite stiff German resistance and heavy losses at the code-named Omaha Beach and Juno Beach. Allied air supremacy prevented rapid German reinforcements, and discord between Adolf Hitler and his generals stalled crucial counterattacks. Though delayed by heavy fighting near Cherbourg and around Caen, the Allied ground troops broke out of the beachheads in mid-July and began a rapid advance across northern France. The Normandy Campaign is traditionally considered to have concluded with the liberation of Paris on Aug. 25, 1944.

Pearl Harbor attack

(Dec. 7, 1941) Surprise aerial attack by the Japanese on the U.S. naval base at Pearl Harbor on Oahu island, Hawaii, that precipitated U.S. entry into World War II. In the decade preceding the attack, U.S.-Japanese relations steadily worsened, especially after Japan entered into an alliance with the Axis powers (Germany and Italy) in 1940, and by late 1941 the U.S. had severed practically all commercial and financial relations with Japan. On November 26 a Japanese fleet sailed to a point some 275 mi (440 km) north of Hawaii, and from there about 360 planes were launched. The first dive-bomber appeared over Pearl Harbor at 7:55 AM (local time) and was followed by waves of torpedo planes, bombers, and fighters. Due to lax reconnaissance and the fact that many vessels were undermanned since it was a Sunday morning, the base was unable to mount an effective defense. The *Arizona* was completely destroyed; the *Oklahoma* capsized; the *California*, *Nevada*, and *West Virginia* sank; more than 180 aircraft were destroyed; and numerous vessels were damaged. In addition, more than 2,300 military personnel were killed. The "date which will live in infamy," as U.S. Pres. Franklin Roosevelt termed it, unified the American public and swept away any earlier support of neutrality. On Dec. 8, 1941, Congress declared war on Japan.

Persian Gulf War, First

Or Gulf War (1990–91) International conflict triggered by Iraq's invasion of Kuwait in August 1990. Though justified by Iraqi leader Saddam

Hussein on grounds that Kuwait was historically part of Iraq, the invasion was presumed to be motivated by Iraq's desire to acquire Kuwait's rich oil fields and expand its power in the region. The United States, fearing Iraq's broader strategic intentions and acting under UN auspices, eventually formed a broad coalition, which included a number of Arab countries, and began massing troops in northern Saudi Arabia. When Iraq ignored a UN Security Council deadline for it to withdraw from Kuwait, the coalition began a large-scale air offensive (Jan. 16–17, 1991). Saddam responded by launching ballistic missiles against neighboring coalition states as well as Israel. A ground offensive by the coalition (February 24–28) quickly achieved victory. Estimates of Iraqi military deaths range up to 100,000; coalition forces lost about 300 troops. The war also caused extensive damage to the region's environment. The Iraqi regime subsequently faced widespread popular uprisings, which it brutally suppressed. A UN trade embargo remained in effect after the end of the conflict, pending Iraq's compliance with the terms of the armistice. The foremost term was that Iraq destroy its nuclear-, biological-, and chemical-weapons programs. The embargo continued into the 21st century and ceased only after the Second Persian Gulf War.

Persian Gulf War, Second

(2003) International conflict that took place between Iraq and a combined force of troops from the United States and Great Britain, with smaller contingents from several other countries. The trade embargo and weapons-inspection process that the UN imposed on Iraq following the First Persian Gulf War (1990–91) had partly fallen into abeyance by 2001. U.S. Pres. George W. Bush argued that the September 11 attacks on the U.S. in that same year highlighted the threat to U.S. security posed by hostile countries such as Iraq. Encouraged by Bush and British Prime Minister Tony Blair, the UN issued Security Council Resolution 1441 in November 2002, demanding that Iraq readmit weapons inspectors and comply with all previous resolutions. Although Iraqi did readmit inspectors, Bush and Blair declared in early 2003 (despite objections by many world leaders) that Iraq was continuing to hinder UN inspections and that it still retained proscribed weapons. On March 20, seeking no further UN resolutions, the U.S. and Britain (with token representation from other countries) launched a series of air attacks on Iraq, and a ground invasion followed. Iraqi military and paramilitary forces were rapidly defeated. Within a few more days, all major cities had fallen, and by May 1 major combat operations had been completed. Guerrilla assaults on occupying forces continued thereafter, hindering Iraq's recovery.

Pompeii

Ancient city, southern Italy, southeast of Naples. Founded in the 6th century BC (or earlier) by Oscan-speaking descendants of the Neolithic inhabitants of Campania, Pompeii came under Greek and Etruscan influence and then was occupied by the Samnites, an Italic tribe, in the late 5th century BC. The city was allied with Rome and colonized by 80 BC. It was damaged by an earthquake in AD 63 and was completely destroyed by the eruption of Mount Vesuvius in 79. Volcanic debris buried the town and protected the ruins for years. Archaeological excavations, begun in 1748, have uncovered much of the city, including forums, temples, baths, theaters, and hundreds of private homes.

Temple of Apollo, Pompeii, Italy, with Mount Vesuvius in the background

September 11 attacks

Series of airline hijackings and suicide bombings against U.S. targets perpetrated by 19 militants associated with the Islamic extremist group al-Qaeda. The attacks were planned well in advance; the militants—most of whom were from Saudi Arabia—traveled to the U.S. beforehand, where a number received commercial flight training. Working in small groups, the hijackers boarded four domestic airliners in groups of five (a 20th participant was alleged) on Sept. 11, 2001, and took control of the planes soon after takeoff. At 8:46 AM (local time), the terrorists piloted the first plane into the north tower of the World Trade Center in New York City. A second plane struck the south tower some 15 minutes later. Both structures erupted in flames and, badly damaged, soon collapsed. A third plane struck the southwest side of the Pentagon near Washington, D.C., at 9:40, and within the next hour the fourth crashed in Pennsylvania after its passengers—aware of events via cellular telephone—attempted to overpower their assailants. Some 2,750 people were killed in New York, 184 at the Pentagon, and 40 in Pennsylvania. All 19 terrorists died.

slavery

Forced labor for little or no pay under the threat of violence. Slavery has existed on nearly every continent, including Asia, Europe, Africa, and the Americas, and throughout most of recorded history. The ancient Greeks and Romans accepted the institution of slavery, as did the Mayas, Incas, Aztecs, and Chinese. Until European involvement in the trade, however, slavery was a private and domestic institution. Beginning in the 16th century, a more public and "racially" based type of slavery was established when Europeans began importing slaves from Africa to the New World. An estimated 11 million people were taken from Africa during the transatlantic slave trade. By the mid-19th century the slave population in the U.S. had risen to more than four million, although slave imports had been banned from 1809. Most of the Africans sent to the United States worked on cotton or rice plantations in the South, their status governed by slave codes. Almost 40 percent of captives transported from Africa to the Americas were taken to Brazil, where harsh conditions required the constant replenishing of slaves. Following the rise of abolitionism, Britain outlawed slavery in its colonies in 1833, and France did the same in 1848. During the American Civil War, slavery was abolished in the Confederacy by the Emancipation Proclamation (1863), which was decreed by Pres. Abraham Lincoln. Brazil was the last to abolish slavery, doing so in 1888. Official policy notwithstanding, slavery continues to exist in many parts of the world. Many contemporary slaves are women and children forced into prostitution or working at hard labor or in sweatshops. Debt bondage is common, affecting millions of people, and slaves are often traded for material goods.

Timbuktu

(French; Tombouctou) Town (pop., 1998: 32,000), Mali, on the southern edge of the Sahara near the Niger River. Founded c. AD 1100 by Tuareg nomads, it became an important post on the trans-Saharan caravan routes. After it was incorporated within the Mali empire, probably in the late 13th century, it became a center of Islamic culture (*c.* 1400–1600). It reached its apex as a commercial and cultural center under Songhai rule *c.* 1500 but declined rapidly after being conquered by Moroccan forces in the late 16th century. The French captured it in 1894. It became part of independent Mali in 1960. The city was designated a UNESCO World Heritage site in 1988.

Titanic

British luxury passenger liner that sank on April 15, 1912, en route to New York from Southampton, England, on its maiden voyage. More than 1,500 of its 2,200 passengers were lost. The largest and most

The *Titanic*

luxurious ship afloat, it had a double-bottomed hull divided into 16 watertight compartments. Because four of these could be flooded without endangering its buoyancy, it was considered unsinkable. Shortly before midnight on April 14, it collided with an iceberg southeast of Cape Race, Newfoundland; five compartments ruptured and the ship sank. As a result, new rules were drawn up requiring that the number of places in lifeboats equal the number of passengers (the *Titanic* had only 1,178 lifeboat places for 2,224 passengers) and that all ships maintain a 24-hour radio watch for distress signals (a ship less than 20 mi [32 km] away had not heard the *Titanic*'s distress signal because no one had been on duty). The International Ice Patrol was established to monitor icebergs in shipping lanes. In 1985 the wreck was found lying upright in two pieces at a depth of 13,000 ft (4,000 m) and was explored by American and French scientists using an unmanned submersible.

Trail of Tears

Forced migration of the Cherokee Indians in 1838–39. In 1835, when gold was discovered on Cherokee land in Georgia, a small minority of Cherokee ceded all tribal land east of the Mississippi for $5 million. The U.S. Supreme Court invalidated the deal, but the ruling was ignored by state officials and Pres. Andrew Jackson refused to enforce it. The subsequent eviction and 116-day forced march of thousands of Cherokee to Oklahoma was badly mismanaged, and inadequate food supply, frigid weather, and the cruelty of escorting troops led to the death of about 4,000 Cherokee.

Tutankhamen

Orig. Tutankhaten (flourished 14th century BC) Egyptian pharaoh (r. 1333–23 BC) of the 18th dynasty. When he took the throne at about age eight, he was advised to move back to Memphis from Akhetaton, the city of his father-in-law and predecessor, Akhenaton. During his reign the traditional religion was restored after the changes made by Akhenaton. Shortly before he died, while still in his teens, he sent troops to Syria to aid an ally against a group connected with the Hittites. Because his name was among those stricken from the royal lists during the 19th dynasty, his tomb's location was forgotten and his burial chamber was not opened until 1922, when it was discovered by Howard Carter (1873–1939). Its treasures made Tutankhamen perhaps the best-known of the pharaohs despite his early death and limited accomplishments.

Tutankhamen, gold funerary mask found in the king's tomb, 14th century BC; in the Egyptian Museum, Cairo

Ultra

Allied intelligence project that, in tapping the very highest-level communications among the armed forces of Germany and Japan, contributed to the Allied victory in World War II. In the early 1930s Polish cryptographers first broke the code of Germany's cipher machine Enigma. In 1939 they turned their information over to the Allies, and Britain established the Ultra project at Bletchley Park to intercept and decipher Enigma messages. The Japanese also had a modified version of the Enigma, known as "Purple" by the Americans, who were able to duplicate it well before Pearl Harbor. The intercept of signals helped Allied forces win the

Battle of Britain and the Battles of the Coral Sea and Midway and led to the destruction of a large part of the German forces following the Allied landing in Normandy.

Underground Railroad

Secret system in northern U.S. states to help escaping slaves. Its name derived from the need for secrecy and the railway terms used in the conduct of the system. Various routes in 14 states, called lines, provided safe stopping places (stations) for the leaders (conductors) and their charges (packages) while fleeing north, sometimes to Canada. The system developed in defiance of the Fugitive Slave Acts and was active mainly from 1830 to 1860. An estimated 40,000 to 100,000 slaves used the network. Assistance was provided mainly by free blacks, including Harriet Tubman, and philanthropists, church leaders, and abolitionists. Its existence aroused support for the antislavery cause and convinced Southerners that the North would never allow slavery to remain unchallenged.

Vietnam War

(1955–75) Protracted effort by South Vietnam and the U.S. to prevent North and South Vietnam from being united under communist leadership. After the First Indochina War, Vietnam was partitioned to separate the warring parties until free elections could be held in 1956. Ho Chi Minh's popular Viet Minh party from the north was expected to win the elections, which the leader in the south, Ngo Dinh Diem, refused to hold. In the war that ensued, fighters trained in the north (the Viet Cong) fought a guerrilla war against U.S.-supported South Vietnamese forces; North Vietnamese forces later joined the fighting. At the height of U.S. involvement, there were more than half a million U.S. military personnel in Vietnam. The Tet Offensive of 1968, in which the Viet Cong and North Vietnamese attacked 36 major South Vietnamese cities and towns, marked a turning point in the war. Many in the U.S. had come to oppose the war on moral and practical grounds, and Pres. Lyndon B. Johnson decided to shift to a policy of "de-escalation." Peace talks were begun in Paris. Between 1969 and 1973 U.S. troops were withdrawn from Vietnam, but the war was expanded to Cambodia and Laos in 1970. Peace talks, which had reached a stalemate in 1971, started again in 1973, producing

a cease-fire agreement. Fighting continued, and there were numerous
truce violations. In 1975 the North Vietnamese launched a full-scale
invasion of the south. The south surrendered later that year, and in 1976
the country was reunited as the Socialist Republic of Vietnam. More
than two million people (including 58,000 Americans) died over the
course of the war, about half of them civilians.

Viking

Or Norseman. Member of the Scandinavian seafaring warriors who
raided and colonized wide areas of Europe from the 9th to the 11th
century. Overpopulation at home, ease of conquest abroad, and their
extraordinary capacity as shipbuilders and sailors inspired their adventures. In 865 Vikings conquered East Anglia, Northumbria, and much of
Mercia. Wessex under Alfred the Great made a truce in 878 that led to
Danish control of much of England. Alfred defeated fresh Viking armies
(892–899), and his son continued his reconquest, recovering lands in
Mercia and East Anglia by 924; Viking Northumbria fell in 954. Renewed
raids in 980 brought England into the empire of Canute, and it remained
as such until 1042, when native rule was restored. The Vikings permanently affected English social structure, dialect, and names. In the
western seas, Vikings had settled in Iceland by 900, whence they traveled
to Greenland and North America. They invaded Ireland in 795, establishing kingdoms at Dublin, Limerick, and Waterford. The Battle of Clontarf
(1014) ended the threat of Scandinavian rule. France suffered periodic
Viking raids but no domination. In Russia Vikings briefly dominated

Novgorod, Kiev, and other centers, but they were quickly absorbed by the Slav population. As traders they made commercial treaties with the Byzantines (912, 945), and they served as mercenaries in Constantinople. Viking activity ended in the 11th century.

Villa, Pancho

Orig. Doroteo Arango (born June 5, 1878, Hacienda de Rio Grande, San Juan del Rio, Mex.—died June 20, 1923, Parral) Mexican guerrilla leader. He was orphaned at a young age and spent his adolescence as a fugitive, having murdered a landowner in revenge for an assault on his sister. An advocate of radical land reform, he joined Francisco Madero's uprising against Porfirio Díaz. His División del Norte joined forces with Venustiano Carranza to overthrow Victoriano Huerta (1854–1916), but he soon broke with the moderate Carranza and in 1914 was forced to flee with Emiliano Zapata. In 1916, to demonstrate that Carranza did not control the north, he raided a town in New Mexico. A U.S. force led by Gen. John Pershing was sent against him, but his popularity and knowledge of his home territory made him impossible to capture. He was granted a pardon after Carranza's overthrow (1920) but was assassinated three years later.

Washington, George

(Born Feb. 22, 1732, Westmoreland County, Va., U.S.—died Dec. 14, 1799, Mount Vernon) American Revolutionary commander-in-chief (1775–83) and first president of the U.S. (1789–97). Born into a wealthy family, he was educated privately. In 1752 he inherited his brother's estate at Mount Vernon, including 18 slaves; their ranks grew to 49 by 1760, though he disapproved of slavery. In the French and Indian War he was commissioned as colonel and sent to the Ohio Territory. After Edward Braddock was killed, Washington became commander of all Virginia forces, entrusted with defending the western frontier (1755–58). He resigned to manage his estate and in 1759 married Martha Dandridge Custis (1731–1802), a widow. He served in the House of Burgesses (1759–74), where he supported the colonists' cause, and later in the Continental Congress (1774–75). In 1775 he was elected to command the Continental Army. In the ensuing American Revolution, he proved a brilliant commander and a stalwart leader, despite several defeats. With the war effectively ended by the capture of Yorktown (1781), he resigned his commission and returned to Mount Vernon (1783). He was a delegate to and presiding officer of the Constitutional Convention (1787) and helped secure ratification of the Constitution in Virginia. When the state electors met to select the first president (1789), Washington was the unanimous choice. He formed a cabinet to balance sectional and political differences but was committed to a strong central government. Elected to a second term, he followed a middle course between the political factions that later became the Federalist Party and the Democratic Party. He proclaimed a policy of neutrality in the war between Britain and France (1793) and sent troops to suppress the Whiskey Rebellion (1794). He declined to serve a third term (thereby setting a 144-year precedent) and retired in 1797 after delivering his "Farewell Address." Known as the "father of his country," he is universally regarded as one of the greatest figures in U.S. history.

World War I

Or First World War (1914–18) International conflict between the Central Powers—Germany, Austria-Hungary, and Turkey—and the Allied Powers—mainly France, Britain, Russia, Italy, Japan, and (from 1917) the U.S. After a Serbian nationalist assassinated Archduke Francis Ferdinand of Austria in June 1914, a chain of threats and mobilizations resulted in a general war between the antagonists by mid-August. Prepared to fight a war on two fronts, based on the Schlieffen Plan, Germany first swept through neutral Belgium and invaded France. After the First Battle of the Marne (1914), the Allied defensive lines were stabilized in France, and a war of attrition began. Fought from lines of trenches and supported by modern artillery and machine guns, infantry assaults gained little ground and were enormously costly in human life, especially at the Battles of Verdun and the Somme (1916). On the Eastern Front, Russian forces initially drove deep into East Prussia and German Poland (1914) but were stopped by German and Austrian forces at the Battle of Tannenberg and forced back into Russia (1915). After several offensives, the Russian army failed to break through the German defensive lines. Russia's poor performance and enormous losses caused widespread domestic discontent that led to the Russian Revolution of 1917. Other fronts in the war included the Dardanelles Campaign, in which British and Dominion forces were unsuccessful against Turkey; the Caucasus and Iran (Persia), where Russia fought Turkey; Mesopotamia and Egypt, where British forces fought the Turks; and northern Italy, where Italian and Austrian troops fought the costly Battles of the Isonzo. At sea, the German and British fleets fought the inconclusive Battle of Jutland, and Germany's use of the submarine against neutral shipping eventually brought the U.S. into the war in 1917. Though Russia's armistice with Germany in December 1917 released German troops to fight on the Western Front, the Allies were reinforced by U.S. troops in early 1918. Germany's unsuccessful offensive in the Second Battle of the Marne was countered by the Allies' steady advance, which recovered most of France and Belgium by October 1918 and led to the November Armistice. Total casualties were estimated at 10 million dead, 21 million wounded, and 7.7 million missing or imprisoned.

World War II

Or Second World War (1939–45) International conflict principally between the Axis Powers—Germany, Italy, and Japan—and the Allied Powers—France, Britain, the U.S., the Soviet Union, and China. Political and economic instability in Germany, combined with bitterness over its defeat in World War I and the harsh conditions of the Treaty of Versailles, allowed Adolf Hitler and the Nazi Party to rise to power. In the mid-1930s Hitler began secretly to rearm Germany, in violation of the treaty. He signed alliances with Italy and Japan to oppose the Soviet Union and intervened in the Spanish Civil War in the name of anticommunism. Capitalizing on the reluctance of other European powers to oppose him by force, he sent troops to occupy Austria in 1938 and to annex Czechoslovakia in 1939. After signing the German-Soviet Nonaggression Pact, Germany invaded Poland on Sept. 1, 1939. Two days later France and Britain declared war on Germany. Poland's defeat was followed by a period of military inactivity on the Western Front. At sea, Germany conducted a damaging submarine campaign by U-boat against merchant shipping bound for Britain. By early 1940 the Soviet Union had divided Poland with Germany, occupied the Baltic states, and subdued Finland in the Russo-Finnish War. In April 1940 Germany overwhelmed Denmark and began its conquest of Norway. In May German forces swept through The Netherlands and Belgium on their blitzkrieg invasion of France, forcing it to capitulate in June and establish the Vichy France regime. Germany then launched massive bombing raids on Britain in preparation for a cross-Channel invasion, but, after losing the Battle of Britain, Hitler postponed the invasion indefinitely. By early 1941 Hungary, Romania, and Bulgaria had joined the Axis, and German troops quickly overran Yugoslavia and Greece in April. In June Hitler abandoned his pact with the Soviet Union and launched a massive surprise invasion of Russia, reaching the outskirts of Moscow before Soviet counterattacks and winter weather halted the advance. In East Asia Japan expanded its war with China and seized European colonial holdings. In December 1941 Japan attacked U.S. bases at Pearl Harbor and in the Philippines. The U.S. declared war on Japan, and the war became truly global when the other Axis Powers declared war on the U.S. Japan quickly invaded and occupied most of Southeast Asia, Burma, The Netherlands, East Indies, and many Pacific islands. After the crucial U.S. naval victory at the Battle of Midway (1942), U.S. forces began to advance up the chains of islands toward Japan. In the North Africa Campaigns the British and Americans defeated Italian and German forces by 1943. The Allies then invaded Sicily and Italy, forcing the overthrow of the fascist government in July 1943, though fighting against the Germans continued in Italy until 1945. In the Soviet Union the Battle of Stalingrad (1943) marked the end of the German advance, and Soviet reinforcements in great numbers gradually pushed the German armies back. The massive Allied invasion of Western Europe began with the Normandy Campaign in western France (1944), and the Allies' steady advance ended in the occupation of Germany in 1945. After Soviet troops pushed German forces out of the Soviet Union, they advanced into Poland, Czechoslovakia, Hungary, and Romania and had occupied the eastern third of Germany by the time the surrender of Germany was signed on May 8, 1945. In the Pacific an Allied invasion of the Philippines (1944) was followed by the successful Battle of Leyte Gulf and the costly Battles of Iwo Jima and Okinawa (1945). Atomic bombs were dropped on Hiroshima and Nagasaki in August 1945, and Japan's formal surrender on September 2 ended the war. Estimates of total military and civilian casualties varied from 35 million to 60 million killed, including about 6 million Jews who died in the Holocaust. Millions more civilians were wounded and made homeless throughout Europe and East Asia.

Religion, Philosophy, and Ideas

The Earl of Chesterfield, in his famous letters to his son and godson, stated, "Religion is by no means a proper subject of conversation in a mixed company," something the Crusades, the Hundred Years' War, and the whole nasty business with Mary, Queen of Scots, seem to have born out. H.L. Mencken, not always the most charitable of men, wrote, "We must respect the other fellow's religion, but only in the sense and to the extent that we respect his theory that his wife is beautiful and his children smart." Schopenhauer dismissed religion as "the masterpiece of the art of animal training," but John Cardinal Newman, in *Apologia pro Vita Sua*, agreed with St. Augustine that "faith is the pursuit of faith" despite the evidence:

> To consider the world in its length and breadth, its various history, the many races of man, their starts, their fortunes, their mutual alienation, their conflicts; and then their ways, habits, governments, forms of worship; their enterprises, their aimless courses, their random achievements and acquirements, the impotent conclusion of long-standing facts, the tokens so faint and broken, of a superintending design, the blind evolution of what turn out to be great powers or truths,

the progress of things, as if from unreasoning elements, not toward final causes, the greatness and littleness of man, his far-reaching aims, his short duration, the curtain hung over his futurity, the disappointments of life, the defeat of good, the success of evil, physical pain, mental anguish, the prevalence and intensity of sin, the pervading idolatries, the corruptions, the dreary hopeless irreligion, that condition of the whole race, so fearfully yet exactly described in the Apostle's words, "having no hope and without God in the world"—all this is a vision to dizzy and appall; and inflicts upon the mind the sense of a profound mystery, which is absolutely beyond human solution.

Cardinal Newman seems to agree with St. Augustine that "faith is the pursuit of faith," despite the evidence against it provided by the works of man.

Amish

Member of a conservative Christian group in North America known as the Old Order Amish Mennonite Church. The Amish originated in 1693–97 as followers of the Mennonite elder Jakob Ammann (1644?–c. 1730) in Switzerland, Alsace, and Germany. He taught that lying was grounds for excommunication (which meant being shunned by all other Mennonites), that clothing should be uniform and beards untrimmed, and that the state church should be avoided. Migration to North America and assimilation eliminated the Amish in Europe. They settled in Pennsylvania in the 18th century. After 1850 they split into "Old Order" (traditional) and "New Order" (now the Mennonite churches). Old Order Amish now live in Pennsylvania, Ohio, Indiana, Iowa, Illinois, and Kansas. Adults are baptized and admitted to formal church membership between ages 17 and 20. Services are in Pennsylvania Dutch (a German dialect) and some English. Though similar in theology to Mennonites, Amish wear modest, old-fashioned clothing and generally reject modern technology, including automobiles and telephones.

anti-Semitism

Hostility toward or discrimination against Jews as a religious group or "race." Although the term *anti-Semitism* has wide currency, it is regarded by some as a misnomer, implying discrimination against all Semites, including Arabs and other peoples who are not the targets of anti-Semitism as it is usually understood. In antiquity, hostility to the Jews emerged because of religious differences, a situation worsened as a result of the competition with Christianity. By the 4th century, Christians tended to see Jews as an alien people whose repudiation of Christ had condemned them to perpetual migration. Jews were denied citizenship and its rights in much of Europe in the Middle Ages (though some societies were more tolerant) or were forced to wear distinctive clothing, and there were forced expulsions of Jews from several regions in that period. Developed during the Middle Ages were many of the stereotypes of Jews (e.g., the blood libel, alleged greed, conspiracy against humankind) that have persisted into the modern era. The Enlightenment and the French Revolution brought a new religious freedom to Europe in the 18th century but did not reduce anti-Semitism, because Jews continued to be regarded as outsiders. In the

19th century violent discrimination intensified, and so-called "scientific racism" emerged, which based hostility to the Jews on their supposed biological characteristics and replaced religion as the primary basis for anti-Semitism. In the 20th century the economic and political dislocations caused by World War I intensified anti-Semitism, and racist anti-Semitism flourished in Nazi Germany. Nazi persecution of the Jews led to the Holocaust, in which an estimated six million Jews were exterminated. Despite the defeat of the Nazis in World War II, anti-Semitism remained a problem in many parts of the world into the 21st century.

Aristotle

(Born 384 BC, Stagira—died 322 BC, Chalcis) Greek philosopher and scientist whose thought determined the course of Western intellectual history for two millenia. He was the son of the court physician to Amyntas III, grandfather of Alexander the Great. In 367 he became a student at the Academy of Plato in Athens; he remained there for 20 years. After Plato's death in 348/347, he returned to Macedonia, where he became tutor to the young Alexander. In 335 he founded his own school in Athens, the Lyceum. His intellectual range was vast, covering most of the sciences and many of the arts. He worked in physics, chemistry, biology, zoology, and botany; in psychology, political theory, and ethics; in logic and metaphysics; and in history, literary theory, and rhetoric. He invented the study of formal logic, devising for it a finished system, known as syllogistic, that was considered the sum of the discipline until the 19th century; his work in zoology, both observational and theoretical, was not surpassed until the 19th century. His ethical and political theory, especially his conception of the ethical virtues and of human flourishing ("happiness"), continue to exert great influence in philosophical debate. He wrote prolifically; his major surviving works include the *Organon, De Anima* ("On the Soul"), *Physics, Metaphysics, Nicomachean Ethics, Eudemian Ethics, Magna Moralia, Politics, Rhetoric,* and *Poetics,* as well as other works on natural history and science.

Bible

Sacred scriptures of Judaism and Christianity. The Jewish scriptures consist of the Torah (or Pentateuch), the Neviim ("Prophets"), and the

Ketuvim ("Writings"), which together constitute what Christians call the Old Testament. The Pentateuch and Joshua relate how Israel became a nation and came to possess the Promised Land. The Prophets describe the establishment and development of the monarchy and relate the prophets' messages. The Writings include poetry, speculation on good and evil, and history. The Roman Catholic and Eastern Orthodox Bible includes additional Jewish writings called the Apocrypha. The New Testament consists of early Christian literature. The Gospels tell of the life, person, and teachings of Jesus. The Acts of the Apostles relates the earliest history of Christianity. The Epistles (Letters) are correspondence of early church leaders (chiefly St. Paul) and address the needs of early congregations. Revelation is the only canonical representative of a large genre of early Christian apocalyptic literature.

Buddha

Orig. Siddhartha Gautama (flourished *c.* 6th–4th century, born Kapilavastu, Shakya republic, Kosala kingdom—died Kusinara, Malla republic, Magadha kingdom) Indian spiritual leader and founder of Buddhism. The term *buddha* (Sanskrit; "enlightened one") is a title rather than a name, and Buddhists believe that there are an infinite number of past and future buddhas. The historical Buddha, referred to as the Buddha Gautama or simply as the Buddha, was born a prince of the Shakyas, on the India-Nepal border. He is said to have lived a sheltered life of luxury that was interrupted when he left the palace and encountered an old man, a sick man, and a corpse. Renouncing his princely life, he spent seven years seeking out teachers and trying various ascetic practices, including fasting, to gain enlightenment. Unsatisfied with the results, he meditated beneath the bodhi tree, where, after temptations by Mara, he realized the Four Noble Truths and achieved enlightenment. At Sarnath he preached his first sermon to his companions, outlining the Eightfold Path, which offered a middle way between self-indulgence and self-mortification and led to the liberation of nirvana. The five ascetics who heard this sermon became his first disciples and were admitted as bhiksus (monks) into the sangha, or Buddhist order. His mission fulfilled, the Buddha died after eating poisonous mushrooms served to him by accident and escaped the cycle of rebirth; his body was cremated, and stupas were built over his relics.

Buddhism

Major world religion and philosophy founded in northeastern India in the 5th century BC. Based on the teachings of Siddhartha Gautama, called the Buddha, Buddhism takes as its goal the escape from suffering and from the cycle of rebirth: the attainment of nirvana. It emphasizes meditation and the observance of certain moral precepts. The Buddha's teachings were transmitted orally by his disciples; during his lifetime he established the Buddhist monastic order (sangha). He adopted some ideas from the Hinduism of his time, notably the doctrine of karma, but also rejected many of its doctrines and all of its gods. In India, the emperor Ashoka promoted Buddhism during the 3rd century BC, but it declined in succeeding centuries and was nearly extinct there by the 13th century. It spread south and flourished in Sri Lanka and Southeast Asia, and it moved through Central Asia and Tibet to China, Korea, and Japan. In the 19th century, Buddhism spread to Europe and the United States, and it became increasingly popular in the West in the second half of the 20th century. Buddhism's main teachings are summarized in the Four Noble Truths, of which the fourth is the Eightfold Path. Buddhism's two major branches, Mahayana and Theravada, have developed distinctive practices and unique collections of canonical texts. In the early 21st century, the various traditions of Buddhism together had more than 375 million followers.

capital punishment

Or death penalty. Execution of an offender sentenced to death after conviction by a court of law of a criminal offense. Capital punishment for murder, treason, arson, and rape was widely employed in ancient Greece, and the Romans also used it for a wide range of offenses. It also has been sanctioned at one time or another by most of the world's major religions. In 1794 the U.S. state of Pennsylvania became the first jurisdiction to restrict the death penalty to first-degree murder, and in 1846 another U.S. state, Michigan, abolished capital punishment for all murders and other common crimes. In 1863 Venezuela became the first country to abolish capital punishment for all crimes. Portugal was the first European country to abolish the death penalty (1867). By the mid-1960s some 25 countries had abolished the death penalty for murder. During the last third of the 20th century, the number of abolitionist countries increased more than threefold. Despite the movement toward abolition, many countries have retained capital punishment, and some have extended its scope. In the U.S., three-fourths of the states and the federal government retain the death penalty, and death sentences are regularly carried out in China, Saudi Arabia, Singapore, and Iran. Supporters of the death penalty claim that life imprisonment is not an effective deterrent to criminal behavior. Opponents maintain that the death penalty has never been an effective deterrent—that errors sometimes lead to the execution of innocent persons and that capital punishment is imposed inequitably, mostly on the poor and on racial minorities.

Christianity

Religion stemming from the teachings of Jesus in the 1st century AD. Its sacred scripture is the Bible, particularly the New Testament. Its principal tenets are that Jesus is the Son of God (the second person of the Holy Trinity), that God's love for the world is the essential component of his being, and that Jesus died to redeem humankind. Christianity was originally a movement of Jews who accepted Jesus as the messiah, but the movement quickly became predominantly Gentile. The early church was shaped by St. Paul and other Christian missionaries and theologians; it was persecuted under the Roman Empire but supported by Constantine I, the first Christian emperor. In medieval and early modern Europe, Christian thinkers such as St. Augustine, Thomas Aquinas, and Martin Luther contributed to the growth of Christian theology, and beginning in the 15th century missionaries spread the faith throughout much of the world. The major divisions of Christianity are Roman Catholicism, Eastern Orthodoxy, and Protestantism. Nearly all Christian churches have an ordained clergy, members of which are typically though not universally male. Members of the clergy lead group worship services and are viewed as intermediaries between the laity and the divine in some churches. Most Christian churches administer two sacraments, baptism and the Eucharist. In the early 21st century there were more than two billion adherents of Christianity throughout the world, found on all continents.

Christmas

Christian festival celebrated on December 25, commemorating the birth of Jesus. December 25 had already been identified by Sextus Julius

Africanus in AD 221 as the day on which Christmas would be celebrated, and it was celebrated in Rome by AD 336. During the Middle Ages Christmas became extremely popular, and various liturgical celebrations of the holiday were established. The practice of exchanging gifts had begun by the 15th century. The Yule log, cakes, and fir trees derive from German and Celtic customs. Christmas today is regarded as a family festival with gifts brought by Santa Claus. As an increasingly secular festival, it has come to be celebrated by many non-Christians.

communism

Political theory advocating community ownership of all property, the benefits of which are to be shared by all according to the needs of each. The theory was principally the work of Karl Marx and Friedrich Engels. Their "Communist Manifesto" (1848) further specified a "dictatorship of the proletariat," a transitional stage Marx called socialism; communism was the final stage in which not only class division but even the organized state—seen by Marx as inevitably an instrument of oppression—would be transcended. That distinction was soon lost, and "communist" began to apply to a specific party rather than a final goal. Vladimir Ilich Lenin maintained that the proletariat needed professional revolutionaries to guide it. Joseph Stalin's version of communism was synonymous to many with totalitarianism. Mao Zedong mobilized peasants rather than an urban proletariat in China's communist revolution. European communism lost most of its following with the collapse of the Soviet Union (1991).

Confucianism

Scholarly tradition and way of life propagated by Confucius in the 6th–5th century BC and followed by the Chinese for more than two millennia. Though not organized as a religion, it has deeply influenced East Asian spiritual and political life in a comparable manner. The core idea is *ren* ("humaneness," "benevolence"), signifying excellent character in accord with *li* (ritual norms), *zhong* (loyalty to one's true nature), *shu* (reciprocity), and *xiao* (filial piety). Together these constitute *de* (virtue). Mencius, Xunzi, and others sustained Confucianism, but it was not influential until Dong Zhongshu emerged in the 2nd century BC. Confucianism was then recognized as the Han state cult, and the Five Classics became the core of education. In spite of the influence of Daoism and Buddhism, Confucian ethics have had the strongest influence on the moral fabric of Chinese society. A revival of Confucian thought in the 11th century produced Neo-Confucianism, a major influence in Korea during the Choson dynasty and in Japan during the Tokugawa period.

creationism

Theory that matter, the various forms of life, and the world were created by God out of nothing. Biblical creationists believe that the story told in Genesis of God's six-day creation of all things is literally correct. Scientific creationists believe that a creator made all that exists, but they may not hold that the Genesis story is a literal history of that creation. Creationism grew as a result of the advancement of the theory of evolution after the 1859 publication of Charles Darwin's *On the Origin of Species*. Within two decades most of the scientific community had accepted some form of organic evolution, and most churches eventually followed suit. Some conservative religious groups, however, have argued that Darwinian evolution alone cannot account for the complexity of the living world and have insisted that certain biblical descriptions of creation are revealed scientific truth. In the early 20th century, some areas in the U.S. banned the teaching of Darwinian theory, which led to the famous Scopes Trial (the so-called "Monkey Trial") of 1925. Many creationists now work toward ensuring that schools and textbooks present evolution as a theory that is no more provable than biblical creation.

Dalai Lama

Head of the dominant Dge-lugs-pa order of Tibetan Buddhism. The first of the line was Dge-'dun-grub-pa (1391–1475), founder of a monastery in central Tibet. His successors were regarded as his reincarnations and, like himself, manifestations of the bodhisattva Avalokitesvara. The second head of the order established the 'Brasspungs monastery near Lhasa as its base, and the third received the title Dalai ("Ocean") from Altan Khan. The fifth, Ngag-dbang-rgya-mtsho (1617–1682), established the supremacy of the Dge-lugs-pa over other orders. The 13th Dalai Lama, Thub-bstan-rgya-mtsho (1875–1933), held temporal and spiritual power after the Chinese were expelled in 1912. The 14th and current Dalai Lama, Bstan-'dzin-rgya-mtsho (b. 1935), was enthroned in 1940 but fled in 1959 with 100,000 followers after a failed revolt against the Chinese, who had gained control of Tibet in 1950–51. His government-in-exile is in Dharmsala, India. A respected figure worldwide, he was awarded the 1989 Nobel Peace Prize in recognition of his "constructive and forward-looking proposals" for solving world problems.

Dead Sea Scrolls

Caches of ancient, mostly Hebrew, manuscripts found at several sites on the northwestern shore of the Dead Sea (1947–56). The writings date from between the 3rd century BC and the 2nd century AD and total 800–900 manuscripts in 15,000 fragments. Many scholars believe that those deposited in 11 caves near the ruins of Qumran belonged to a sectarian community whom most scholars believe were Essenes, though other scholars suggest Sadducees or Zealots. The community rejected the rest of the Jewish people and saw the world as sharply divided between good and evil. They cultivated a communal life of ritual purity, called the "Union," led by a messianic "Teacher of Righteousness." The Dead Sea Scrolls as a whole represent a wider spectrum of Jewish belief and may have been the contents of libraries from Jerusalem hidden during the war of AD 66–73. They also cast new light on the emergence of Christianity and the relationship of early Christian and Jewish religious traditions.

deconstruction

Method of philosophical and literary analysis, derived mainly from the work of Jacques Derrida, that questions the fundamental conceptual distinctions, or "oppositions," in Western philosophy through a close examination of the language and logic of philosophical and literary texts. Such oppositions are characteristically "binary" and "hierarchical," involving a pair of terms in which one member of the pair is assumed to be primary or fundamental, the other secondary or derivative; examples include nature/culture, speech/writing, and mind/body. To "deconstruct" an opposition is to explore the tensions and contradictions between the hierarchical ordering assumed in the text and other aspects of the text's meaning,

especially its figurative or performative aspects. The deconstruction
"displaces" the opposition by showing that neither term is primary; the
opposition is a product, or "construction," of the text rather than something given independently of it. The speech/writing opposition, according
to which speech is "present" to the speaker or author and writing "absent,"
is a manifestation of what Derrida calls the "logocentrism" of Western
culture—i.e., the general assumption that there is a realm of "truth" existing prior to and independent of its representation by linguistic signs. In
polemical discussions about intellectual trends of the late 20th century,
deconstruction was sometimes used pejoratively to suggest nihilism and
frivolous skepticism. In popular usage the term has come to mean a critical dismantling of tradition and traditional modes of thought.

Dewey, John

(Born Oct. 20, 1859, Burlington, Vt., U.S.—died June 1, 1952, New York,
N.Y.) U.S. philosopher and educator who was one of the founders of

pragmatism, a pioneer in functional psychology, and a leader of the Progressive movement in U.S. education. He received a Ph.D. (1884) from Johns Hopkins University and taught 10 years at the University of Michigan before moving to the University of Chicago. Influenced by G. Stanley Hall and William James, he developed an instrumentalist theory of knowledge that conceived of ideas as tools for the solution of problems encountered in the environment. Believing the experimental methods of modern science provided the most promising approach to social and ethical problems, he applied this view to studies of democracy and liberalism. He asserted that democracy provided citizens with the opportunity for maximum experimentation and personal growth. His writings on education, notably *The School and Society* (1899) and *The Child and the Curriculum* (1902), emphasized the interests of the child and the use of the classroom to cultivate the interplay between thought and experience. At Chicago he created laboratory schools to test his theories. His work in psychology focused on the total organism in its efforts to adjust to the environment. In 1904 Dewey joined the Columbia University faculty. In 1925 he published his magnum opus, *Experience and Nature.*

Dreaming, the

Or Dream-Time. In the religion of the Australian Aborigines, the mythological time of the Creation. In the Dreaming the environment was shaped and humanized by mythic beings, many of whom took animal or human form. Some could change form at will. They took long journeys and created human life and the social order. In Aboriginal belief, these beings are eternal and continue to exist, although they may have traveled beyond the lands of the people who sing about them or may have metamorphosed into natural features such as rocky outcrops or water holes. The landscape is thus sacred to Aboriginal peoples.

Easter

Major festival of the Christian church year, celebrating the resurrection of Jesus on the third day after his crucifixion. In Western churches it falls on a Sunday between March 22 and April 25, depending on the date of the first full moon after the spring equinox. This time span was fixed after the Council of Nicaea (AD 325). In the Eastern Orthodox calendar, which uses a different calculation, it often falls later. A joyful festival and a time of redemption, Easter brings an end to the long period of penance that constitutes Lent. The word is sometimes said to have been derived from Eostre, a Germanic goddess of spring, but other origins of the term more closely associated with Christian traditions have been proposed. Easter has acquired a number of religious and popular customs. The Easter worship service is one of the high points of the Christian calendar, and since the late 2nd century Easter has also been a time for baptism. The painting of eggs and tales of a rabbit who decorates and hides eggs are among the folk customs associated with the holiday.

existentialism

Philosophical movement oriented toward two major themes, the analysis of human existence and the centrality of human choice. Existentialism's chief theoretical energies are thus devoted to questions about ontology and decision. It traces its roots to the writings of Søren Kierkegaard and Friedrich Nietzsche. As a philosophy of human existence, existentialism found its best 20th-century exponent in Karl Jaspers; as a philosophy of human decision, its foremost representative was Jean-Paul Sartre. Sartre finds the essence of human existence in freedom—in the duty of self-determination and the freedom of choice—and therefore spends much time describing the human tendency toward "bad faith," reflected in humanity's perverse attempts to deny its own responsibility and flee from the truth of its inescapable freedom.

Hanukkah

In Judaism, a holiday celebrating the rededication of the Second Temple of Jerusalem in 164 BC, after its desecration three years earlier by order of Antiochus IV Epiphanes. The Maccabees recaptured Jerusalem and reconsecrated the Temple after leading a successful revolt against Syrian rule. The lighting of the menorah recalls the story that a one-day supply of oil burned miraculously in the Temple for eight days until new oil could be obtained. Sometimes called the Feast of Dedication or Feast of Lights, it is celebrated for eight days in December, during which the ceremonial candles are lit and children play games and receive gifts. Originally a minor holiday, it has become more lavishly celebrated as a result of its proximity to Christmas.

hate crime

In law, a crime directed at a person or persons on the basis of characteristics such as race, religion, ethnicity, or sexual orientation. The concept emerged in the U.S. in the late 1970s, and since then laws have been passed in many U.S. states mandating additional penalties for violent crimes motivated by bias or bigotry against particular groups. Several other Western countries, including Australia, Britain, and Canada, have adopted laws designed to curb violent crime against racial and religious minorities. For example, German law forbids public incitement and instigation of racial hatred, including the distribution of Nazi propaganda.

Hinduism

Oldest of the world's major religions. It evolved from the Vedic religion of ancient India. The major branches of Hinduism are Vaishnavism and Shaivism, each of which includes many different sects. Though the various sects each rely on their own set of scriptures, they all revere the ancient Vedas, which were brought to India by Aryan invaders after 1200 BC. The philosophical Vedic texts called the Upanishads explored the search for knowledge that would allow mankind to escape the cycle of reincarnation. Fundamental to Hinduism is the belief in a cosmic principle of ultimate reality called Brahman and its identity with the individual soul, or atman. All creatures go through a cycle of rebirth, or samsara, which can be broken only by spiritual self-realization, after which liberation, or moksha, is attained. The principle of karma determines a being's status within the cycle of rebirth. The greatest Hindu deities are Brahma, Vishnu, and Shiva. The numerous other Hindu gods are mostly viewed as incarnations or epiphanies of the main deities, though some are survivors of the pre-Aryan era. The major sources of classical mythology are the *Mahabharata* (which includes the *Bhagavadgita*, the most important religious text of Hinduism), the *Ramayana*, and the *Puranas*. The hierarchical social structure of the caste system is also important in Hinduism; it is supported by the principle of dharma. In the 20th century Hinduism blended with Indian nationalism to become a powerful political force in Indian politics. In the early 21st century there were more than 850 million Hindus worldwide.

Islam

Major world religion founded by Muhammad in Arabia in the early 7th century AD. The Arabic word *islam* means "submission"—specifically submission to the will of the one God, called Allah in Arabic. Islam is a strictly monotheistic religion, and its adherents, called Muslims, regard the Prophet Muhammad as the last and most perfect of God's messengers, who include Adam, Abraham, Moses, Jesus, and others. The sacred scripture of Islam is the Quran, which contains God's revelations to Muhammad. The sayings and deeds of the Prophet recounted in the sunna are also an important source of belief and practice in Islam. The religious obligations of all Muslims are summed up in the Five Pillars of Islam, which include belief in God and his Prophet and obligations of prayer, charity, pilgrimage, and fasting. The fundamental concept in Islam is the Sharia, or Law, which embraces the total way of life commanded by God. Observant Muslims pray five times a day and join in community worship on Fridays at the mosque, where worship is led by an imam. Every believer is required to make a pilgrimage to Mecca, the holiest city, at least once in a lifetime, barring poverty or physical incapacity. The month of Ramadan is set aside for fasting. Alcohol and pork are always forbidden, as are gambling, usury, fraud, slander, and the making of images. In addition to celebrating the breaking of the fast of Ramadan, Muslims celebrate Muhammad's birthday and his ascension into heaven. The Id al-Adha festival inaugurates the season of pilgrimage to Mecca. Muslims are enjoined to defend Islam against unbelievers through jihad. Divisions occurred early in Islam, brought about by disputes over the succession to the caliphate. About 90 percent of Muslims belong to the Sunnite branch. The Shiites broke away in the 7th century and later gave rise to other sects, including the Ismailis. Another significant element in Islam is the mysticism known as Sufism. Since the 19th century the concept of the Islamic community has inspired Muslim peoples to cast off Western colonial rule, and in the late 20th century fundamentalist movements threatened or toppled a number of secular Middle Eastern governments. In the early 21st century, there were more than 1.2 billion Muslims in the world.

Jainism

Religion of India established in the 6th century BC. It was founded by Vardhamana, who was called Mahavira, as a reaction against the Vedic religion, which required animal sacrifices. Jainism's core belief is ahimsa, or noninjury to all living things. Jainism has no belief in a creator god, though there are a number of lesser deities for various aspects of life. Jains believe their religion is eternal and hold that it was revealed in stages by a number of Conquerors, of whom Mahavira was the 24th. Living as an ascetic, Mahavira preached the need for rigorous penance and self-denial as the means of perfecting human nature, escaping the cycle of rebirth, and attaining moksha, or liberation. Jains view karma as an invisible material substance that interferes with liberation and can be dissolved only through asceticism. By the end of the 1st century AD the Jains had split into two sects, each of which later developed its own canon of sacred writings: the Digambaras, who held that an adherent should own nothing, not even clothes, and that women must be reborn as men before they can attain moksha; and the more moderate Svetambaras, who retained a few possessions such as a robe, an alms bowl, a whisk broom, and a *mukhavastrika* (a piece of cloth held over the mouth to protect against the ingestion and killing of small insects). In keeping with their principle of reverence for life, Jains are known for their charitable works, including building shelters for animals. Jainism preaches universal tolerance and does not seek to make converts. In the early 21st century Jainism had some 4.5 million followers.

Jerusalem

(Hebrew, Yerushalayim; Arabic, Al-Quds) City (pop., 2005 est.: 704,900), capital of Israel. Located in the heart of historic Palestine, it is nestled between the West Bank and Israel. The Old City is a typical walled Middle Eastern enclosure; the modern city is an urban agglomeration of high-rises and housing complexes. It is holy to Judaism as the site of the Temple of Jerusalem, to Christianity because of its association with Jesus, and to Islam because of its connection with the Miraj (the Prophet Muhammad's ascension to heaven). Jewish shrines include the Western Wall. Islamic holy places include the Dome of the Rock. In 1000 BC David made it the capital of Israel. Razed by the Babylonians in the 6th century BC, it thereafter enjoyed only brief periods of independence. The Romans devastated it in the 1st and 2nd centuries AD, banishing the Jewish population. From 638 it was ruled by various Muslim dynasties, except for short periods during the Crusades when it was controlled by Christians. Rule by the Ottoman Empire ended in 1917, and the city became the capital of the British mandate of Palestine. It was thereafter the subject of competing Zionist and Palestinian national aspirations. Israel claimed the city as its capital after the Arab-Israeli War in 1948 and took the entire city during the Six-Day War of 1967. Its status as Israel's capital has remained a point of contention: official recognition by the international community has largely been withheld pending final settlement of regional territorial rights.

Jesus

In Christianity, the son of God and the second person of the Holy Trinity. Christian doctrine holds that by his crucifixion and resurrection he paid for the sins of all mankind. His life and ministry are recounted in the four Gospels of the New Testament. He was born a Jew in Bethlehem before the death of Herod the Great in 4 BC, and he died while Pontius Pilate was Roman governor of Judaea (AD 28–30). His mother, Mary, was married to Joseph, a carpenter of Nazareth. Of his childhood after the birth narratives in Matthew and Luke, nothing is known, except for one visit to Jerusalem with his parents. He began his ministry about age 30, becoming a preacher, teacher, and healer. He gathered disciples in the region of Galilee, including the 12 Apostles, and preached the imminent arrival of the Kingdom of God. His moral teachings, outlined in the Sermon on the Mount, and his reported miracles won him a growing number of followers who believed that he was the promised messiah. On Passover he entered Jerusalem on a donkey, where he shared the Last Supper with his disciples and was betrayed to the Roman authorities by Judas Iscariot. Arrested and tried, he was condemned to death as a political agitator and was crucified and buried. Three days later visitors to his tomb found it empty. According to the Gospels, he appeared several times to his disciples before ascending into heaven.

The Deposition of Christ, oil on canvas by Caravaggio, 1602–04; in the Vatican Museum

John Paul II

Orig. Karol Wojtyla (born May 18, 1920, Wadowice, Pol.—died April 2, 2005, Vatican City) Pope (1978–2005), the bishop of Rome and head of the Roman Catholic church, the first non-Italian pope in 455 years and the first ever from a Slavic country. He studied for the priesthood at an underground seminary in Kraków during World War II and was ordained in 1946. He earned a doctorate in philosophy in Rome (1948) and returned home to serve in a parish, earning a second

John Paul II, 1979

doctorate (also 1948), in sacred theology, from the Jagiellonian University. He became archbishop of Kraków in 1964 and cardinal in 1967. Elected pope after the 33-day pontificate of John Paul I (b. 1912—d. 1978), he became known for his energy, charisma, and intellect as well as for his conservative theological views and fervent anticommunism. In 1981 John Paul was shot in St. Peter's Square by a Turkish gunman, but he recovered, resumed his work, and forgave his would-be assassin. His trips abroad attracted some of the largest crowds ever assembled. His nonviolent activism spurred movements that contributed to the peaceful dissolution of the Soviet Union in 1991. He championed economic and political justice in developing nations. In naming 44 cardinals from five continents (February 2001), John Paul reached out to cultures around the world. He also canonized more saints, from more parts of the world, than had any other pope. His ecumenical efforts, including meetings with Jewish, Muslim, and Eastern Orthodox religious leaders, were widely praised, though he often drew criticism for his traditionalist views on issues of gender and sexuality. Although afflicted with Parkinson's disease since the early 1990s, John Paul remained active and made a historic trip to Jerusalem in March 2000, during which he sought to improve relations between the Roman Catholic Church and Jews.

Judaism

Religious beliefs and practices of the Jews. One of the three great monotheistic world religions, Judaism began as the faith of the ancient Hebrews, and its sacred text is the Hebrew Bible, particularly the Torah.

Fundamental to Judaism is the belief that the people of Israel are God's chosen people, who must serve as a light for other nations. God made a covenant first with Abraham and then renewed it with Isaac, Jacob, and Moses. The worship of Yahweh (God) was centered in Jerusalem from the time of David. The destruction of the First Temple of Jerusalem by the Babylonians (586 BC) and the subsequent exile of the Jews led to hopes for national restoration under the leadership of a messiah. The Jews were later allowed to return by the Persians, but an unsuccessful rebellion against Roman rule led to the destruction of the Second Temple in AD 70 and the Jews' dispersal throughout the world in the Jewish Diaspora. Rabbinic Judaism emerged to replace the beliefs and practices associated with the Temple at Jerusalem, as the Jews carried on their culture and religion through a tradition of scholarship and strict observance. The great body of oral law and commentaries were committed to writing in the Talmud and Mishna. The religion was maintained despite severe persecutions by many nations.

Two branches of Judaism emerged in the Middle Ages: the Sephardic, centered in Spain and culturally linked with the Babylonian Jews; and the Ashkenazic, centered in France and Germany and linked with the Jewish culture of Palestine and Rome. Elements of mysticism also appeared, notably the esoteric writings of the Kabbala and, in the 18th century, the movement known as Hasidism. The 18th century was also the time of the Jewish Enlightenment (Haskala). Conservative and Reform Judaism emerged in 19th-century Germany as an effort to modify the strictness of Orthodox Judaism. By the end of the 19th century Zionism had appeared as an outgrowth of reform. European Judaism suffered terribly during the Holocaust, when millions were put to death by the Nazis, and the rising flow of Jewish emigrants to Palestine led to the declaration of the State of Israel in 1948. In the early 21st century there were nearly 15 million Jews worldwide.

Muhammad

Or Mohammed (born *c.* 570, Mecca, Arabia—died June 8, 632, Medina) Arab prophet who established the religion of Islam. The son of a merchant of the ruling tribe, he was orphaned at age six. He married a rich widow, Khadijah, with whom he had six children, including Fatimah, a daughter. According to tradition, in 610 he was visited by the angel Gabriel, who informed Muhammad that he was the messenger of God.

His revelations and teachings, recorded in the Quran, are the basis of Islam. He began to preach publicly c. 613, urging the rich to give to the poor and calling for the destruction of idols. He gained disciples but also acquired enemies, whose plan to murder Muhammad forced him to flee Mecca for Medina in 622. This flight, known as the Hijrah, marks the beginning of the Islamic era. Muhammad's followers defeated a Meccan force in 624; they suffered reverses in 625 but repelled a Meccan siege of Medina in 627. He won control of Mecca by 629 and of all Arabia by 630. He made his last journey to Mecca in 632, establishing the rites of the hajj, or pilgrimage to Mecca. He died later that year and was buried at Medina. His life, teachings, and miracles have been the subjects of Muslim devotion and reflection ever since.

Nicholas, Saint

Or Santa Claus (flourished 4th century, Myra, Lycia, Asia Minor; feast day December 6) Minor saint associated with Christmas. Probably bishop of Myra, he is reputed to have provided dowries for three poor girls to save them from prostitution and to have restored to life three children who had been chopped up by a butcher. He became the patron saint of Russia and Greece, of charitable fraternities and guilds, and of children, sailors, unmarried girls, merchants, and pawnbrokers. After the Reformation his cult disappeared in all the Protestant countries of Europe except Holland, where he was known as Sinterklaas. Dutch colonists brought the tradition to New Amsterdam (now New York City), and English-speaking Americans adopted him as Santa Claus, who is believed to live at the North Pole and to bring gifts to children at Christmas.

Passover

In Judaism, the holiday commemorating the liberation of the Hebrews from slavery in Egypt. Before sending a plague to destroy the firstborn of the Egyptians, God instructed Moses to tell the Israelites to place a special mark above their doors as a signal for the angel of death to pass over (i.e., spare the residents). The festival of Passover begins on the 15th and ends on the 22nd (in Israel, the 21st) day of the month of Nisan (March or April). During Passover only unleavened bread may be eaten, symbolizing the Hebrews' suffering in bondage and the haste with which they left Egypt. On the first night of Passover, a Seder is held, and the Haggadah is read aloud.

Plato

Orig. Aristocles (born 428/427 BC, Athens, or Aegina, Greece—died 348/347 BC, Athens) Greek philosopher, who with his teacher Socrates and his student Aristotle laid the philosophical foundations of Western culture. His family was highly distinguished; his father claimed descent from the last king of Athens, and his mother was related to Critias and Charmides, extremist leaders of the oligarchic terror of 404. Plato (whose acquired name refers to his broad forehead, and thus his range of knowledge) must have known Socrates from boyhood. After Socrates was put to death in 401, Plato fled Athens for Megara, then spent the next 12 years in travel. Upon his return, he founded the Academy, an institute of scientific and philosophical research, where Aristotle was one of his students. Building on but also departing from Socrates's thought, he developed a profound and wide-ranging philosophical system, subsequently known as Platonism. His thought has logical, epistemological, and metaphysical aspects, but much of its underlying motivation is ethical. It is presented in his many dialogues, in most of which Socrates plays a leading role.

Quran

Or Koran. Sacred scripture of Islam, regarded by Muslims as the infallible word of God, revealed to Muhammad. The book, first compiled in its authoritative form in the 7th century, consists of 114 chapters (*surahs*) of varying length, written in Arabic. The earliest *surahs* call for moral and religious obedience in light of the coming Day of Judgment; the ones written later provide directives for the creation of a social structure that will support the moral life called for by God. The Quran also provides detailed accounts of the joys of paradise and the terrors of hell. Muslims believe that the God who spoke to Muhammad is the God worshiped by Jews and Christians but that the revelations received by those religions are incomplete. Emphasis on the stern justice of God is tempered by frequent references to his mercy and compassion. The Quran demands absolute submission (*islam*) to God and his word, and it serves as the primary source of Islamic law. It is regarded as immutable in both form and content; traditionally translation was forbidden. The translations available today are regarded as paraphrases to facilitate understanding of the actual scripture.

Ramadan

In Islam, a holy month of fasting, the ninth month of the Muslim year, commemorating the revelation of the Quran to Muhammad. As an act of atonement, Muslims are required to fast and abstain from sexual activity during the daylight hours of Ramadan. Determined according to the lunar calendar, Ramadan can fall in any season of the year. The Ramadan fast is considered one of the Five Pillars of Islam, and the end of the fast is celebrated as one of the important religious holidays of Islam.

Shinto

Indigenous religion of Japan. Based on the worship of spirits known as *kami*, Shinto has no founder and no official scripture, though its mythology is collected in the *Kojiki* ("Records of Ancient Matters") and *Nihon shoki* ("Chronicles of Japan"), written in the 8th century. The term *Shinto* ("Way of the *Kami*") came into use to distinguish indigenous Japanese beliefs from Buddhism, which had been introduced into Japan in the 6th century. At Shinto's core are beliefs in the *kami*'s mysterious creating and harmonizing power. According to Shinto myths, in the beginning a certain number of *kami* simply emerged, and a pair of *kami*, Izanagi and Izanami, gave birth to the Japanese islands, as well as to the *kami* who became ancestors of the various clans. The Japanese imperial family claims descent from Izanagi's daughter, the sun goddess Amaterasu. All *kami* are said to cooperate with one another, and life lived in accordance with their will is believed to produce a mystical power that gains their protection, cooperation, and approval. Through veneration and observation of prescribed rituals at shrines (e.g., ritual purity), practitioners of Shinto can come to understand and live in accordance with divine will. In the early 21st century, Shinto had nearly 2.8 million followers.

Sikhism

Indian monotheistic religion founded in the late 15th century by Guru Nanak. Most of its 18 million members, called Sikhs, live in the Punjab, the site of their holiest shrine, the Golden Temple, and the center of Sikh authority, the Akal Takht. The *Adi Granth* is the canonical scripture of Sikhism. Its theology is based on a supreme God who governs with justice and grace. Human beings, irrespective of caste and gender distinctions, have the opportunity to become one with God. The basic human flaw of self-centeredness can be overcome through proper reverence for God, commitment to hard work, service to humanity, and sharing the fruits of one's labor. Sikhs consider themselves disciples of the 10 Gurus. They accept the Hindu ideas of samsara and karma, and they view themselves as the Khalsa, a chosen race of soldier-saints committed to a Spartan code of conduct and a crusade for righteousness. The emblems of the Khalsa, called the five Ks, are *kes* (uncut hair), *kangha* (a comb), *kachha* (long shorts), *kirpan* (a sword), and *karka* (a steel bracelet).

Smith, Joseph

(Born Dec. 23, 1805, Sharon, Vt., U.S.—died June 27, 1844, Carthage, Ill.) Founder of the Church of Jesus Christ of Latter-day Saints (Mormon church). He began experiencing visions as a teenager in Palmyra, N.Y. In 1827 he claimed that an angel had directed him to buried golden plates containing God's revelation; these he translated into the *Book of Mormon* (1830). He led converts to Ohio, Missouri, and Illinois, where he established the town of Nauvoo (1839), which soon became the state's largest town. Imprisoned for treason after his efforts to silence Mormon dissenters led to mob violence, he was murdered by a lynch mob that stormed the jail where he was held. His work was continued by Brigham Young.

Joseph Smith, detail from an oil painting by an unknown artist; in the Community of Christ Temple and Auditorium complex, Independence, Missouri

Socrates

(Born *c.* 470 BC, Athens—died 399 BC) Greek philosopher whose way of life, character, and thought exerted a profound influence on ancient and modern philosophy. Because he wrote nothing, information about his personality and doctrine is derived chiefly from depictions of his conversations and other information in the dialogues of Plato, in the *Memorabilia* of Xenophon, and in various writings of Aristotle. He fought bravely in the Peloponnesian War and later served in the Athenian *boule* (assembly). Socrates considered it his religious duty to call his fellow citizens to the examined life by engaging them in philosophical conversation. His contribution to these exchanges typically consisted of a series of probing questions that cumulatively revealed his interlocutor's complete ignorance of the subject under discussion; such cross-examination used as a pedagogical technique has been called the "Socratic method." Though Socrates characteristically professed his own ignorance regarding many of the (mainly ethical) subjects he investigated (e.g., the nature of piety), he did hold certain convictions with confidence, including that: (1) human wisdom begins with the recognition of one's own ignorance; (2) the unexamined life is not worth living; (3) ethical virtue is the only thing that matters; and (4) a good person can never be harmed, because whatever misfortune he may suffer, his virtue will remain intact. His students and admirers included, in addition to Plato, Alcibiades, who betrayed Athens in the Peloponnesian War, and Critias (*c.* 480–403 BC), who was one of the Thirty Tyrants imposed on Athens after its defeat by Sparta. Because he was connected with these two men, but also because his habit of exposing the ignorance of his fellow citizens had made him widely hated and feared, Socrates was tried on charges of impiety and corrupting the youth and condemned to death by poisoning (the poison probably being hemlock) in 399 BC. He submitted to the sentence willingly. Plato's *Apology* purports to be the speech that Socrates gave in his own defense. As depicted in the *Apology*, Socrates's trial and death raise vital questions about the nature of democracy, the value of free speech, and the potential conflict between moral and religious obligation and the laws of the state.

Talmud

In Judaism, the systematic amplification and analysis of passages of the Mishna, the Gemara, and other oral law, including the Tosefta. Two

Socrates was a plebian; he couldn't help it, he was just born that way, being the son of a stonemason and a midwife. He was mercilessly mocked by the comic dramatists of Athens, who portrayed him as a bug-eyed buffoon, and a lowlife to boot. The exception was Xenophon, the patrician historian, who sat at Socrates's feet so he wouldn't miss a word; because Socrates never wrote any of it down, it was a necessity. Soon there was a small crowd at his feet, including Plato, who, coming from one of the best families in town, had to do it on the sly. They would volley *eidos* (ideas) back and forth, having discourses far into the night (although it was strictly platonic)—giving as good as getting when it came to the nature of "good" and "beautiful" and "being" and many things we'll never know about. Socrates liked to ask questions and question answers, which is probably what most Athenians found so annoying about him. But Plato hung on every word and made the Socratic monologues into Platonic dialogues, giving himself all the good parts in *Laches, Euthyphro,* and *Charmides* (Plato was brilliant, but not as a titlist), rendering Socrates's "what is this, what is that?" to the page. In 399 BC Socrates was prosecuted for impiety, a rather loose charge barely disguising the fact that the hoi polloi got him and the hoity toity didn't. Using the admittedly poor tactic of putting his accusers on trial, Socrates was convicted 280 votes to 221 (with Plato in the gallery to record it for his *Apology*) and that same year asked, "what is poison?" and answered, "hemlock."—M.F.

Talmuds exist, produced by two different groups of Jewish scholars: the Babylonian Talmud (*c.* AD 600) and the Palestinian Talmud (*c.* AD 400). The Babylonian Talmud is more extensive and thus more highly esteemed. Both Talmuds formulate their own hermeneutics to convey their theological system by defining the Torah and by demonstrating its perfection and comprehensive character. The Talmud remains a text of central importance, particularly in Orthodox Judaism. Intensive modern Talmudic scholarship is pursued in Israel and the U.S.

Teresa (of Calcutta), Blessed Mother

Orig. Agnes Gonxha Bojaxhiu (born Aug. 27, 1910, Skopje, Maced., Ottoman Empire—died Sept. 5, 1997, Calcutta, India; beatified Oct. 19, 2003) Roman Catholic nun, founder of the Order of the Missionaries of Charity. The daughter of a grocer, she became a nun and went to India as a young woman. After studying nursing, she moved to the slums of Calcutta (Kolkata); in 1948 she founded her order, which served the blind, the aged, the disabled, and the dying. In 1963 the Indian government awarded her the Padmashri ("Lord of the Lotus") for her services to the people of India, and in 1971 Pope Paul VI awarded her the first Pope John XXIII Peace Prize. In 1979 she received the Nobel Prize for Peace. Although in her later years she suffered from a worsening heart condition, Mother Teresa continued to serve the poor and sick and also spoke out against divorce, contraception, and abortion. Her order included hundreds of centers in more than 90 countries, with some 4,000 nuns and hundreds of thousands of lay workers. She was succeeded by the Indian-born Sister Nirmala. The process to declare her a saint began within two years of her death, and Pope John Paul II issued a special dispensation to expedite the process. She was beatified on Oct. 19, 2003, reaching the ranks of the blessed in the shortest time in the church's history.

Torah

Or Pentateuch. In Judaism, the divine revelations to Israel; specifically, the first five books of the Bible: Genesis, Exodus, Leviticus, Numbers, and Deuteronomy. By tradition their authorship has been ascribed to Moses, but biblical scholarship has shown that they were written and compiled at a much later date, probably in the 9th–5th century BC, though drawing on much older traditions. The Scroll of the Torah (Sefer Torah) is kept in the Synagogue Ark. The term *Torah* (but not *Pentateuch*) is often applied to the whole Hebrew Scripture (i.e., the later books of the Old Testament), or, even more generally, to that and other Jewish sacred literature and oral tradition.

Valentine, Saint

(Died 3rd century, Rome; feast day February 14) Christian martyr whose legend inspired the lover's holiday Valentine's Day. According to tradition, he was a Roman priest and physician who died during the persecution of Christians by the emperor Claudius II Gothicus and was buried on the Via Flaminia. The priest signed a letter to his jailer's daughter, whom he had befriended and with whom he had fallen in love, "from your Valentine." The legend of the bishop of Terni, Italy—also called Valentine and also martyred in Rome—may refer to the same person.

Feldman's Religion, Philosophy, and Ideas

Quiz?

1. Why was Jean-Paul Sartre nauseous?
   (a) the usual existential angst
   (b) colitis
   (c) because he was always being compared to his cousin, Albert Schweitzer

(a) Although admittedly flip, this pretty much sums up the existential dilemma of the protagonist of nausea who says things like *I live alone, entirely alone. I never speak to anyone, never; I receive nothing, I give nothing...* When you live alone you no longer know what it is to tell something: the plausible disappears at the same time as the fiends. You let events flow past; suddenly you see people pop up who speak and who go away, you plunge into stories without beginning or end: you make a terrible witness. But in compensation, one misses nothing, no improbability or, story too tall to be believed in cafes. When this came out in 1964, it pretty much put existentialism on the map.

2. How did the Israelites manage to lose 10 of 12 tribes?
   (a) through intermarriage
   (b) they didn't lose them; they're just not talking to one another
   (c) they were deported to God knows where by the Assyrians after conquering the Northern Kingdom of Israel in the 8th century BC.

(c) Although I wouldn't rule out the others. They are rumored to have gone to what is now Iran, Afghanistan, Tajikistan, Turkmenistan, and/or Uzbekistan. This move left only the tribes of Benjamin and Judah, the latter of which is the tribe you see today, albeit with many variations.

3. Not that I'm a curmudgeon, but why is St. Valentine's Day really for the birds?
   (a) because you are a curmudgeon
   (b) because St. Valentine was martyred by pecking
   (c) because the holiday is not so much about St. Valentine as the medieval belief that February 14 was when birds mated

(c) And for life, at least among the waterfowl. There were actually at least two St. Valentines, all martyred, none of whom is the clear heir to the title. Chaucer, however, pretty much summed up popular feeling about February 14 when he wrote, "For this was sent on Seynt Valentyne's day, Whan every foul cometh ther to choose his mate." That's "foul," not "foole."

witchcraft and sorcery

Use of alleged supernatural powers, usually to control people or events. Sorcery is sometimes distinguished from witchcraft in that sorcery may be practiced by anyone with the appropriate knowledge, using charms, spells, or potions, whereas witchcraft is considered to result from inherent mystical power and to be practiced by invisible means. Modern witches, however, claim that their craft is learned, and therefore another distinction between witchcraft and sorcery is that sorcery is always used with evil intent. Controversies over witchcraft and sorcery have been especially prevalent in close-knit communities experiencing decline or misfortune and embroiled in petty social conflict and scapegoating. In ancient Greece, witchcraft was mentioned as early as Homer. The best-known sorceress in Classical times was the legendary Medea. The Roman Horace describes two witches in his *Satires*. The Bible contains several references to witches, notably the Witch of Endor consulted by Saul (1 Samuel 28). The early Church Fathers held that witchcraft was a delusion and denounced its practice. In the Middle Ages, witchcraft was believed to involve demonic possession. It was also associated with heresy and so came within the scope of the Inquisition. In the witch-hunts of the 16th–17th centuries, European courts frequently regarded witches and sorcerers alike as candidates for burning. Although estimates of the number killed vary widely, it is likely that between 40,000 and 60,000 people were executed and many more were tortured and imprisoned during the witch hunts. In the 20th century the modern witchcraft movement, Wicca, was established and promoted respect for nature and a pantheistic worldview. Belief in witchcraft is apparent in traditional societies throughout the world. The Navajo protect themselves against witches with sand or pollen paintings, and in African societies people seek aid from medical doctors and witch doctors, the former for treatment of the "external" causes of the illness and the latter for the "internal."

Yom Kippur

(English; "Day of Atonement") Jewish religious holiday, observed on the 10th day of the lunar month of Tishri (in late September or early October). It concludes the 10 days of repentance that begin with Rosh Hashanah. Its purpose is to purify the individual and community by forgiving the sins of others and by repenting one's own sins against God. Before the destruction of the Temple of Jerusalem, the high priest performed a sacrificial ceremony that concluded with the death of a scapegoat. Today it is marked by fasting and abstention from sex. Its eve, when the Kol Nidre is recited, and the entire day of Yom Kippur, are spent in prayer and meditation.

zombie

In Vodun, a dead person who is revived after burial and compelled to do the bidding of the reviver, including criminal acts and heavy manual labor. It is believed that actual zombies are living persons under the influence of powerful drugs, including burundanga (a drug reportedly used by Colombian criminals) and drugs derived from poisonous toads and puffer fish.

Science, Technology, and Life

Science! The problem with it is that although it profoundly affects our lives, increasingly, only scientists can understand it. Don Herbert, a Mr. Wizard in his day, would be hard-pressed to explain the esoterica of today's physics, genetics, nanotechnology, cosmology, microbiology, or quantum mechanics to kids in his garage. Take string theory—three dimensions is pushing it, but we should think in 11? How would you even illustrate that on the final exam, which counts for half of your grade? What is the matter with the dark-matter people? They can't come up with most of the mass of the universe—how can you not find anything that big? What happens when you get sucked over the event horizon into a black hole—is it at least painless? Aren't machines made out of carbon atoms going to be extremely difficult to service? Why would anyone want to clone sheep—don't they look enough alike? The questions are endless, and the answers, which we probably couldn't understand anyway, are slow in coming.

This means that we have to take science on faith, and the irony is almost too much for one layman to bear in an age when faith and science seem to be at one another's throats (not a recent development, really, with Copernicus just now getting his dispensation). Darwin was a profoundly religious man who might well have a fish on his trunk without his name in it today, and Einstein believed that God would not play dice with the universe, even if Stephen Hawking does.

munodeficiency Syndrome (AIDS)

e of the immune system caused by HIV. AIDS is
fection, during which time the individual devel-
al infections and cancers, including *Pneumocystis*
umonia, cytomegalovirus (CMV), lymphoma, and Kaposi
oma. The first AIDS cases were identified in 1981, HIV was isolated in 1983, and blood tests were developed by 1985. According to
the UN's 2004 report on AIDS, some 38 million people are living with
HIV, approximately five million people become infected annually, and
about three million people die each year from AIDS. Some 20 million
people have died of the disease since 1981. Sub-Saharan Africa
accounts for some 70 percent of all HIV infections. Rates of infection
are lower in other parts of the world, but the epidemic is spreading
rapidly in Eastern Europe, India, South and Southeast Asia, Latin
America, and the Caribbean.

artificial intelligence (AI)

Ability of a machine to perform tasks thought to require human
intelligence. Typical applications include game playing, language
translation, expert systems, and robotics. Although pseudo-intelligent
machinery dates back to antiquity, the first glimmerings of true
intelligence awaited the development of digital computers in the
1940s. AI, or at least the semblance of intelligence, has developed in
parallel with computer processing power, which appears to be the
main limiting factor. Early AI projects, such as playing chess and
solving mathematical problems, are now seen as trivial compared to
visual pattern recognition, complex decision making, and the use of
natural language.

atom

Smallest unit into which matter can be divided and still retain the
characteristic properties of an element. The word derives from the
Greek *atomos* ("indivisible"), and the atom was believed to be indivisible until the early 20th century, when electrons and the nucleus were
discovered. It is now known that an atom has a positively charged

nucleus that makes up more than 99.9 percent of the atom's mass but only about 1/100,000 of its volume. The nucleus is composed of positively charged protons and electrically neutral neutrons, each about 2,000 times as massive as an electron. Most of the atom's volume consists of a cloud of electrons that have very small mass and negative charge. The electron cloud is bound to the nucleus by the attraction of opposite charges. In a neutral atom, the protons in the nucleus are balanced by the electrons. An atom that has gained or lost electrons becomes negatively or positively charged and is called an ion.

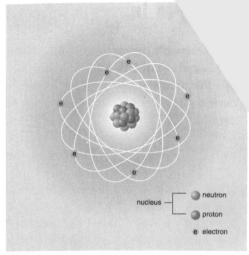

The classical "planetary" model of an atom

big bang

Model of the origin of the universe, which holds that it emerged from a state of extremely high temperature and density in an explosive expansion 10–15 billion years ago. Its two basic assumptions—that Albert Einstein's general theory of relativity correctly describes the gravitational interaction of all matter and that an observer's view of the universe does not depend on direction of observation or on location—make it possible to calculate physical conditions in the universe back to a very early time called the Planck time (after Max Planck). According to the model proposed by George Gamow in the 1940s, the universe expanded rapidly from a highly compressed early state, with a steady decrease in density and temperature. Within seconds, matter predominated over antimatter and certain nuclei formed. It took another million years before atoms could form and electromagnetic radiation could travel through space unimpeded. The abundances of hydrogen, helium, and lithium and the discovery of cosmic background radiation support the model, which also explains the redshifts of the light from distant galaxies as resulting from the expansion of space.

It's hard to picture a time before there was a big bang (it's so much a part of our lives now), but before Al Friedmann in 1922, most of us still thought that the stars were ornaments God had hung on the tree and just left up all year. Friedmann, a brilliant Russian mathematician in the post-revolution still-honeymoon days, said that space and time were isotropic, with all points traveling uniformly in all directions fleeing a dramatic event of some magnitude. Einstein at this time was saying the universe was static, so he was by no means perfect. Friedmann's calculations were reworked into Big Bang 1 by one of his former students at Leningrad U, George Gamow, who, along with Edward Teller, a man with no small interest in big bangs, held that the universe began with a nuclear explosion Teller could only dream of and from a device that could fit inside an overnight bag. Who left the bag and why was not their field. Après bang, atomic nuclei streamed from ground zero like pea shot colliding and recombining with other nuclei clumping together into an early test version of matter.

Here's where it gets hairy. First off, you need to accept the Cosmological Principle, or you're not going anywhere: how you look at the universe in no way depends on where you are or which way you look. This makes for an edgeless universe from a source coming not from one spot but from everywhere—and simultaneously. Then you've got your Planck time to consider, being the smallest and first unit of time. The laws of physics, if not the union of physicists, do not allow them to look past the first Planck; who knows, it could look entirely different on the other side.—M.F.

bird flu

Or avian influenza. Viral respiratory disease, mainly of birds including poultry and waterbirds but also transmissible to humans. Symptoms in humans include fever, sore throat, cough, headache, and muscle aches. Severe infections can result in life-threatening complications such as pneumonia and acute respiratory illness. The first known human cases occurred in Hong Kong in 1997, resulting in six deaths. Deadly outbreaks among poultry in several countries in eastern and central Asia between 2003 and mid-2005 were accompanied by more than 100 human cases, about half of them fatal. The causative agents are virus subtypes related to the human influenza type A viruses, the most virulent and contagious being the H5N1 subtype. A specific protective vaccine for this virus remains to be developed. Studies suggest that some antiviral drugs that work against human influenza may be effective in treating bird flu in humans.

black hole

Cosmic body with gravity so intense that nothing, not even light, can escape. It is suspected to form in the death and collapse of a star that has retained at least three times the Sun's mass. Stars with less mass evolve into white dwarf stars or neutron stars. Details of a black hole's structure are calculated from Albert Einstein's general theory of relativity: a "singularity" of zero volume and infinite density pulls in all matter and energy that comes within an event horizon, defined by the Schwarzschild radius, around it. Black holes cannot be observed directly because they are small and emit no light. However, their enormous gravitational fields affect nearby matter, which is drawn in and emits X rays as it collides at high speed outside the event horizon. Some black holes may have nonstellar origins. Astronomers speculate that supermassive black holes at the centers of quasars and many galaxies are the source of energetic activity that is observed. Stephen W. Hawking theorized the creation of numerous tiny black holes, possibly no more massive than an asteroid, during the big bang. These primordial "mini black holes" lose mass over time and disappear as a result of Hawking radiation. Although black holes remain theoretical, the case for their existence is supported by many observations of phenomena that match their predicted effects.

blue whale

Mottled, blue-gray baleen whale (*Balaenoptera musculus*), also called sulfur-bottom whale because of the yellowish diatoms on some individuals. The largest of all animals, the blue whale reaches a maximum length of about 100 ft (30 m) and a maximum weight of 150 tons (136,000 kg). It is found alone or in small groups in all oceans. In summer it feeds on krill in polar waters, and in winter it moves toward the equator to breed. It was once the most important of the commercially hunted baleen whales, and its populations were greatly reduced. Listed as an endangered species, it is now protected.

cancer

Uncontrolled multiplication of abnormal cells. Cancerous cells and tissues have abnormal growth rates, shapes, sizes, and functioning.

Cancer may progress in stages from a localized tumor (confined to the site of origin) to direct extension (spread into nearby tissue or lymph nodes) and metastasis (spread to more distant sites via the blood or lymphatic system). This malignant growth pattern distinguishes cancerous tumors from benign ones. Cancer is also classified by grade, the extent to which cell characteristics remain specific to their tissue of origin. Both stage and grade affect the chances of survival. Genetic factors and immune status affect susceptibility. Triggers include hormones, viruses, smoking, diet, and radiation. Cancer can begin in almost any tissue, including blood and lymph. When it metastasizes, it remains a cancer of its tissue of origin. Early diagnosis and treatment increase the chance of cure. Treatment may include chemotherapy, surgery, and radiation therapy.

Copernicus, Nicolaus

(Polish; Mikolaj Kopernik) (born Feb. 19, 1473, Toruń, Pol.—died May 24, 1543, Frauenburg, East Prussia) Polish astronomer. He was educated at Kraków, Bologna, and Padua, where he mastered all the knowledge of the day in mathematics, astronomy, medicine, and theology. Elected a canon of the cathedral of Frauenburg in 1497, he took advantage of his financial security to begin his astronomical observations. His publication in 1543 of *Six Books Concerning the Revolutions of the Heavenly Orbs* marked a landmark of Western thought. Copernicus had first conceived of his revolutionary model decades earlier but delayed publication because, while it explained the retrograde motion of the planets (and resolved their order), it raised new problems that had to be explained, required verification of old observations, and had to be presented in a way that would not provoke the religious authorities. The book did not see print until he was on his deathbed. By attributing to Earth a daily rotation around its own axis and a yearly revolution around a stationary Sun, he developed an idea that had far-reaching implications for the rise of modern science. He asserted, in contrast to Platonic instrumental-ism, that astronomy must describe the real, physical system of the world. Only with Johannes Kepler was Copernicus's model fully trans-formed into a new philosophy about the fundamental structure of the universe.

designer drug

Synthetic version of a controlled narcotic substance. Designer drugs usually are synthesized for the first time in an attempt to create a chemical whose molecular structure differs only slightly from that of some well-known controlled substance but whose effects are essentially the same. Because of the difference in molecular structure, the designer drug, unlike the controlled substance, ordinarily will not be specifically listed as illicit by law-enforcement organizations. Many designer drugs are manufactured in clandestine laboratories, often by amateurs; for this reason they are sometimes more dangerous than the drugs they are intended to replace. One of the best-known is MDMA (3,4-methylene-dioxymethamphetamine), a variation of methamphetamine, popularly called Ecstasy. Nonnarcotic synthetic chemical compounds designed to interact with specific proteins and enzymes in order to combat disease also have been called designer drugs.

dinosaur

Any of the extinct reptiles that were the dominant land animals during most of the Mesozoic Era (248–65 million years ago). The various species appeared at different times, and not all overlapped. The shape of the teeth reveal whether a given dinosaur was a carnivore or herbivore. Dinosaurs are classified as either ornithischians or saurischians, based on pelvic girdle structure. Most had a long tail, which they held straight out, apparently to maintain balance. Most, if not all, were egg layers. Some were probably warm-blooded. Dinosaur fossils have been found on every continent, including Antarctica. Most types of dinosaurs flourished until late in the Cretaceous Period (65 million years ago), then disappeared within the next million years. Two theories for the cause

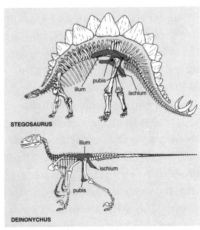

Skeletons of an ornithischian dinosaur (*Stegosaurus*) and a saurischian dinosaur (*Deinonychus*)

122

of this mass extinction, following some 140 million years of existence, are that mountain-building cycles altered habitat and changed climate or that an asteroid hit the Earth, resulting in immense dust clouds that blocked sunlight for several years. Birds are thought to be living descendants of the dinosaurs.

DNA

Or deoxyribonucleic acid. One of two types of nucleic acid (the other is RNA); a complex organic compound found in all living cells and many viruses. It is the chemical substance of genes. Its structure, with two strands wound around each other in a double helix to resemble a twisted ladder, was first described (1953) by Francis Crick and James D. Watson. Each strand is a long chain (polymer) of repeating nucleotides: adenine (A), guanine (G), cytosine (C), and thymine (T). The two strands contain complementary information: A forms hydrogen bonds only with T, C only with G. When DNA is copied in the cell, the strands separate and each serves as a template for assembling a new complementary strand; this is the key to stable heredity. DNA in cells is organized into dense protein-DNA complexes called chromosomes. In eukaryotes these are in the nucleus, and DNA also occurs in mitochondria and chloroplasts (if any). Prokaryotes have a single circular chromosome in the cytoplasm. Some prokaryotes and a few eukaryotes have DNA outside the chromosomes in plasmids.

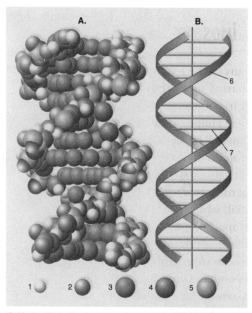

DNA double helix. A. Molecular model of DNA. The molecules include (1) hydrogen, (2) oxygen, (3) carbon and nitrogen in the linked nitrogenous bases, (4) carbon in the sugar deoxyribose, and (5) phosphorus. B. Schematic representation of DNA. The twisted ladder shape consists of (6) nitrogenous base pairs joined by hydrogen bonds, on (7) a sugar-phosphate backbone.

Earth

Third planet in distance outward from the Sun. Believed to be about 4.6 billion years old, it is some 92,960,000 mi (149,600,000 km) from the Sun. It orbits the Sun at a speed of 18.5 mi (29.8 km) per second, making one complete revolution in 365.25 days. As it revolves, it rotates on its axis once every 23 hours 56 minutes 4 seconds. The fifth largest planet of the solar system, it has an equatorial circumference of 24,902 mi (40,076 km). Its total surface area is roughly 197,000,000 sq mi (509,600,000 sq km), of which about 29 percent is land. Earth's atmosphere consists of a mixture of gases, chiefly nitrogen and oxygen. Its only natural satellite, the Moon, orbits the planet at a distance of about 238,860 mi (384,400 km). Earth's surface is traditionally subdivided into seven continental masses: Africa, Antarctica, Asia, Australia, Europe, North America, and South America. These continents are surrounded by four major bodies of water: the Arctic, Atlantic, Indian, and Pacific oceans. Broadly speaking, Earth's interior consists of two regions: a core composed largely of molten, iron-rich metallic alloy and a rocky shell of silicate minerals comprising both the mantle and crust. Fluid motions in the electrically conductive outer core generate a magnetic field around Earth that is responsible for the Van Allen radiation belts. According to the theory of plate tectonics, the crust and upper mantle are divided into a number of large and small plates that float on and travel independently of the lower mantle. Plate motions are responsible for continental drift and seafloor spreading and for most volcanic and seismic activity on Earth.

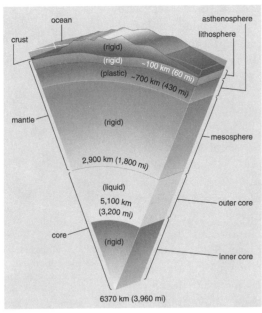

Earth's layers

Earth impact hazard

The danger of collision with asteroids and comets whose orbits carry them near Earth. Space around Earth contains vast numbers of objects in a range of sizes, but only the largest, which strike very rarely on average, are thought to pose a great danger. Scientists believe that such an impact may have caused the mass extinction of dinosaurs and other species at the end of the Cretaceous Period 65 million years ago. In addition to creating tremendous immediate destruction, a large impact could throw great clouds of debris into the atmosphere, cutting off sunlight and causing a prolonged temperature drop—an "impact winter" (similar to a nuclear winter) that would kill plant life and bring on worldwide famine. The amount of damage depends primarily on the colliding object's mass and relative velocity. The energy released, expressed in millions of tons (megatons) of TNT, falls between about 10 megatons and 1 billion megatons, corresponding to objects roughly 160 ft (50 m) to 12 mi (20 km) across. The last destructive impact known, the Tunguska event, occurred over Siberia in 1908. Since the 1990s, search programs have scanned for objects on possible collision courses. Should a collision appear likely, nonexplosive projectiles or, in extreme cases, nuclear weapons might succeed in redirecting the object away from Earth.

earthquake

Sudden shaking of the ground caused by a disturbance deeper within the crust of the Earth. Most earthquakes occur when masses of rock straining against one another along fault lines suddenly fracture and slip. The Earth's major earthquakes occur mainly in belts coinciding with the margins of tectonic plates. These include the Circum-Pacific Belt, which affects New Zealand, New Guinea, Japan, the Aleutian Islands, Alaska, and the western coasts of North and South America; the Alpide Belt, which passes through the Mediterranean region eastward through Asia; oceanic ridges in the Arctic, Atlantic, and western Indian oceans; and the rift valleys of East Africa. The "size," or magnitude, of earthquakes is usually expressed in terms of the Richter scale, which assigns levels from 1.0 or lower to 8.0 or higher. The largest quake ever recorded (Richter magnitude 9.5) occurred off the coast of Chile in 1960. The "strength" of an earthquake is rated in intensity scales such as the Mercalli scale, which assigns qualitative measures of damage to terrain and structures that range from "not felt" to "damage nearly total." The most destructive quake of modern times occurred in 1976, when the city of Tangshan, China, was leveled and more than 250,000 people were killed.

Ecstasy

Euphoria-inducing stimulant and hallucinogen. It is a derivative of the amphetamine family and a relative of the stimulant methamphetamine. Taken in pill form, it has a chemical relationship to the psychedelic drug mescaline. Developed in 1913 as an appetite suppressant, the drug was not originally approved for release. In the 1950s and 1960s, it began to be used in psychotherapy. The drug increases the production of the neurotransmitter serotonin and blocks its reabsorption in the brain; it also increases the amount of the neurotransmitter dopamine. Stimulation of the central nervous system gives users feelings of increased energy and lowers social inhibitions. By the 1980s, parties and dances that featured Ecstasy use (known as "raves") became popular. Despite its ban in the U.S. and the rest of the world, the drug retained a huge following, and it played an important role in the youth subculture, similar to that of LSD during the 1960s.

evolution

Biological theory that animals and plants have their origin in other preexisting types and that the distinguishable differences are due to modifications in successive generations. It is one of the keystones of modern biological theory. In 1858 Charles Darwin and Alfred Russel Wallace jointly published a paper on evolution. The next year Darwin presented his major treatise *On the Origin of Species by Means of Natural Selection*, which revolutionized all later biological study. The

A pair of red deer stags (Cervus elaphus) competing for possession of a female in the rutting season

Natural selection is the engine driving evolution, the attack on all that many deem holy, first launched in a broadside by Charles Darwin, mild-mannered country squire and naturalist, and radicalized by his going around the world in 50 months collecting specimens that showed that genetic variations in species occur over time, and only the best peas (with apologies to Mendel) get to be Birdseye. What was he thinking on that fateful trip on the *Beagle*, sailing for the Galapagos—that no one would notice the ape at the wheel? The gale that little brig sailed into rages yet: in the fall of 2005, a good 147 years after man evolved, the Museum of Natural History in New York was unable to find a corporate sponsor for its exhibit on Darwin, because business leaders didn't want to be seen "as taking sides," the similarities between a CEO and a silverback being a little too obvious.

Darwin said, prior to publishing, "This is a death sentence," although it's ambiguous whether he meant for religion or for himself. He did send review copies to the experts of the day with notes like, "you will long to crucify me," so I have to go with the latter. His anguish over the reaction to *On the Origin of Species by Means of Natural Selection* (1859) gave him ulcers and caused him to devolve to the moors in Yorkshire where, after randomly selecting a wife, he lived in a kind of self-exile while completing his definitive study of hermaphroditic barnacles, which, strangely, elicited little controversy.—M.F.

heart of Darwinian evolution is the mechanism of natural selection. Surviving individuals, which vary in some way that enables them to live longer and reproduce, pass on their advantage to succeeding generations. In 1937 Theodosius Dobzhansky applied Mendelian genetics to Darwinian theory, contributing to a new understanding of evolution as the cumulative action of natural selection on small genetic variations in whole populations. Part of the proof of evolution is in the fossil record, which shows a succession of gradually changing forms leading up to those known today. Structural similarities and similarities in embryonic development among living forms also point to common ancestry. Molecular biology (especially the study of genes and proteins) provides the most detailed evidence of evolutionary change. Though the theory of evolution is accepted by nearly the entire scientific community, it has sparked much controversy from Darwin's time to the present; many of the objections have come from religious leaders and thinkers who believe that elements of the theory conflict with literal interpretations of the Bible.

Global Positioning System (GPS)

Precise satellite-based navigation and location system originally developed for U.S. military use. GPS is a fleet of more than 24 communications satellites that transmit signals globally around the clock. With a GPS receiver, one can quickly and accurately determine the latitude, the longitude, and in most cases the altitude of a point on or above Earth's surface. A single GPS receiver can find its own position in seconds from GPS satellite signals to an accuracy of one meter; accuracy within one centimeter can be achieved with sophisticated military-specification receivers. This capability has reduced the cost of acquiring spatial data for making maps while increasing cartographic accuracy. Other applications include measuring the movement of polar ice sheets or even finding the best automobile route between given points.

global warming

Increase in the global average surface temperature resulting from enhancement of the Greenhouse Effect, primarily by air pollution. In 2001 the UN Intergovernmental Panel on Climate Change estimated that by 2100 global average surface temperatures would increase 2.5 to 10.4 °F (1.4 to 5.8 °C), depending on a range of scenarios for greenhouse gas emissions. Many scientists predict that such an increase would cause polar ice caps and mountain glaciers to melt rapidly, significantly raising the levels of coastal waters, and would produce new patterns and extremes of drought and rainfall, seriously disrupting food production in certain regions. Other scientists maintain that such predictions are overstated. The 1992 Earth Summit and the 1997 Kyoto Protocol to the United Nations Framework Convention on Climate Change attempted to address the issue of global warming, but in both cases the efforts were hindered by conflicting national economic agendas and disputes between developed and developing nations over the cost and consequences of reducing emissions of greenhouse gases.

gravitation

Universal force of attraction that acts between all bodies that have mass. Though it is the weakest of the four known forces, it shapes the structure and evolution of stars, galaxies, and the entire universe. The laws of gravity describe the trajectories of bodies in the solar system and the motion of objects on Earth, where all bodies experience a downward gravitational force exerted by Earth's mass, the force experienced as weight. Isaac Newton was the first to develop a quantitative theory of gravitation, holding that the force of attraction between two bodies is proportional to the product of their masses and inversely proportional to the square of the distance between them. Albert Einstein proposed a whole new concept of gravitation, involving the four-dimensional continuum of space-time, which is curved by the presence of matter. In his general theory of relativity, he showed that a body undergoing uniform acceleration is indistinguishable from one that is stationary in a gravitational field.

Greenhouse Effect

Warming of the Earth's surface and lower atmosphere caused by water vapor, carbon dioxide, and other trace gases in the atmosphere. Visible light from the Sun heats the Earth's surface. Part of this energy is radiated back into the atmosphere in the form of infrared radiation, much of which is absorbed by molecules of carbon dioxide and water vapor in the atmosphere and reradiated toward the surface as more heat. (Despite the name, the Greenhouse Effect is different from the warming in a greenhouse, where panes of glass allow the passage of visible light but hold heat inside the building by trapping warmed air.) The absorption of infrared radiation causes the Earth's surface and lower atmosphere to warm more than they otherwise would, making the Earth's surface habitable. An increase in atmospheric carbon dioxide caused by

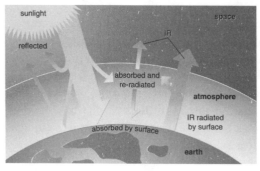

Some incoming sunlight is reflected by the Earth's atmosphere and surface, but most is absorbed by the surface, which is warmed. Infrared (IR) radiation is then emitted from the surface. Some IR radiation escapes to space, but some is absorbed by the atmosphere's greenhouse gases and reradiated in all directions, some to space and some back toward the surface, where it further warms the surface and lower atmosphere.

widespread combustion of fossil fuels may intensify the Greenhouse Effect and cause long-term climatic changes. Likewise, an increase in atmospheric concentrations of other trace greenhouse gases such as chlorofluorocarbons, nitrous oxide, and methane resulting from human activities may also intensify the Greenhouse Effect. From the beginning of the Industrial Revolution through the end of the 20th century, the amount of carbon dioxide in the atmosphere increased 30 percent and the amount of methane more than doubled. It is also estimated that the U.S. is responsible for about one-fifth of all human-produced greenhouse-gas emissions.

Hippocrates

(Born *c.* 460 BC, island of Cos, Greece—died *c.* 377 BC, Larissa, Thessaly) Greek physician regarded as the father of medicine. Plato, his contemporary, referred to him twice and implied that he was famous as a physician. Meno, a pupil of Aristotle, stated that Hippocrates believed that disease was caused by the excreted vapors of undigested food. His philosophy was to see the body as a whole. He apparently traveled widely in Greece and Asia Minor, practicing and teaching. The "Hippocratic Collection" supposedly belonged to the library of a medical school (probably at Cos) and then to the Library of Alexandria. An unknown proportion of the 60 or so surviving manuscripts—the earliest dating from the 10th century

Hippocrates, Roman bust copied from a Greek original, c. 3rd century BC; in the collection of the Antichità Di Ostia, Italy

AD—are actually by Hippocrates. The collection deals with anatomy, clinical subjects, diseases of women and children, prognosis, treatment, surgery, and medical ethics. The Hippocratic Oath (not actually written by Hippocrates), also part of the Hippocratic Collection, is divided into two major sections, the first setting out the physician's obligations to his students and his pupils' duties to him, the second pledging him to prescribe only beneficial treatments, refrain from causing harm or hurt, and live an exemplary life.

Everyone thinks of the oath, but there is, in fact, a "Hippocratic Collection," some 60 volumes of which survived the destruction of the great library at Alexandria. The works constituted the library of the medical school at Cos, where Hippocrates, described by Plato as a great healer of small stature, held sway. The volumes are almost certainly the works of many authors, the first specialists, perhaps, each holding forth on an area of expertise: anatomy, pediatrics, diseases of women, prognosis, treatment, billing, medical ethics, and a variety of clinical subjects. The seven books on epidemics stand out, along with *Airs, Waters, and Places*, which expands on the Hippocratic view that disease was caused by undigested residues produced by an unsuitable diet exuding pestilent vapors, which we know to be true today. The oath itself, which famously asks the physician to at least not make things worse, begins by holding the doctor accountable first, not to his patients, but to his teacher: "to live my life in partnership with him," especially regarding fee sharing. One could, therefore, view the Hippocratic Oath as an oath to Hippocrates.—M.F.

International Space Station (ISS)

Space station assembled from modules in Earth orbit largely by the U.S. and Russia, with assistance and components from a multinational consortium. The project, which began as a U.S. effort, was long delayed by funding and technical problems. Originally called Freedom in the 1980s, it was redesigned in the 1990s to reduce costs and expand international involvement, at which time it was renamed. In-orbit construction started in late 1998 with the launches of a Russian control module and a U.S.-built connecting node, which were linked in orbit by space shuttle astronauts. In mid-2000 a habitat and control-center module was added, and later in the year the ISS received its first resident crew, two Russians and an American. Other elements were subsequently joined to the station, with the overall plan calling for a complex of laboratories and habitats crossed by a long truss supporting four large solar power arrays. Station construction involved at least 16 countries, including Canada, Japan, Brazil, and 11 members of the European Space Agency. Much of the early work aboard the ISS would focus on long-term life-sciences and material-sciences research in the weightless environment. It was expected to serve as the basis for human operations in Earth orbit for at least the first quarter of the 21st century.

Jupiter

Fifth planet from the Sun, the largest nonstellar object in the solar system. It has 318 times the mass and more than 1,400 times the volume of Earth. Its enormous mass gives it nearly 2.5 times the gravity of Earth (measured at the top of Jupiter's atmosphere), and it exerts strong effects on other members of the solar system. It is responsible for the Kirkwood gaps in the asteroid belt and changes in the orbits of comets; it may act as a "sweeper," pulling in bodies that might otherwise collide with other planets. Jupiter has more than 60 moons and a diffuse ring system discovered in 1979 by the Voyager spacecraft. The planet is a gas giant, composed mainly of hydrogen and helium in proportions near those of the Sun, which it orbits every 11.9 years at an average distance of 483 million mi (778 million km). Its rapid rotation (9 hr 55.5 min) acts on electric currents to give it the largest magnetic field of any of the planets and causes intense storms, including one that has lasted hundreds of years (the Great Red Spot). Little is known of its interior, but it is presumed to have a deep layer of metallic hydrogen and a dense core. Its central temperature is estimated to be 45,000 °F (25,000 °C); it radiates twice as much heat as it receives from the Sun, probably largely heat left over from its formation.

laser

Device that produces an intense beam of coherent light (light composed of waves having a constant difference in phase). Its name, an acronym derived from "light amplification by stimulated emission of radiation," describes how its beam is produced. The first laser, constructed in 1960 by Theodore Maiman (born 1927) based on earlier work by Charles H. Townes, used a rod of ruby. Light of a suitable wavelength from a flashlight excited the ruby atoms to higher energy levels. The excited atoms decayed swiftly to slightly lower energies (through phonon reactions) and then fell more slowly to the ground state, emitting light at a specific wavelength. The light tended to bounce back and forth between the polished ends of the rod, stimulating further emission. The laser has found valuable applications in microsurgery, compact-disc players, communications, and holography, as well as for drilling holes in hard materials, alignment in tunnel drilling, long-distance measurement, and mapping fine details.

leprosy

Or Hansen disease. Chronic disease of the skin, peripheral nerves, and mucous membranes of the nose, throat, and eyes, caused by the bacterium *Mycobacterium leprae*. In tuberculoid leprosy, cells of the immune system crowd into infected areas of the skin, forming hard nodules, or tubercles, that spread along nerve fibers. This type of reaction commonly leads to claw hand, gross deformity of the foot, and paralysis of muscles of the face, eye, and neck. In the lepromatous type, bacilli multiply freely in deep layers of the skin and spread widely through lymphatic channels and along nerve fibers, causing thickening and corrugation of the skin, raising soft nodules on the ears, nose, and cheeks, and sometimes destroying the septum of the nose and the palate. Leprosy has a long history. Until the 20th century, infected people were ostracized from society or at best segregated and cared for in isolated leper colonies. Today the disease is entirely curable through multidrug therapy, though tissue damage caused before drug treatment cannot be reversed. Some 600,000 new cases arise every year, mostly in Asia, Africa, Central and South America, and the Pacific Islands. About 60 percent of new cases occur in India.

Mars

Fourth planet from the Sun, named after the Roman god of war. Its mean distance from the Sun is 141 million mi (227 million km). Its day is 24.6 Earth hours and its year about 687 Earth days. It has two small moons, Phobos and Deimos. Mars's equatorial diameter is 4,220 mi (6,792 km), about half that of Earth, and it is less dense than Earth. Its mass is about one-tenth of Earth's and its surface gravity about one-third as strong. No magnetic field has been detected on Mars, suggesting, as does its low density, the absence of a substantial metallic core. Like Earth, it has seasons and an atmosphere, but its average daytime surface temperature is only −10 °F (−20 °C). Mars's thin atmosphere is mainly carbon dioxide, with some nitrogen and argon and traces of water vapor. Spacecraft images show a cratered surface, with volcanoes, lava plains, flood channels, and canyons, many large by Earth standards; Olympus Mons, for example, is the largest known volcano in the solar system. Wind is an important element on Mars, sculpting features such as dunes and occasionally causing global dust storms. In the distant past Mars appears to have had a denser, warmer atmosphere and much more water than at present. Images from the Mars Global Surveyor spacecraft suggest that some liquid water may have flowed near the planet's surface in relatively recent times. No life has been detected on the planet.

Mercury

Innermost planet of the solar system. Its average distance from the Sun is about 36 million mi (58 million km), but its highly elliptical orbit carries it 7.5 million mi (12 million km) nearer to and farther from the Sun. It is the second-smallest major planet (after Pluto), having a diameter of about 3,030 mi (4,880 km) and a mass about one-eighteenth of Earth's. With the shortest period of revolution (only 88 Earth days) and the highest average orbital speed (30 mi/second, or 48 km/second) of any planet, it is aptly named after the fleet-footed Roman messenger god. It spins very slowly, making one complete rotation relative to the stars every 59 Earth days, while its solar day (from one sunrise to the next) is 176 Earth days, owing to its revolution around the Sun. Its surface is heavily cratered. Its most impressive feature is perhaps the 800-mi (1,300-km) Caloris Basin, formed by a huge meteorite impact. Mercury also has steep cliffs that extend for hundreds of miles. The discovery of a magnetic field in its vicinity suggests it has a large iron core, which would account for a mean density almost as high as Earth's. Its atmosphere is negligible; its surface gravity, about one-third that of Earth's, holds an exceedingly tenuous layer of gases. Temperatures at its surface change dramatically, ranging from a high that can exceed 800 °F (425 °C) on the sunward side to a low of about –290 °F (–180 °C) at the end of its night.

monkeypox

Viral disease of both animals and humans that causes symptoms similar to those of smallpox, though less severe. The monkeypox virus is usually found in primates and rodents in Central and West Africa but has spread to other parts of the world through the export of infected small mammals. It can be transmitted to humans through an animal bite and from person to person through prolonged close contact. Symptoms of the disease include fever, headache, general malaise and fatigue, and swollen lymph nodes. A rash of raised bumps appears on the infected person's face and body. Treatment is limited to alleviating symptoms. Outbreaks are contained by isolating patients and controlling the trade of animals.

Moon

Sole natural satellite of Earth, which it orbits from west to east at a mean distance of about 238,900 mi (384,400 km). It is less than one-third the size of Earth (diameter about 2,160 mi, or 3,476 km, at its equator), about one-eightieth as massive, and about two-thirds as dense. Its surface gravity is about one-sixth that of Earth, and its gravitational pull is largely responsible for Earth's tides. The Moon shines by reflected sunlight, but its albedo is only 7.3 percent. It rotates on its axis in about 29.5 days, in exactly the time it takes to orbit Earth, and it therefore always presents the same face to Earth. However, that face is lit by the Sun at different angles as the Moon revolves around Earth, causing it to display different phases over the month, from new to full. Most astronomers believe that the Moon formed from a cloud of fragments ejected into Earth orbit when a Mars-sized body struck the proto-Earth early in the solar system's history. Its surface has been studied by telescope since Galileo first observed it in 1609 and firsthand by a total of 12 U.S. astronauts during the six successful lunar landing missions of the Apollo program. The dominant process affecting the surface has been impacts, both from micrometeorite bombardment, which grinds rock fragments into fine dust, and from meteorite strikes, which produced the craters profusely scattered over its surface mostly early in its history, more than four billion years ago. The maria are huge, ancient lava flows. In the late 1990s unmanned spacecraft found possible signs of water ice

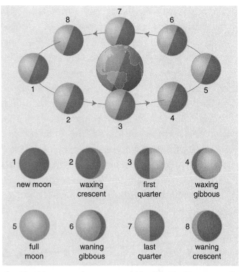

As the Moon revolves around the Earth, the amount of its illuminated half seen from the Earth slowly increases and decreases (waxes and wanes)

Nanotechnology is one word now, so that tells you some-thing, namely that this thing could happen, is happening. Nanowhiskers, billions of which are already imbedded in your fabrics, are defeating staining once and for all, even as we speak.

Soon, nano elevators will take molecules to whatever floor they want in compounds, nano robotic internists will float in your bloodstream just like in *Fantastic Voyage*—only without the young Raquel Welch—and the nano Jumbotron will not be an oxymoron. Nano anti-terrorists will sniff our very air, nano meat-inspectors our meat, nano scrubbers will trap our particulates, and nano factories with nano machines run by nano workers working for nano money will produce tiny little goods. Nano is big.

Nanotechnology is the answer to the question of why anyone would go into materials science. It was Richard Feynman who in 1959 first suggested that *Encyclopædia Britannica* could fit on the head of a pin, even though it would look more impressive on the shelf. Norio Taniguchi came up with the term in 1974, and Eric Drexler popularized the idea in 1986 with *Engines of Creation: The Coming Era of Nanotechnology...* Nanoscience, a department in search of a chair, brings together the hydrogen-bonding people with the Van der Waals–force–attraction people, and the hydrophobicists with the hydrophilicists with the tiny little future hanging in the balance.—M.F.

---

near the Moon's poles. More generally, a moon is any natural satellite orbiting a planet or other nonstellar body.

nanotechnology

Manipulation of atoms, molecules, and materials to form structures on the scale of nanometers (billionths of a meter). These nanostructures typically exhibit new properties or behaviors due to quantum mechanics. In 1959 Richard Feynman first pointed out some potential quantum benefits of miniaturization. A major advancement was the invention of molecular-beam epitaxy by Alfred Cho and John Arthur at Bell Laboratories in 1968 and its development in the 1970s, which enabled the controlled deposition of single atomic layers. Scientists have made some progress at building devices, including computer components, at nanoscales. Faster progress has occurred in the incorporation of nanomaterials in other products, such as stain-resistant coatings for clothes and invisible sunscreens.

Neptune

Eighth planet from the Sun, discovered in 1846 and named for the Roman god of the sea. It has an average distance from the Sun of 2.8 billion mi (4.5 billion km), taking nearly 164 years to complete one orbit and rotating every 16.11 hours. Neptune has more than 17 times Earth's mass, 58 times its volume, and 12 percent stronger gravity at the top of its atmosphere. It has an equatorial diameter of 30,775 mi (49,528 km). Neptune consists largely of hydrogen and helium. It has no solid surface; its interior is believed to consist of a fluid mixture of rock, ices, and gas. Its atmosphere contains substantial amounts of methane gas, whose absorption of red light causes Neptune's deep blue-green color. The Voyager 2 space probe in 1989 discovered winds of more than 1,570 mi/hour (700 m/second), the fastest known for any of the Sun's planets, and dark spots that appear to be storms similar to Jupiter's Great Red Spot. Neptune receives little solar radiation, but it radiates substantially more energy than it receives, which indicates an internal heat source. Neptune's weak magnetic field traps charged particles in a belt around the planet. Neptune has a system of rings, made up largely of dust-size particles, and at least 13 moons; the largest is Triton, almost as big as Earth's Moon.

oxygen

Gaseous chemical element, chemical symbol O, atomic number 8. It constitutes 21 percent (by volume) of air and more than 46 percent (by weight) of Earth's crust, where it is the most plentiful element. It is a colorless, odorless, tasteless gas, occurring as the diatomic molecule O_2. In respiration, it is taken up by animals and some bacteria (and by plants in the dark), which give off carbon dioxide (CO_2). In photosynthesis, green plants assimilate carbon dioxide in the presence of sunlight and give off oxygen. The small amount of oxygen that dissolves in water is essential for the respiration of fish and other aquatic life. Oxygen takes part in combustion and in corrosion but does not itself burn. It has valence 2 in compounds; the most important is water. It forms oxides and is part of many other molecules and functional groups, including nitrate, sulfate, phosphate, and carbonate; alcohols, aldehydes, carboxylic acids, and ketones; and peroxides. Obtained for industrial use by distillation of liquefied air, oxygen is used in steelmaking and other metallurgical processes and in the chemical industry. Medical uses include respiratory therapy, incubators, and inhaled anesthetics. Oxygen is part of all gas mixtures for manned spacecraft, scuba divers, workers in closed environments, and hyperbaric chambers. It is also used in rocket engines as an oxidizer (in liquefied form) and in water- and waste-treatment processes.

Pangea

Or Pangaea. Hypothetical protocontinent proposed by Alfred Wegener in 1912 as part of his theory of continental drift. Pangea (from Greek: *pangaia*, "all earth") supposedly covered about half the Earth and was completely surrounded by a world ocean called Panthalassa. Late in the Triassic Period (248–206 million years ago), Pangea began to break apart. Its segments, Laurasia (composed of all the present-day northern continents) and Gondwana (the present-day southern continents) gradually receded, resulting in the formation of the Atlantic Ocean.

periodic table

Organized array of all the chemical elements in approximately increasing order of their atomic weight. The elements show a periodic recurrence of certain properties, first discovered in 1869 by Dmitry I. Mendeleyev. Those in the same column (group) of the table as usually arranged have similar properties. In the 20th century, when the structure of atoms was understood, the table was seen to precisely reflect increasing order of atomic number. Members of the same group in the table have the same number of electrons in the outermost shells of their atoms and form bonds of the same type, usually with the same valence; the noble gases, with full outer shells, generally do not form bonds. The periodic table has thus greatly deepened understanding of bonding and chemical behavior. It also allowed the prediction of new elements, many of which were later discovered or synthesized.

photosynthesis

Process by which green plants and certain other organisms transform light into chemical energy. In green plants, light energy is captured by chlorophyll in the chloroplasts of the leaves and used to convert water, carbon dioxide, and minerals into oxygen and energy-rich organic compounds (simple and complex sugars) that are the basis of both plant and animal life. Photosynthesis consists of a number of photochemical and enzymatic reactions. It occurs in two stages. During the light-dependent stage (light reaction), chlorophyll absorbs light energy, which excites some electrons in the pigment molecules to higher energy levels; these leave the chlorophyll and pass along a series of molecules, generating formation of NADPH (an enzyme) and high-energy ATP molecules. Oxygen, released as a by-product, passes into the atmosphere through pores in the leaves. NADPH and ATP drive the second stage, the dark reaction (or Calvin cycle, discovered by Melvin Calvin), which does not require light. During this stage glucose is generated using atmospheric carbon dioxide. Photosynthesis is crucial for maintaining life on Earth; if it ceased, there would soon be little food or other organic matter on the planet, and most types of organisms would disappear.

plate tectonics

Theory that the Earth's lithosphere (the crust and upper portion of the mantle) is divided into about 12 large plates and several small ones that float on and travel independently over the asthenosphere. The theory revolutionized the geological sciences in the 1960s by combining the

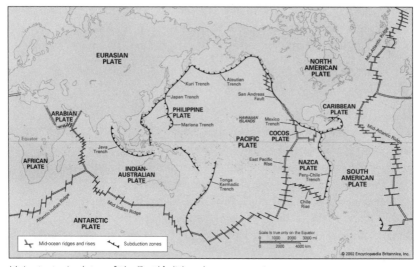

Major tectonic plates of the Earth's lithosphere

earlier idea of continental drift and the new concept of seafloor spreading into a coherent whole. Each plate consists of rigid rock created by upwelling magma at oceanic ridges, where plates diverge. Where two plates converge, a subduction zone forms, in which one plate is forced under another and into the Earth's mantle. The majority of the earthquakes and volcanoes on the Earth's surface occur along the margins of tectonic plates. The interior of a plate moves as a rigid body, with only minor flexing, few earthquakes, and relatively little volcanic activity.

Pluto

Ninth planet from the Sun. It was discovered in 1930 by Clyde W. Tombaugh (1906–97) and named after the Greek god of the underworld. It is usually the outermost of the known planets, averaging about 3.7 billion mi (5.9 billion km) from the Sun (within the Kuiper belt), but its eccentric orbit brings it closer to the Sun than Neptune for 22 years during its 248-year orbit. Its axis is tipped 120°, so it rotates nearly on its side and "backward" once every 6.39 days, locked synchronously with the orbit of its single moon, Charon, discovered in 1978. Pluto has a diameter of about 1,455 mi (2,340 km), roughly two-thirds that of the Moon, and has less than 1 percent of Earth's mass and only about 6 percent of its surface gravity. Its estimated average surface temperature is near –390 °F (–235 °C). Its thin atmosphere contains nitrogen, methane, and perhaps other heavier gases. Pluto is thought to be made of frozen gases with a significant fraction of rocky material. Its size, composition, and orbital location in the Kuiper belt have sparked debate over its classification as a major planet.

Ptolemy

(Latin; Claudius Ptolemaeus) (born c. AD 100—died c. AD 170) Greek astronomer and mathematician. He worked principally in Alexandria. It is often difficult to determine which findings in his great astronomical book, the *Almagest*, are Ptolemy's and which are Hipparchus's. The Sun, Moon, planets, and stars, he believed, were attached to crystalline spheres, centered on Earth, which turned to create the cycles of day and night, the lunar month, and so on. In order to explain retrograde motion of the planets, he refined a complex geometric model of cycles within cycles that was highly successful at predicting the planets' positions in the sky. The

Earth-centered Ptolemaic system became dogmatically asserted in Western Christendom until the Sun-centered Copernican system replaced it. His *Geography* contained an estimate of the size of Earth, a description of its surface, and a list of places located by latitude and longitude. Ptolemy also dabbled in mechanics, optics, and music theory.

quark

Any of a group of subatomic particles thought to be among the fundamental constituents of matter—more specifically, of protons and neutrons. The concept of the quark was first proposed independently by Murray Gell-Mann (recipient of the Nobel Prize in Physics in 1969 and a member of Britannica's Board of Directors) and George Zweig; its name was taken from James Joyce's novel *Finnegans Wake*. Quarks include all particles that interact by means of the strong force. They have mass and spin, and they obey the Pauli exclusion principle. They have never been resolved into smaller components, and they never occur alone. Their behavior is explained by the theory of quantum chromodynamics, which provides a means of calculating their basic properties. There are six types of quarks, called up, down, strange, charm, bottom, and top. Only the up and down quarks are needed to make protons and neutrons; the others occur in heavier, unstable particles.

Feldman-ISM

There are seven dwarves, but only six quarks: up, down, charm, strange, top, and bottom, with Murray Gell-Mann as Snow White. Gell-Mann, already hyphenated and in Yale at 15, hypothesized "strangeness," a quantum property that explains why certain mesons, particles with an equal number of quarks and anti-quarks, decay. Quarks are the constituent parts of the subatomic particles that make up matter bound together by strong force into protons and neutrons. Gell-Mann came up with the Eightfold Way to classify mesons and baryons (heavier atomic particles) and speculated on the existence of even more basic components that he named quarks (see *Finnegans Wake*). As of this writing, quarks are as fundamental as matter gets, having no apparent structure and therefore no moving parts; they hate to be alone, even if it means going in tandem with an antiquark. They come in flavors. Quarks have been seen to exchange mass-less gluons which transmit the force that holds them together; they tend to cling—the trick now will be to knock one free to observe it nekkid.—M.F.

robotics

Design, construction, and use of machines (robots) to perform tasks traditionally done by human beings. Robots are widely used in such industries as automobile manufacture to perform simple repetitive tasks and in industries where work must be performed in environments hazardous to humans. Many aspects of robotics involve artificial intelligence; robots may be equipped with the equivalent of human senses such as vision, touch, and the ability to sense temperature. Some are even capable of simple decision making, and current robotics research is geared toward devising robots with a degree of self-sufficiency that will permit mobility and decision making in an unstructured environment. Today's industrial robots do not resemble human beings; a robot in human form is called an android.

Severe Acute Respiratory Syndrome (SARS)

Highly contagious respiratory illness characterized by a persistent fever, headache, and bodily discomfort, followed by a dry cough that may progress to great difficulty in breathing. SARS appeared in November 2002 in Guangdong province, China, and was brought to Hong Kong in February 2003. As it spread from there to other countries of East Asia and the world, health authorities instituted an unprecedented series of control measures, including quarantines and prohibitions on travel, and in June 2003 the global outbreak was declared to be contained. By that time more than 8,000 cases had been reported, and some 800 people had died. SARS is believed to be caused by a mutant coronavirus, a type usually associated with pneumonia and the common cold. A specific vaccine has not been developed. Treatment is usually restricted to easing the patient's symptoms—providing mechanical ventilation if necessary—until the illness has run its course.

Saturn

Sixth planet from the Sun, named for the Roman god of sowing and seed. The second largest nonstellar object in the solar system after Jupiter, it is about 95 times as massive as Earth and has more than 700 times its volume. Saturn's outer layers are gaseous, mainly hydrogen. Models of its interior suggest a rock-and-ice core surrounded by a shallow layer of liquid metallic hydrogen encased by an envelope of molecular hydrogen. Its mean density, about 70 percent that of water, is the lowest of any known object in the solar system. Saturn has at least 47 moons (including Titan, the largest) and an extensive ring system, with several main sections visible from Earth with a telescope. Saturn's rings, first observed in 1610 by Galileo, are made up of countless separate particles ranging mainly from inches to many feet in size but also including dust in some regions. Water ice probably constitutes most of the ring material. Saturn's day is about 10.6 hours; its year is 29.4 Earth years. Its rapid rotation, acting on electric currents in the core, generates a strong magnetic field and large magnetosphere. Saturn's fast spin also makes it the most flattened (oblate) of the planets; its polar diameter of 67,560 mi (108,728 km) is 10 percent smaller than its equatorial diameter. Its average distance from the Sun is 887 million mi (1.43 billion km).

Silicon Valley

Industrial strip, west-central California. Located between San Jose and Palo Alto in the San Jose and Santa Clara valleys, its (unofficial) name derives from the extensive use of silicon in the region's electronics industries. The U.S. government invested heavily in the region's industry following World War II, a second economic surge occurred with the proliferation of personal computers in the 1980s, and a third surge followed the growth of the Internet in the 1990s.

sociobiology

Systematic study of the biological basis of social behavior. The concept was popularized by Edward O. Wilson in his *Sociobiology* (1975) and by Richard Dawkins in *The Selfish Gene* (1976). Sociobiology attempts to understand and explain animal (and human) social behavior in the light of natural selection and other biological processes. A central tenet is that the transmission of genes through successful reproduction is the central motivator in animals' struggle for survival and that animals will behave in ways that maximize their chances of transmitting their genes to succeeding generations. Though sociobiology has contributed insights into animal behavior (such as altruism in social insects and male-female differences in certain species), it remains controversial when applied to human social behavior.

space shuttle

Formally Space Transportation System (STS). Partially reusable rocket-launched vehicle developed by NASA to go into Earth orbit, transport people and cargo between Earth and orbiting spacecraft, and glide to a runway landing on Earth. The first flight of a space shuttle into orbit took place in 1981. The shuttle consists of a winged orbiter that carries crew and cargo; an expendable external tank of liquid fuel and oxidizer for the orbiter's three main rocket engines; and two large, reusable solid-propellant booster rockets. The orbiter lifts off vertically like an expendable launch vehicle but makes an unpowered descent similar to a glider. Each orbiter was designed to be reused up to 100 times. For manipulating cargo and other materials outside the orbiter, astronauts use a remotely controlled robot arm or exit the orbiter wearing spacesuits. On some missions, the shuttle carries a European-built pressurized research facility called Spacelab in its cargo bay. Between 1981 and 1985, four shuttle orbiters were put into service: *Columbia* (the first in orbit), *Challenger*, *Discovery*, and *Atlantis*. *Challenger* exploded in 1986 during launch, killing all seven astronauts aboard; it was replaced in 1992 by *Endeavour*. From 1995 to 1998, NASA conducted shuttle missions to the Russian space station Mir to prepare for the construction of the International Space Station (ISS). Beginning in 1998, the shuttle was used extensively to ferry components, supplies, and crews to the ISS. In 2003 *Columbia* disintegrated while returning from a space mission, claiming the lives of its seven-person crew.

Sputnik

Any of a series of Earth-orbiting spacecraft whose launching by the Soviet Union inaugurated the space age. *Sputnik 1*, the world's first artificial satellite (October 1957), remained in orbit until early 1958, when it reentered Earth's atmosphere and burned up. *Sputnik 2* carried a dog, Laika, the first living creature to orbit Earth; because *Sputnik 2* was not designed to sustain life, Laika did not survive the flight. Eight more missions with similar satellites carried out experiments on various animals to test life-support systems and reentry procedures and to furnish data on space temperatures, pressures, particles, radiation, and magnetic fields.

stem cell

In living organisms, an undifferentiated cell that can produce other cells that eventually make up specialized tissues and organs. There are two major types of stem cells, embryonic and adult. Embryonic stem cells are located in the inner mass of a blastocyst (an embryo at a very early stage of development), and they eventually give rise to every cell type of the adult organism. Adult stem cells are found in some tissues in the adult body, such as the epidermis of the skin, the lining of the small intestine, and the bone marrow, where they serve in the regeneration of old or worn tissue. In cancer treatment, blood-forming adult stem cells are routinely harvested from bone marrow, stored, and then reinfused into patients to replace blood cells destroyed by chemotherapy or radiation therapy. This potential for replacing damaged tissues has aroused great interest in using embryonic stem cells to treat a number of other conditions, such as Parkinson disease, severe burns, and damage to the spinal cord. Mouse embryonic stem cells are widely used to create genetically modified mice that serve as models for investigating human disease. However, the use of human embryonic stem cells, which requires destroying the blastocysts from which they are obtained, has raised objections by those who feel blastocyst-stage embryos are human beings. The first human stem cell line was created in 1998, using cells harvested from embryos produced through in vitro fertilization. The use of human embryonic stem cells is allowed in some countries and prohibited or restricted in others.

string theory

Any of a number of theories in particle physics that treat elementary particles as infinitesimal one-dimensional "stringlike" objects rather than dimensionless points in space-time. Different vibrations of the strings correspond to different particles. Introduced in the early 1970s in attempts to describe the strong force, string theories became popular in the 1980s when it was shown that they might provide a fully self-consistent quantum field theory that could describe gravitation as well as the weak, strong, and electromagnetic forces. The development of a unified quantum field theory is a major goal in theoretical particle physics, but inclusion of gravity usually leads to difficult problems with infinite quantities in the calculations. The most self-consistent string theories propose 11 dimensions; four correspond to the three ordinary spatial dimensions and time, while the rest are curled up and not perceptible.

Sun

Star around which the components of the solar system revolve. It is about five billion years old and is the dominant body of the system, with more than 99 percent of its mass. It converts five million tons of matter into energy every second by nuclear fusion reactions in its core, producing neutrinos and solar radiation. The small amount of this energy that penetrates Earth's atmosphere provides the light and heat that support life. A sphere of luminous gas 864,950 mi (1,392,000 km) in diameter, the Sun has about 330,000 times the mass of Earth. Its core temperature is close to 27 million °F (15 million °C) and its surface temperature about 10,000 °F (6,000 °C). The Sun, a spectral type G (yellow) star, has fairly average properties for a main-sequence star. It rotates at different rates at different latitudes; one rotation takes 36 days at the poles but only 25 days at the equator. The visible surface, or photosphere, is in constant motion, with the number and position of sunspots changing in a regular solar cycle. External phenomena include magnetic activity extending into the chromosphere and corona, solar flares, solar prominences, and the solar wind. Effects on Earth include auroras and disruption of radio communications and power-transmission lines. Despite its activity, the Sun appears to have remained relatively unchanged for billions of years.

tropical cyclone

Severe atmospheric disturbance in tropical oceans. Tropical cyclones have very low atmospheric pressures in the calm, clear center (the eye) of a circular structure of rain, cloud, and very high winds. In the Atlantic and Caribbean they are called hurricanes; in the Pacific they are known as typhoons. Because of the Earth's rotation, tropical cyclones rotate

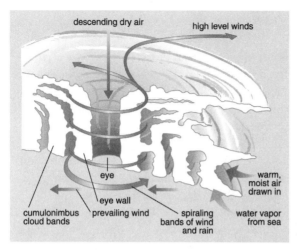

Cross section of a
tropical cyclone

clockwise in the Southern Hemisphere and counterclockwise in the
Northern. They may be 50–500 mi (80–800 km) in diameter, and sustained winds in excess of 100 mph (160 kph) are common. In the eye,
however, the winds drop abruptly to light breezes or even complete
calm. The lowest sea-level pressures on Earth occur in or near the eye.

tsunami

Or seismic sea wave or tidal wave. Catastrophic ocean wave, usually
caused by a submarine earthquake. Underwater or coastal landslides or
volcanic eruptions also may cause tsunamis. The term *tsunami* is
Japanese for "harbor wave." The term *tidal wave* is a misnomer, because
the wave has no connection with the tides. Perhaps the most destructive
tsunami ever occurred in 2004 in the Indian Ocean, after an earthquake
struck the seafloor off the Indonesian island of Sumatra. More than
200,000 people were killed in Indonesia, Thailand, India, Sri Lanka, and
other countries as far away as Somalia on the Horn of Africa.

Turing, Alan (Mathison)

(Born June 23, 1912, London, Eng.—died June 7, 1954, Wilmslow,
Cheshire) English mathematician and logician. He studied at the
University of Cambridge and at Princeton's Institute for Advanced Study.
In his seminal 1936 paper "On Computable Numbers," he proved that

there cannot exist any universal algorithmic method of determining truth in mathematics and that mathematics will always contain undecidable (as opposed to unknown) propositions. That paper also introduced the Turing machine. He believed that computers eventually would be capable of thought indistinguishable from that of a human and proposed a simple test to assess this capability. His papers on the subject are widely acknowledged as the foundation of research in artificial intelligence. He did valuable work in cryptography during World War II, playing an important role in breaking the Enigma code used by Germany for radio communications. After the war he taught at the University of Manchester and began work on what is now known as artificial intelligence. In the midst of this groundbreaking work, Turing was found dead in his bed, poisoned by cyanide. His death followed his arrest for a homosexual act (then a crime) and sentence to 12 months of hormone "therapy."

Uranus

Or Ouranus. Seventh planet from the Sun. It was discovered in 1781 by William Herschel and named for the Greek god personifying heaven. A blue-green gas giant, it has almost 15 times the mass of Earth and more than 50 times its volume. It is less dense than Earth; the gravity at the top of its atmosphere is 11 percent weaker. Its equatorial diameter is 31,800 mi (51,100 km). Uranus has 10 sharply defined narrow, dark rings, with broad dust bands between them; the rings consist mainly of boulder-size chunks of dark material. Uranus also has at least 27 moons (most named after Shakespearean characters) and a magnetic field about as strong as Earth's. The planet rotates once every 17 hours around an axis that, unusually, is almost parallel to the ecliptic; from Earth it appears to spin on its side. It takes 84 years to orbit the Sun, at a mean distance of 1.78 billion mi (2.87 billion km). It has no solid surface; its fluid interior is thought to consist of a mixture of rock, ices, and gas, with little or no rocky core. Its upper atmosphere is mostly hydrogen and helium; the blue-green color comes from absorption of red light by the small amount of methane present.

Venus

Second major planet from the Sun. Named for the Roman goddess, Venus is, after the Moon, the most brilliant natural object in the night sky. Venus

Feldman's Science, Technol...

1. String theory is
   (a) the Yamaha method of violin instruction
   (b) an 11-dimensional universe with infinitesimal string-like thingies in lieu of points
   (c) a Seattle grunge band of the early 1990s

(b) In the theory that makes the Mad Hatter's tea party look li... luncheon, your basic massless strings are exactly one Planck lon... each according to its own particle nature. String theory got supe... Stewart did (and in London, as well, at Queen Mary College) when t... to cover all bases of supersymmetry, that being symmetry between... with half-spin) and bosons (particles that spin all the way) giving su... on the GUT, the grand unifying theory of physics incorporating every t... brother. Eleven dimensions seems like a lot until you realize that most... and not bothering anyone.

2. With the possibility of orchids and tomatoes all year round, ... Greenhouse Effect be a good thing?

Not really, although the gradual warming of the planet doesn't sound unapp... in the upper Midwest (although putting New York, San Diego, and Banglades... water doesn't seem to be the way to go about it). The Greenhouse Effect wa... described by Fourier in 1824 as a natural effect of the atmosphere vis-a-vis t... ture patterns on the earth. The study of the unnatural effects of fossil-fuel-g... carbon dioxide came of age in the 1970s, quickly warming up into a political hot... due to the implications for development, manufacturing, transportation, and life... general: like, total. Robert May, of the Royal Society, told the UN recently that gl... warming is comparable to weapons of mass destruction that *actually exist* (emph... mine), noting rising sea levels, decreasing availability of fresh water, a chilling effect... agriculture, and an increasing number and destructiveness of floods, droughts, and... hurricanes. The Kyoto Protocol, which seeks to cut greenhouse gases, has been signe... and ratified by some 160 countries, save the number one emitter, the United States.

and thic...
Venus h...
more th...
and ro...
and tw...
also h...
The i...
dens...
no i...

Vi...

Fir...
FI...
in...
as...
v...
n...

comes closer to Earth—about 26 million mi (42 million km)—than any other planet. Its orbit around the Sun is nearly circular at a distance of about 67 million mi (108 million km) and takes 225 days; its rotation, in retrograde motion, takes even longer (243 days). As viewed from Earth, Venus undergoes phase changes similar to the Moon's, going through one cycle of phases in 584 days. It is seen only near sunrise or sunset and has long been known as both the morning star and the evening star. Venus is a near twin of Earth in size and mass but is completely enveloped by thick clouds of concentrated sulfuric acid droplets. Its surface gravity is about 90 percent that of Earth. Its atmosphere is more than 96 percent carbon dioxide, with a pressure about 95 times Earth's. The dense atmosphere

k cloud layers trap incoming solar energy so efficiently that
s the highest surface temperature of any of the Sun's planets,
an 860 °F (460 °C). Radar imaging indicates that the surface is dry
ky, consisting mostly of gently rolling plains, broad depressions,
o large elevated regions analogous to continents on Earth; Venus
s impact craters, extensive lava fields, and massive shield volcanos.
terior is thought to be similar to that of Earth, with a metal core, a
rocky mantle, and a less-dense rocky crust. Unlike Earth, Venus has
trinsic magnetic field.

gra

st oral drug for male impotence, generic name sildenafil. Before the
A approved Viagra in 1998, impotence was treated with surgical
plants, suppositories, pumps, and drugs injected into the penis. Taken
a pill shortly before sexual intercourse, Viagra selectively dilates blood
ssels in the penis, improving blood flow and allowing a natural sexual
esponse. It works in about 70 percent of cases; it should not be used
y anyone taking nitroglycerin or with heart problems, hypotension,
hypertension, recent stroke, or certain eye disorders.

West Nile virus

Virus, belonging to the family Flaviviridae, that can cause encephalitis
(inflammation of the brain). West Nile is predominantly a fatal infection
of birds but can be transmitted to humans by mosquitoes. Most human
infections are inapparent or mild, causing a flu-like illness that lasts only
a few days. A minority develop encephalitis, characterized by headache,
fever, neck stiffness, and muscle weakness, that has proved fatal in some
cases. There is no cure. In severe cases, intensive medical care, involving
intravenous fluids and respiratory support, is necessary. The virus was
originally confined to Africa, the Middle East, and Southeast Asia but has
spread to Europe and North America.

The World and Its Wonders

While Earth would have been perfectly lovely without us, mankind has stuck more than a few perennials of its own making into the garden. The Seven Wonders of the World are a good place to start, even though only one on the list, the pyramids at Giza, survives today. Nebuchadrezzar II, for all he did to Daniel and others, knew how to revitalize an inner city, making the Hanging Gardens ziggurat in Babylon the tourist destination in ancient Mesopotamia. His wife nagged him to do it, but still. Phidias outdid himself with his rendition of Zeus at Olympia— some said Zeus came out second to the statue, 40 feet high and strewn with gold, ivory, ebony, and enough jewels to stock all the pawnshops of antiquity. Zeus stood with right hand outstretched with a mere 10-foot statue of Nike in his palm. They found Phidias's workshop, but no schematics or models; the statue, after being plucked, was scrapped in 426 AD.

King "as rich as" Croesus had the money to throw at the Temple of Artemis in 550 BC; the Artemesium alone measured 350 by 180 feet and was covered by the finest friezes, statuary, bas-reliefs, and gold leaf money could buy. Pliny the Elder said he had seen a few things in his time, but nothing like the Mausoleum of Halicarnassus. Mausolus was actually his name, and he was a tyrant, although not so much that his loving sister and wife (one and the same) didn't want him to have the very best, commissioning the greatest Greek artists to come up with something that said "monumental." Four hundred and eleven feet around, with 36 columns supporting a 24-step pyramid topped by a marble four-horse chariot, it was never accused of being understated. It was probably destroyed in an earthquake with the stones improving more than a few local hovels. The Colossus of Rhodes, actually Helios, the sun god, whose 105-foot frame guarded the harbor, gave armies the impression that everybody in Rhodes was that size. An earthquake caused the mighty to fall, although they left the scrap on the shore for the longest time until the prices went up for bronze. And, if it's lighthouses you're into, look no further than the one at Pharos, off Alexandria, Egypt, more than 350 feet of lighthouse—three stories of lighthouse—from square to octagon to cylinder, with a spiral ramp up to the fire pit summit. In the Middle Ages, a sultan put a mosque on top. It stood from the 3rd century BC to the 14th century AD, when, you guessed it, earthquakes converted the seventh wonder of the world into building materials.

Amazon River

(Portuguese; Rio Amazonas) River, northern South America. It is the largest river in the world in volume and area of drainage basin; only the Nile River of eastern and northeastern Africa exceeds it in length. It originates within 100 mi (160 km) of the Pacific Ocean in the Peruvian Andes Mountains and flows some 4,000 mi (6,400 km) across northern Brazil into the Atlantic Ocean. Its Peruvian length is called the Marañón River; the stretch of river from the Brazilian border to the mouth of the Negro River is the Solimões River. Its more than 1,000 known tributaries rise in the Guiana Highlands, the Brazilian Highlands, and (principally) the Andes; seven of these are longer than 1,000 mi (1,600 km), and the Madeira River exceeds 2,000 mi (3,200 km). The Amazon can accommodate large freighters as far upriver as the city of Manaus, Braz., 1,000 mi (1,600 km) from the Atlantic. The first European descent was made by Francisco de Orellana in 1541–42; he is said to have given the river its name after reporting battles with tribes of women, whom he likened to the Amazons of Greek legend. Pedro Teixeira achieved the first ascent in 1637–38, but the river remained little explored until the mid-19th century. Many indigenous peoples originally lived along the river, but they moved inland as exploring parties and raiders sought to enslave them. The river was opened to world shipping in the mid-19th century; traffic increased exponentially with the coming of the rubber trade, which reached its height c. 1910 but soon declined. Its basin encompasses the world's most extensive rainforest and is home to an extraordinary diversity of birds, mammals, and other wildlife. Since the 1960s the effects of economic exploitation on the region's ecology and the destruction of the rainforest have generated worldwide concern.

Antarctica

Fifth largest continent on Earth. Antarctica lies concentrically about the South Pole, its landmass almost wholly covered by a vast ice sheet averaging 6,500 ft (2,000 m) thick. It is divided into two subcontinents: East Antarctica, consisting mainly of a high, ice-covered plateau, and West Antarctica, consisting largely of an archipelago of mountainous islands covered with ice. Its land area is about 5.5 million sq mi (14.2 million sq km). The southern portions of the Atlantic, Pacific, and Indian oceans surround it. Antarctica would be circular except for the outflaring

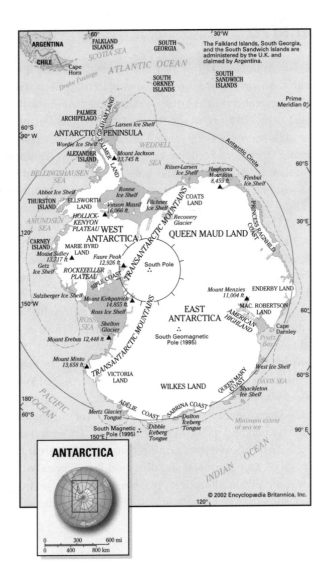

Antarctic Peninsula and two principal bays, the Ross Sea and the
Weddell Sea. East and West Antarctica are separated by the long chain
(1,900 mi [3,000 km]) of the Transantarctic Mountains. The ice sheet
overlaying the continent represents about 90 percent of the world's
glacial ice. By far the coldest continent, it has the world's lowest
recorded temperature, –128.6 °F (–89.2 °C), measured in 1983. The
climate supports only a small community of land plants, but the rich off-
shore food supply sustains penguins and immense seabird rookeries.

There are no permanent human inhabitants. The Russian F.G. von Bellingshausen (b. 1778—d. 1852), the Englishman Edward Bransfield (b. 1795?—d. 1852), and the American Nathaniel Palmer (b. 1799—d. 1877) all claimed first sightings of the continent in 1820. The period to *c.* 1900 was dominated by the exploration of Antarctic and sub-Antarctic seas. The early 20th century, the "heroic era" of Antarctic exploration, produced expeditions deep into the interior by Robert Falcon Scott and later Ernest Shackleton. The South Pole was reached by Roald Amundsen in December 1911 and by Scott in January 1912. The first half of the 20th century was also Antarctica's colonial period. Seven nations claimed sectors of the continent, while many other nations carried out explorations. In the International Geophysical Year of 1957–58, 12 nations established more than 50 stations on the continent for cooperative study. In 1961 the Antarctic Treaty, reserving Antarctica for free and nonpolitical scientific study, entered into full force. A 1991 agreement imposed a ban on mineral exploitation for 50 years.

Channel Tunnel or Eurotunnel

Rail tunnel that runs beneath the English Channel between Folkestone, England, and Sangatte (near Calais), France. A rail tunnel was chosen over proposals for a very long suspension bridge, a bridge-and-tunnel link, and a combined rail-and-road link. The 31-mi (50-km) tunnel, which opened in 1994, consists of three separate tunnels, two for rail traffic and a central tunnel for services and security. Trains, which carry motor vehicles as well as passengers, can travel through the tunnel at speeds as high as 100 mph (160 kph).

China

Officially People's Republic of China. Country, eastern Asia. Area: 3,696,100 sq mi (9,572,900 sq km). Population (2005 est.): 1,304,369,000. Capital: Beijing. It is the world's most populous country, the Han (ethnic Chinese) forming more than nine-tenths of the population. Languages: dialects of Han Chinese, Mandarin being the most important. Religions: traditional beliefs, Buddhism, Christianity, Islam, Daoism (all legally sanctioned). Currency: renminbi (of which the unit is the yuan). China has several topographic regions. The southwestern area contains the Plateau of Tibet, which averages more than 13,000 ft (4,000 m) above sea level; its core area, averaging more than 16,000 ft (5,000 m) in elevation, is called "the Roof of the World" and provides the headwaters for many of Asia's major rivers. Higher yet are the border ranges, the Kunlun Mountains to the north and the Himalayas to the south. China's northwestern region stretches from Afghanistan to the Northeast (Manchurian) Plain. The Tien Shan ("Celestial Mountains") separate China's two major interior basins, the Tarim Basin (containing the Takla Makan Desert) and the Junggar Basin. The Mongolian Plateau contains the southernmost part of the Gobi Desert. The lowlands of the eastern region include the Sichuan Basin, which runs along the Yangtze River (Chang Jiang); the Yangtze divides the eastern region into northern and southern parts. The Tarim is the major river in the northwest. China's numerous other rivers include the Huang He (Yellow River), Xi, Sungari (Songhua), Zhu (Pearl), and Lancang, which becomes the Mekong in Southeast Asia. The country is a single-party people's republic with one legislative house. The chief of state is the president, and the head of government is the premier.

The discovery of Peking man in 1927 dates the advent of early hominins (human ancestors) to the Paleolithic Period. Chinese civilization is thought to have spread from the Huang He valley. The first dynasty for which there is definite historical material is the Shang (*c.* 17th century BC), which had a writing system and a calendar. The Zhou, a subject state of the Shang, overthrew its Shang rulers in the mid-11th century and ruled until the 3rd century BC. Daoism and Confucianism were founded in this era. A time of conflict, called the Warring States period, lasted from the 5th century BC until 221 BC. Subsequently the Qin (or Chin) dynasty (from whose name China is derived) was established, after its rulers had conquered rival states and created a unified empire. The Han dynasty was established in 206 BC and ruled until AD 220. A time of turbulence followed, and Chinese reunification was achieved with the founding of the Sui dynasty in 581 and continued with the Tang dynasty (618–907). After the founding of the Song dynasty in 960, the capital was moved to the south because of northern invasions. In 1279 this dynasty was overthrown and Mongol (Yuan) domination began. During that time Marco Polo visited Kublai Khan. The Ming dynasty followed the period of Mongol rule and lasted from 1368 to 1644, cultivating antiforeign feelings to the point that China closed itself off from the rest of the world. Peoples from Manchuria overran China in 1644 and established the Qing (Manchu) dynasty. Ever-increasing incursions by Western and Japanese interests led in the 19th century to the Opium Wars, the Taiping Rebellion, and the Sino-Japanese War, all of which weakened the Manchu. The dynasty fell in 1911, and a republic was proclaimed in 1912 by Sun Yat-sen. The power struggles of warlords then weakened the republic. Under Chiang Kai-shek some national unification was achieved in the 1920s, but Chiang broke with the communists, who had formed their own armies. Japan invaded northern China in 1937; its occupation lasted until 1945. The communists gained support after the Long March (1934–35), in which Mao Zedong emerged as their leader. Upon Japan's surrender at the end of World War II, a fierce civil war began; in 1949 the Nationalists fled to Taiwan, and the communists proclaimed the People's Republic of China. The communists undertook extensive reforms, but pragmatic policies alternated with periods of revolutionary upheaval, most notably in the Great Leap Forward and the Cultural Revolution. The anarchy, terror, and economic paralysis of the latter led, after Mao's death in 1976, to a turn to moderation under Deng Xiaoping, who undertook economic reforms and renewed China's ties to the West. The government established diplomatic relations with the U.S. in 1979. Since the late 1970s the economy has been moving from central planning and state-run industries to a mixture of state-owned and private enterprises in manufacturing and services, in the process growing dramatically and transforming Chinese society. The Tiananmen Square incident of 1989 (in which prodemocracy demonstrators were forcibly repressed by the government) was a challenge to an otherwise increasingly stable political environment after 1980. In 1997 Hong Kong reverted to Chinese rule, as did Macau in 1999. China made its Olympic debut at the 1932 Summer Games in Los Angeles. Beijing will host the 2008 Summer Games.

East Timor

Officially Democratic Republic of Timor-Leste. Country occupying the eastern half of the island of Timor, Southeast Asia. Bounded by the Timor Sea and by the western half of Timor, it also includes the enclave of Ambeno (surrounding the town of Pante Makasar on the northwestern coast of Timor) and the islands of Atauro (Kambing) and Jaco. Area: 5,639 sq mi (14,604 sq km). Population (2005 est.): 975,000. Capital: Dili. Languages: Tetum and Portuguese (both official). Religions: Christianity (predominantly Roman Catholic; also Protestant); also Islam, traditional beliefs. Currency: U.S. dollar. The Portuguese first settled on Timor in 1520 and were granted rule over Timor's eastern half in 1860. The Timor political party Fretilin declared East Timor independent in 1975 after Portugal withdrew its troops. It was invaded by Indonesian forces and annexed to Indonesia in 1976. The takeover, which resulted in the deaths of thousands of East Timorese during the next two decades, was disputed by the United Nations. In 1999 an independence referendum won overwhelmingly; though Indonesia officially recognized the referendum, anti-independence militias killed hundreds of people and sent thousands fleeing to the western part of the island before and after the vote. A UN-administered interim authority imposed order and oversaw elections, the promulgation of a constitution, and the return of refugees. East Timor became a sovereign nation in 2002; it is the world's youngest country.

ecoterrorism

Or ecological terrorism *or* environmental terrorism. The destruction, or the threat of destruction, of the environment in order to intimidate or coerce governments. The term has also been applied to crimes committed against companies or government agencies in order to prevent or interfere with activities allegedly harmful to the environment. Ecoterrorism includes threats to contaminate water supplies or to destroy or disable energy utilities, for example, and practices such as the deployment of anthrax. Another form of ecoterrorism, often referred to as environmental warfare, consists of the deliberate and illegal destruction, exploitation, or modification of the environment as a strategy of war or in times of armed conflict. Examples include the U.S. military's use of the defoliant Agent Orange during the Vietnam War and the destruction of Kuwaiti oil wells by retreating Iraqi military forces during the 1991 Persian Gulf War. The activities of some environmental activists also have been described as ecoterrorism. These activities include criminal trespass on the property of logging companies and other firms and obstruction of their operations through sabotage as well as the environmentally harmless modification of natural resources in order to make them unsuitable for commercial use (a practice known as "monkey wrenching").

ethnic cleansing

The creation of an ethnically homogenous geographic area through the elimination of unwanted ethnic groups by deportation, forcible displacement, or genocide. Ethnic cleansing also has involved attempts to remove physical vestiges of the targeted group in the territory through the destruction and desecration of monuments, cemeteries, and houses of worship. Although some critics of the term have claimed that ethnic cleansing is simply a form of genocide, defenders of the usage have noted that, whereas the murder of an ethnic, racial, or religious group is the primary intention of a genocidal policy, the chief goal of ethnic cleansing is the establishment of homogenous lands, which may be achieved by any of a number of methods, including genocide. The term was widely employed in the 1990s to describe the brutal treatment of Bosniacs (Bosnian Muslims), ethnic Serbs in the Krajina region of Croatia, and ethnic Albanians in the Serbian province of Kosovo during the conflicts that erupted in the wake of the disintegration of Yugoslavia.

European Union (EU)

Organization of European countries, formed in 1993 to oversee their economic and political integration. It was created by the Maastricht Treaty and ratified by all members of the European Community (EC), out of which the EU developed. The successful EC had made its members more receptive to greater integration and provided a framework for unified action by member countries in security and foreign policy and for cooperation in police and justice matters. In pursuit of its major goal to create a common monetary system, the EU established the euro, which replaced the national currencies of 12 of the 15 EU members in 2002. Originally confined to Western Europe, the EU enlarged to include several Central and Eastern European countries in the early 21st century. The EU's principal institutions are the European Community, the Council of Ministers (a forum for individual ministries), the European Commission (an administrative bureaucracy), the European Parliament, the European Court of Justice, and the European Central Bank.

Everest, Mount

(Tibetan, Chomolungma; Nepali, Sagarmatha) Peak on the crest of the Himalayas, southern Asia. The highest point on Earth, with a summit at 29,035 ft (8,850 m), it lies on the border between Nepal and Tibet (China). Numerous attempts to climb Everest were made from 1921; the summit

The height of Mt. Everest, the "Goddess Mother of the World," has long been controversial, due to variations in snow level, gravity deviation, and light refraction. It currently stands at 29,035 feet and actually moves a few inches to the northeast and rises a fraction of an inch each year. So at one-million-eight, it's still growing! Toward the top the Yellow Band is the remnant of the primeval Tethys Sea that closed up during the violent tectonic-plate collision of its birth. Everest is so high that it pokes the jet stream; winds at the summit can reach 100 mph, combining with temperatures averaging 33° below to make the Earth's most impressive and deadly wind chill factor. The Sherpas are no fools, and they build their stone huts no higher than 14,000 feet, although in summer they graze livestock as high as 16,000 feet (or did before everyone became a porter). Before Hillary, the Sherpas didn't climb Sagarmatha, believing it to be the sacred home of gods and demons, not to mention the Yeti, which, before mountaineers, was the most threatening humanoid of the Himalayas. Unlike the tons of oxygen containers, waste, tents, and gear left behind by the thousands who have attempted to "climb high and sleep low," refuse that is periodically hauled down, the bodies of close to 100 who didn't make it remain on the slopes, impossible to remove due to their weight. If you're inclined, April and May, before the monsoons, is the time to make the siege, the southern route along the Khumbu icefall being the most common approach (the base camp is at 17,600 feet!) and the one used by Hillary and Norgay in 1953.—M.F.

was finally reached by Edmund Hillary of New Zealand and Tenzing Norgay of Nepal in 1953. In dispute is whether the English explorer George Mallory, whose body was discovered below Everest's peak in 1999, had actually reached the peak earlier, in 1924, and was descending it when he died. The formerly accepted elevation of 29,028 ft (8,848 m), established in the early 1950s, was recalculated in the late 1990s.

genocide

Deliberate and systematic destruction of a racial, religious, political, or ethnic group. The term was coined by Raphael Lemkin, a Polish-born jurist who served as an adviser to the U.S. Department of War during World War II, to describe the premeditated effort to destroy a population. In 1946 the UN General Assembly declared genocide a punishable crime. By this declaration, genocide by definition may be committed by an individual, group, or government, against one's own people or another, in peacetime or in wartime. This last point distinguishes genocide from "crimes against humanity," whose legal definition specifies wartime. Suspects may be tried by a court in the country where the act was committed or by an international court. An example of genocide more recent than the Holocaust is the slaughter of Tutsi people by the Hutu in Rwanda in the 1990s.

globalization

Process by which the experience of everyday life, marked by the diffusion of commodities and ideas, is becoming standardized around the world. Factors that have contributed to globalization include increasingly sophisticated communications and transportation technologies and services, mass migration and the movement of peoples, a level of economic activity that has outgrown national markets through industrial combinations and commercial groupings that cross national frontiers, and international agreements that reduce the cost of doing business in foreign countries. Globalization offers huge potential profits to companies and nations but has been complicated by widely differing expectations, standards of living, cultures and values, and legal systems as well as unexpected global cause-and-effect linkages.

Grameen Bank

In Bangladesh, first bank to specialize in small loans for poor individuals. Originated by economist Muhammad Yunus, the Grameen banking model is based on groups of five prospective borrowers who meet regularly with Grameen Bank field managers. Typically, two of the five prospective borrowers are granted loans. If, after a probationary time period, the first two borrowers meet the terms of repayment, then loans are granted to the remaining group members. Peer pressure acts as a replacement for traditional loan collateral. Grameen became an independent bank in 1983; headquartered in Dhaka, Bangladesh, it has more than 1,000 branches in the country. A typical Grameen loan ranges from $100 to $400. The Grameen model has come to symbolize an efficient means of helping the poor by providing them with opportunities to help themselves. More than 90 percent of Grameen's loan recipients have been women.

Grand Canyon

Extensive canyon system cut by the Colorado River, northwestern Arizona, U.S. Noted for its rock formations and coloration, it is about 0.1–18 mi (0.2–29 km) wide and extends from northern Arizona to Grand Wash Cliffs, near the Nevada border, a distance of about 277 mi (446 km). The deepest section, 56 mi (90 km) long, is within Grand Canyon National Park, which covers the river's length from Lake Powell to Lake Mead. The surrounding plateau is 6,000–9,000 ft (1,800–2,750 m) above sea level, and the canyon is in some places more than 1 mi (1.6 km) deep. The national park, now containing 1,904 sq mi (4,931 sq km), was created in 1919. The former Grand Canyon National Monument, established in 1932, was added, with other lands, in 1975. In 1979 the Grand Canyon was designated a UNESCO World Heritage site.

Great Barrier Reef

Extensive complex of coral reefs, shoals, and islets in the Pacific Ocean, off the northeastern coast of Australia. The largest deposit of coral in the world, it extends for more than 1,250 mi (2,000 km) along the coast of Queensland and has an area of some 135,000 sq mi (350,000 sq km). The reef has been formed over millions of years from the skeletons of a mass of living marine organisms. In addition to at least 300 species of hard coral, marine life includes anemones, worms, gastropods, lobsters, crayfish, prawns, crabs, and a variety of fish. Encrusting red algae form the purplish red algal rim that is one of the reef's characteristic features. A major tourist attraction, nearly all of it is within Great Barrier Reef National Park; the reef was designated a UNESCO World Heritage site in 1981.

Great Wall of China

(Chinese; Wanli Changcheng) Defensive wall, northern China. One of the largest building-construction projects ever carried out, it runs (with all its branches) about 4,500 mi (7,300 km) east to west from the Bo Hai (Gulf of Chihli) to a point deep in Central Asia. Large parts of the fortification date from the 7th to the 4th century BC. In the 3rd century BC the

emperor Shihuangdi connected existing defensive walls into a single
system fortified by watchtowers. These served both to guard the
rampart and to communicate with the capital, Xianyang (near modern
Xi'an) by signal—smoke by day and fire by night. Originally constructed
partly of masonry and earth, it was faced with brick in its eastern
portion. It was rebuilt in later times, especially in the 15th and 16th centuries. The basic wall is about 23–26 ft (7–8 m) high; at intervals towers
rise above it to varying heights. It was designated a UNESCO World
Heritage site in 1987.

Hong Kong

(Chinese; Xianggang *or* Hsiang-kang) Special administrative region of
China (pop., 2005 est.: 6,926,000). Located on China's southern coast, it
consists of the island of Hong Kong and adjacent islets in the South
China Sea (ceded by China to the British in 1842), the Kowloon
Peninsula (ceded in 1860), and the New Territories (leased by the
British from China from 1898 to 1997). The entire territory was
returned to China in 1997. It covers 425 sq mi (1,102 sq km); the New
Territories, lying north of the Kowloon Peninsula and constituting an
enclave in China's Guangdong province, are more than nine-tenths of
the total area. The administrative center of Victoria on Hong Kong

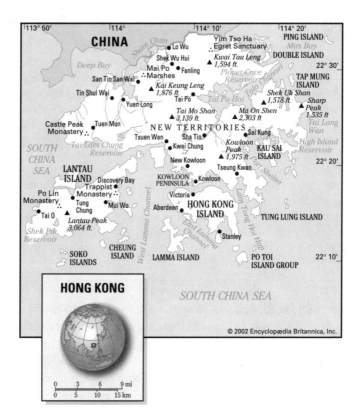

HONG KONG

SOUTH CHINA SEA

0	3	6	9 mi
0	5	10	15 km

island's northwestern coast is also the center of economic activities. Hong Kong has an excellent natural harbor and is one of the world's major trade and financial centers. It has many educational institutions, including the University of Hong Kong (1911). Hong Kong made its Olympic debut at the 1952 Summer Games in Helsinki, Fin.

Indonesia

Officially Republic of Indonesia, formerly Netherlands East Indies. Archipelago country, located off the coast of mainland Southeast Asia. It is comprised of some 17,500 islands, of which about 6,000 are uninhabited. Area: 730,024 sq mi (1,890,754 sq km). Population (2005 est.): 222,781,000. Capital: Jakarta (on Java). Indonesia has more than 300 ethnic groups, which in the western islands fall into three broad divisions: the rice growers of Java and neighboring islands; the Muslim coastal peoples, including the Malays of Sumatra; and the Dayak and other ethnic groups. In the east the distinction is between coastal and interior peoples. Languages: Bahasa Indonesia (official), some 250 languages from different ethnic groups. Religions: Islam; also Christianity, Hinduism, traditional beliefs. Currency: rupiah. The Indonesian archipelago stretches 3,200 miles (5,100 km) from west to east. Major islands include Sumatra, Java (with more than half of Indonesia's population), Bali, Lombok, Sumbawa, about three-fourths of Borneo (Kalimantan), Celebes (Sulawesi), the Moluccas, and the western portions of Timor and New Guinea. The islands are characterized by rugged volcanic mountains and tropical rainforests. Geologically unstable, Indonesia has frequent earthquakes and 220 active volcanoes, including Krakatoa (Krakatau). Roughly one-fifth of its land is arable, and rice is the staple crop. Petroleum, natural gas, timber products, garments, and rubber are major exports. Indonesia is a republic with two legislative houses; its head of state and government is the president.

Austronesian-speaking peoples began migrating to Indonesia about the 3rd millennium BC. Commercial relations were established with Africa about the 1st century AD, and Hindu and Buddhist cultural influences from India began to take hold. Indian traders also brought Islam to the islands, and by the 13th century it was spreading throughout the islands—except Bali, which retained its Hindu religion and culture. Indonesia now has the largest Muslim population of any country. European influence began in the 16th century, and the Dutch gradually established control of Indonesia from the late 17th century until 1942, when the Japanese invaded. Sukarno declared Indonesia's independence in 1945, which the Dutch granted, with nominal union to The Netherlands, in 1949; Indonesia dissolved this union in 1954. The suppression of an alleged coup attempt in 1965 resulted in the deaths of hundreds of thousands of people the government claimed to be communists, and by 1968 Gen. Suharto had taken power. His government forcibly incorporated East Timor into Indonesia in 1975–76, with much loss of life. In the 1990s the country was beset by political, economic, and environmental problems, and Suharto was deposed in 1998. Muslim leader Abdurrahman Wahid was elected president in 1999 but was replaced in 2001 by his vice president, Megawati Sukarnoputri, the eldest daughter of Sukarno. In 2004 she was succeeded by Susilo Bambang Yudhoyono. In 1999 the people of East Timor voted for independence from Indonesia, which was granted; after a period under UN supervision, it achieved full sovereignty in 2002. In 2004 a large tsunami generated by an earthquake off the western coast of Sumatra caused widespread death and destruction. Indonesia made its Olympic debut at the 1952 Summer Games in Helsinki, Fin.

Interpol

Officially International Criminal Police Organization. International organization whose purpose is to fight international crime. Interpol promotes the widest possible mutual assistance between the criminal police authorities of affiliated countries and seeks to establish and develop all institutions likely to contribute effectively to the prevention and suppression of ordinary crime. Though it traces its history to 1914, when a congress of international criminal police, attended by delegates from 14 countries, was held in Monaco, the organization was formally founded in Austria in 1923 with 20 member countries; after World War II its headquarters moved to Paris and, in 1989, to Lyon, France. By the early 21st century, its membership exceeded 180 countries. Interpol pursues criminals who operate in more than one country (e.g., smugglers), those who stay in one country but whose crimes affect other countries (e.g., counterfeiters of foreign currency), and those who commit a crime in one country and flee to another.

North Atlantic Treaty Organization (NATO)

International military alliance created to defend western Europe against a possible Soviet invasion. A 1948 collective-defense alliance between Britain, France, The Netherlands, Belgium, and Luxembourg was recognized as inadequate to deter Soviet aggression, and in 1949 the U.S. and Canada agreed to join their European allies in an enlarged alliance. A centralized administrative structure was set up, and three major commands were established, focused on Europe, the Atlantic, and the English Channel (disbanded in 1994). The admission of West Germany in 1955 led to the Soviet Union's creation of the opposing Warsaw Treaty Organization, or Warsaw Pact. France withdrew from military participation in 1966. Since NATO ground forces were smaller than those of the Warsaw Pact, the balance of power was maintained by superior weaponry, including intermediate-range nuclear weapons. After the Warsaw Pact's dissolution and the end of the Cold War in 1991, NATO withdrew its nuclear weapons and attempted to transform its mission. It involved itself in the Balkan conflicts of the 1990s. Article 5 of the North Atlantic Treaty, stating that an attack on one signatory would be regarded as an attack on the rest, was first invoked in 2001 in response to the September 11 terrorist attacks against the U.S. Additional countries joined NATO in 1999 and 2004 to bring the number of full members to 26.

Nile River

(Arabic; Al-Bahr) River, eastern and northeastern Africa. The longest river in the world, it is about 4,132 mi (6,650 km) long from its remotest headstream (which flows into Lake Victoria) to the Mediterranean Sea. After leaving the lake, it flows generally north through Uganda, The Sudan, and Egypt. Its major tributaries—including the Al-Ghazal (Gazelle) River, the Blue Nile, and the Atbara River—join it before it enters Lake Nasser near the Egypt-Sudan border. Below the Aswan High Dam, which impounds the lake, it continues northward to its delta near Cairo, where it empties into the Mediterranean. The first use of the Nile for irrigation in Egypt began when seeds were sown in the mud left after its annual floodwaters had subsided. It has supported continuous human settlement for at least 5,000 years, and networks of canals and waterworks have been built since the 19th century. The Aswan High Dam, built in 1959–70, provides flood protection, hydroelectric power, and a dependable water supply for both crops and humans. The Nile is also a vital waterway for the transport of people and goods.

Parthenon

Chief temple of Athena on the Acropolis at Athens. Built 447–432 BC by Ictinus and Callicrates under Pericles, it is considered the culmination of the Doric order. Though the white marble temple has suffered damage over the centuries, including the loss of most of its sculpture, its basic

Parthenon, on the Acropolis, Athens, by Ictinus and Callicrates, 447–432 BC

structure remains intact. The colonnade supports an entablature consisting of a plain architrave, a frieze of alternating triglyphs (grooved blocks) and metopes (plain blocks with relief sculpture), and, at the two ends, a triangular pediment. The colonnade consists of eight columns on the ends and 17 on the sides, enclosing a cella; the interior originally held a great gold-and-ivory statue by Phidias. Such architectural devices as entasis of the columns and an upward curvature of the base are used to correct optical illusions. Its sculpture rivaled its architecture. The pediment sculptures represent the birth of Athena and her battle with Poseidon; a continuous frieze shows the annual Panathenaic procession of citizens honoring Athena. The entire work is a marvel of harmony and clarity.

Petronas Towers

Twin stainless-steel-clad skyscrapers, linked by a skybridge, in Kuala Lumpur, Malaysia. Designed by Cesar Pelli (b. 1926) and completed in 1998, the circular, step-tapered towers house the headquarters of Malaysia's national petroleum company. Each tower is 88 stories high, has a structural frame of high-strength, steel-reinforced concrete, and reaches a height of 1,483 ft (451.9 m)—a figure that includes a pinnacle and steel spire atop each. In 1996, after achieving their full height, the towers were considered the world's tallest buildings, surpassing the then-tallest Sears Tower; they, in turn, were superseded in 2003 by the Taipei 101 (Taipei Financial Center) building in Taipei, Taiwan, that rose to 1,667 ft (508 m).

pyramid

Ancient monumental structure constructed of or faced with stone or brick and having a rectangular base and four sloping triangular sides meeting at an apex. Pyramids have been built at various times and places; the best-known are those of Egypt and of Central and South America. The pyramids of ancient Egypt were royal tombs. Each contained an inner sepulchral chamber that housed the deceased (usually mummified) ruler, members of his entourage, and artifacts. The rest of the pyramid complex consisted of a large enclosure, an adjacent mortuary temple, and a causeway leading down to a pavilion. About 80 royal pyramids survive in Egypt, the greatest being those at Giza.

American pyramids include the pyramids of the Sun and Moon at
Teotihuacán, the Castillo at Chichén Itzá, and various Inca and Chimú
structures in Andean settlements. These pyramids were generally built
of earth and faced with stone; they are typically stepped pyramids and
are topped by a platform or temple structure used for rituals, including human sacrifice.

San Marino

Officially Republic of San Marino. Country, central Italian peninsula,
southern Europe. It is located near the Adriatic Sea and is surrounded by
Italy. Area: 24 sq mi (62 sq km). Population (2002 est.): 27,700. Capital:
San Marino. Most of the people are Italian. Language: Italian (official).
Religion: Roman Catholicism. Currency: Italian lira. The territory has an
irregular rectangular form with a maximum length of 8 mi (13 km). It is
crossed by streams that flow into the Adriatic Sea. It is dominated by
Mount Titano, 2,424 ft (739 m) high, on which the capital, the town of

San Marino, is located, surrounded by triple walls. The economy is based on private enterprise and includes tourism, commerce, agriculture, crafts, and fine printing, particularly of postage stamps. San Marino is a republic with one legislative house; its heads of state and government are two captains-regent. According to tradition, it was founded in the early 4th century AD by St. Marinus. By the 12th century it had developed into a commune and remained independent despite challenges from neighboring rulers, including the Malatesta family in nearby Rimini. San Marino survived the Renaissance as a relic of the self-governing Italian city-state and remained an independent republic after the unification of Italy in 1861–70. It is one of the smallest republics in the world and may be the oldest one in Europe. At the beginning of the 21st century its citizens enjoyed a high standard of living.

Seven Wonders of the World

Preeminent architectural and sculptural achievements of antiquity, as listed by various Greco-Roman observers. Included on the best-known list were the Pyramids of Giza (the oldest of the wonders and the only one substantially in existence today), the Hanging Gardens of Babylon (a series of landscaped rooftop terraces on a ziggurat, ascribed to either Nebuchadnezzar II or the semilegendary Queen Sammu-ramat), the

Statue of Zeus at Olympia (a large gold-and-ivory figure of the god on his throne by Phidias), the Temple of Artemis at Ephesus (a temple, built in 356 BC, famous for its imposing size and the works of art that adorned it), the Mausoleum of Halicarnassus, the Colossus of Rhodes, and the Pharos of Alexandria (a lighthouse built *c.* 280 BC on the island of Pharos off Alexandria, said to have been more than 350 ft, or 110 m, high). These wonders inspired the compilation of many other lists of seven attractions, or "wonders," by later generations.

Singapore

Officially Republic of Singapore. Island country, Southeast Asia. Situated off the southern tip of the Malay Peninsula, it comprises Singapore island and 60 islets. Area: 264 sq mi (683 sq km). Population (2002 est.): 4,204,000. Capital: Singapore. Three-fourths of the people are of Chinese ethnicity; most of the rest are Malays and Indians. Languages: English, Chinese (Mandarin), Malay, Tamil (all official).

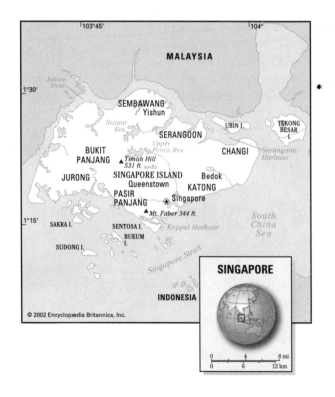

Religions: primarily Confucianism, Buddhism, and Daoism; also Islam, Christianity, Hinduism. Currency: Singapore dollar. Nearly two-thirds of the island's hilly landscape lies less than 50 ft (15 m) above sea level; it has a hot, humid climate. Although only about 2 percent of its land is arable, it is among the most productive fruit and vegetable cropland in the world. The economy is based largely on international trade and finance; there are more than 100 commercial banks, most of which are foreign, and the headquarters of the Asian Dollar Market is located there. The port is one of the largest in the world, and the country is one of the world's leading petroleum refiners. It has the highest per capita income of any Southeast Asian country. Singapore is a republic with one legislative house; its chief of state is the president, and the head of government is the prime minister. Long inhabited by fishermen and pirates, it was an outpost of the Sumatran empire of Shrivijaya until the 14th century, when it passed to Java and then Siam. It became part of the Malacca empire in the 15th century. In the 16th century the Portuguese controlled the area; they were followed by the Dutch in the 17th century. In 1819 it was ceded to the British East India Company, becoming part of the Straits Settlements and the center of British colonial activity in Southeast Asia. During World War II the Japanese occupied the island (1942–45). In 1946 it became a crown colony. It achieved full internal self-government in 1959, became part of Malaysia in 1963, and gained independence in 1965. Singapore is influential in the affairs of the Association of Southeast Asian Nations (ASEAN). The country's dominant voice in politics for 30 years after independence was Lee Kuan Yew. Its economy was affected during the Asian economic crises that began in the mid-1990s, but it recovered more easily than many of its neighbors did.

Statue of Liberty National Monument

Historic site in New York Harbor, New York, and New Jersey, U.S. Covering 58 ac (23 ha), it includes the Statue of Liberty (on Liberty Island [formerly Bedloe's Island]) and nearby Ellis Island. The colossal statue, *Liberty Enlightening the World*, was sculpted by Frédéric-Auguste Bartholdi and dedicated in 1886. This 305-ft (93-m) statue of a woman holding a tablet and upraised torch was given to the U.S. by France and commemorates the friendship of the two countries; a plaque at the pedestal's entrance is inscribed with the sonnet "The New Colossus" by

Emma Lazarus. The Statue of Liberty was declared a national monument in 1924 and a UNESCO World Heritage site in 1984; Ellis Island, containing the Ellis Island Immigration Museum, was added to the monument in 1965.

Stonehenge

Monumental, circular arrangement of standing stones built in prehistoric times and located near Salisbury, Wiltshire, England. The stones are believed to have been put in place in three main phases c. 3100–c. 1550 BC. The reasons for the building of Stonehenge are unknown, but it is believed to have been a place of worship and ritual. Many theories have been advanced as to its specific purpose (e.g., for the prediction of eclipses), but none has been proved. Stones erected during the second phase of construction (c. 2100 BC) were aligned with the sunrise at the summer solstice, suggesting some ritual connection with that event.

Taj Mahal

Mausoleum complex on the southern bank of the Yamuna River, outside Agra, India. It was built by the Mughal emperor Shah Jahán in memory of his wife, Mumtaz Mahal, who died in 1631. The Taj complex, begun c. 1632, took 22 years to complete. At its center lies a square garden area bounded by two smaller, oblong sections, one comprising the mausoleum and the other an entrance gateway. The mausoleum, of pure-white marble inlaid with semiprecious stones, is flanked by two red sandstone buildings, a mosque on one side, and an identical building for aesthetic balance on the other. It stands on a high marble plinth with a minaret at each corner. It has four identical facades, each with a massive central arch 108 ft (33 m) high, and is surmounted by a bulbous double dome and four domed kiosks. Its interior, with fine, restrained stone decoration, centers on an octagonal chamber containing the marble tombs, enclosed by a perforated marble screen, with sarcophagi below. Regarded as one of the world's most beautiful buildings, it was designated a UNESCO World Heritage site in 1983. Steps have been taken since the late 1990s to reduce air pollution that has damaged the facade of the building.

terrorism

Systematic use of violence to create a general climate of fear in a population and thereby to bring about a particular political objective. It has been used throughout history by political organizations of both the left and the right, by nationalist and ethnic groups, and by revolutionaries. Although usually thought of as a means of destabilizing or overthrowing existing political institutions, terror also has been employed by governments against their own people to suppress dissent; examples include the reigns of certain Roman emperors, the French Revolution, Nazi Germany, the Soviet Union under Stalin, and Argentina during the "dirty war" of the 1970s. Terrorism's impact has been magnified by the deadliness and technological sophistication of modern-day weapons and the capability of the media to disseminate news of such attacks instantaneously throughout the world. The deadliest terrorist attack ever occurred in the United States on Sept. 11, 2001, when members of the al-Qaeda terrorist network hijacked four commercial airplanes and crashed two of them into the twin towers of the World Trade Center complex in New York City and one into the Pentagon building near Washington, D.C.; the fourth plane crashed near Pittsburgh, Pa. The crashes resulted in the collapse of much of the World Trade Center complex, the destruction of part of the southwest side of the Pentagon, and the deaths of some 3,000 people.

United Nations (UN)

International organization founded (1945) at the end of World War II to maintain international peace and security, develop friendly relations among nations on equal terms, and encourage international cooperation in solving intractable human problems. A number of its agencies have been awarded the Nobel Prize for Peace, and the UN was the corecipient, with Kofi Annan, of the prize in 2001. The term originally referred to the countries that opposed the Axis powers. An international organization was discussed at the Yalta Conference in February 1945, and the UN charter was drawn up two months later at the UN Conference on International Organization. The UN has six principal organs: the Economic and Social Council, the United Nations General Assembly, the International Court of Justice, the Secretariat, the United Nations Security Council, and the United Nations Trusteeship Council. It also has 14 specialized agencies—some inherited from its predecessor, the League of Nations (e.g., the International Labour Organization)—and a number of special offices (e.g., the Office of the United Nations High Commissioner for Refugees), programs, and funds (e.g., UNICEF). The UN is involved in economic, cultural, and humanitarian activities and the coordination or regulation of international postal services, civil aviation, meteorological research, telecommunications, international shipping, and intellectual property. Its peacekeeping troops have been deployed in several areas of the world, sometimes for lengthy periods (e.g., they have been in Cyprus since 1964). The UN's world headquarters are in New York City; its European headquarters are in Geneva. In 2005 the UN had 191 member countries. The principal administrative officer of the UN is the secretary-general, who is elected to a five-year renewable term by the General Assembly on the recommendation of the Security Council. The secretaries-general of the UN have been Trygve Lie (1946–53), Dag Hammarskjöld (1953–61), U Thant (1961–71), Kurt Waldheim (1972–81), Javier Pérez de Cuéllar (1982–91), Boutros Boutros-Ghali (1992–96), and Kofi Annan (from 1997).

United States

Officially United States of America. Country, North America. It comprises 48 conterminous states occupying the mid-continent, Alaska at the northwestern extreme of North America, and the island state of Hawaii in the mid-Pacific Ocean. Area, including the U.S. share of the Great Lakes: 3,676,487 sq mi (9,522,058 sq km). Population (2005 est.): 296,748,000. Capital: Washington, D.C. The population includes people of European and Middle Eastern ancestry, African Americans, Hispanics, Asians, Pacific Islanders, American Indians (Native Americans), and Alaska Natives. Languages: English (predominant), Spanish. Religions: Christianity (Protestant, Roman Catholic, other Christians, Eastern Orthodox); also Judaism, Islam, Buddhism, Hinduism. Currency: U.S. dollar. The country encompasses mountains, plains, lowlands, and deserts. Mountain ranges include the Appalachians, Ozarks, Rockies, Cascades, and Sierra Nevada. The lowest point is Death Valley, Calif. The highest point is Alaska's Mount McKinley; within the conterminous states it is Mount Whitney, Calif. Chief rivers are the Mississippi system, the Colorado, the Columbia, and the Rio Grande. The Great Lakes, the Great Salt Lake, Iliamna Lake, and Lake Okeechobee are the largest lakes. The

U.S. is among the world's leading producers of several minerals, including copper, silver, zinc, gold, coal, petroleum, and natural gas; it is the chief exporter of food. Its manufactures include iron and steel, chemicals, electronic equipment, and textiles. Other important industries are tourism, dairying, livestock raising, fishing, and lumbering. The U.S. is a federal republic with two legislative houses; its head of state and government is the president.

The territory was originally inhabited for several thousand years by numerous American Indian peoples who had probably emigrated from Asia. European exploration and settlement from the 16th century began displacement of the Indians. The first permanent European settlement, by the Spanish, was at Saint Augustine, Fla., in 1565. The English settled Jamestown, Va. (1607); Plymouth, Mass. (1620); Maryland (1634); and Pennsylvania (1681). The English took New York, New Jersey, and Delaware from the Dutch in 1664, a year after English noblemen had begun to colonize the Carolinas. The British defeat of the French in 1763 assured Britain political control over its 13 colonies. Political unrest caused by British colonial policy culminated in the American Revolution (1775–83) and the Declaration of Independence (1776). The U.S. was first organized under the Articles of Confederation (1781), then finally under the Constitution (1787) as a federal republic. Boundaries extended west to the Mississippi River, excluding Spanish Florida. Land acquired from France by the Louisiana Purchase (1803) nearly doubled the country's territory. The U.S. fought the War of 1812 against the British and acquired Florida from Spain in 1819. In 1830 it legalized the removal of American Indians to lands west of the Mississippi River. Settlement expanded into the Far West in the mid-19th century, especially after the discovery of gold in California in 1848. Victory in the Mexican War (1846–48) brought the territory of seven more future states (including California and Texas) into U.S. hands. The northwestern boundary was established by treaty with Britain in 1846. The U.S. acquired southern Arizona by the Gadsden Purchase (1853). It suffered disunity during the conflict between the slavery-based plantation economy in the South and the industrial and agricultural economy in the North, culminating in the American Civil War and the abolition of slavery under the 13th Amendment. After Reconstruction (1865–77) the U.S. experienced rapid growth, urbanization, industrial development, and European immigration. In 1887 it authorized allotment of American Indian reservation land to individual tribesmen, resulting in widespread loss of land to whites. Victory in the Spanish-American War brought the U.S. the overseas territories of the Philippines, Guam, and Puerto Rico. By the end of the 19th century, it had further developed foreign trade and acquired other outlying territories, including Alaska, Midway Island, the Hawaiian Islands, Wake Island, American Samoa, and the Panama Canal Zone.

The U.S. participated in World War I in 1917–18. It granted suffrage to women in 1920 and citizenship to American Indians in 1924. The stock market crash of 1929 led to the Great Depression, which New Deal legislation combated by increasing the federal government's role in the economy. The U.S. entered World War II after the Japanese bombing of Pearl Harbor (Dec. 7, 1941). The explosion by the U.S. of an atomic bomb on Hiroshima (Aug. 6, 1945) and another on Nagasaki (Aug. 9, 1945), Japan, brought about Japan's surrender. Thereafter the U.S. was the military and economic leader of the Western world. In the first decade after the war, it aided the reconstruction of Europe and Japan and became embroiled in a rivalry with the Soviet Union known as the Cold War. It participated in the Korean War from 1950–53. In 1952 it granted autonomous commonwealth status to Puerto Rico. Racial segregation in schools was declared unconstitutional in 1954. Alaska and Hawaii were made states in 1959. In 1964 Congress passed the Civil Rights Act and authorized U.S. entry into the Vietnam War. The mid- to late 1960s were marked by widespread civil disorder, including race riots and antiwar demonstrations. The U.S. accomplished the first manned lunar landing in 1969. All U.S. troops were withdrawn from Vietnam in 1973. With the dissolution of the Soviet Union in 1991, the U.S. assumed the status of sole world superpower. The U.S. led a coalition of forces against Iraq in the First Persian Gulf War (1991). Administration of the Panama Canal was turned over to Panama in 1999. After the September 11 attacks on the U.S. in 2001 destroyed the World Trade Center and part of the Pentagon, the U.S. attacked Afghanistan's Taliban government for harboring and refusing to extradite the mastermind of the terrorism, Osama bin Laden. In 2003 the U.S. attacked Iraq, with British support, and overthrew the government of Saddam Hussein.

The U.S. made its Olympic debut at the inaugural Games in 1896 in Athens. The Summer Games have been held in Los Angeles, Calif. (1932, 1984), St. Louis, Mo. (1904), and Atlanta, Ga. (1996); the Winter Games were held in Lake Placid, N.Y. (1932, 1980), Squaw Valley, Calif. (1960), and Salt Lake City, Utah (2002).

Vatican City

In full State of the Vatican City. Independent papal state, southern Europe, within the commune of Rome, Italy. Area: 109 ac (44 ha). Population (2005 est.): 800. Its medieval and Renaissance walls form its boundaries except on the southeast at St. Peter's Square. Within the walls is the world's smallest independent nation-state, with its own diplomatic missions, newspaper, post office, radio station, banking system, army of 100 Swiss Guards, and publishing house. Extraterritoriality of the state extends to Castel Gandolfo and to several churches and palaces in Rome proper. Its independent sovereignty was recognized in the Lateran Treaty of 1929. The pope has absolute executive, legislative, and judicial powers within the city. He appoints the members of the Vatican's government organs, which are separate from those of the Holy See, the name given to the government of the Roman Catholic Church. The many imposing buildings include St. Peter's Basilica, the Vatican Palace, and the Vatican Museums. Frescoes by Michelangelo in the Sistine Chapel, by Pinturicchio in the Borgia Apartment, and by Raphael in the Stanze (rooms in the papal apartments) are also there. The Vatican Library contains a priceless collection of manuscripts from the pre-Christian and Christian eras. The pope and other representatives of the papal state travel widely to maintain international relations.

weapon of mass destruction (WMD)

Weapon with the capacity to inflict death and destruction indiscriminately and on a massive scale. The term has been in currency since at least 1937, when it was used to describe massed formations of bomber aircraft. Today WMDs are nuclear, biological, or chemical weapons—frequently referred to collectively as NBC weapons. Efforts to control the spread of WMDs are enshrined in international agreements such as the Nuclear Non-Proliferation Treaty of 1968, the Biological Weapons Convention of 1972, and the Chemical Weapons Convention of 1993.

World Heritage site

Any of various areas or objects designated as having "outstanding universal value" under the Convention Concerning the Protection of the World

Cultural and Natural Heritage. This convention, adopted by UNESCO in 1972, provides for international cooperation in preserving and protecting cultural and natural treasures throughout the world. Each site on the list is under strict legal protection by the government of the nation in which it is situated. Among the cultural sites are many of the world's most famous buildings. The ratio of cultural to natural sites on the list is roughly three to one.

World Trade Organization (WTO)

International organization based in Geneva that supervises world trade. It was created in 1995 to replace the General Agreement on Tariffs and Trade (GATT). Like its predecessor, it aims to lower trade barriers and encourage multilateral trade. It monitors members' adherence to GATT agreements and negotiates and implements new agreements. Critics of the WTO, including many opponents of economic globalization, have charged that it undermines national sovereignty by promoting the interests of large multinational corporations and that the trade liberalization it encourages leads to environmental damage and declining living standards for low-skilled workers in developing countries. By the early 21st century, the WTO had more than 145 members.

Trailblazers

C lark was the short one; Lewis was the lanky former private secretary to Thomas Jefferson, who seemed not at all the type to forge the transcontinental American wilderness in the days when the west was anything past the Blue Ridge Mountains of Virginia. Jefferson saw something in Meriwether, though, and groomed him into his explorer alter ego to find out what really was out there and send as much of it back as Monticello could hold (and Jefferson was always expanding it). Lewis did do quite a bit of hunting around Charlottesville, but that's still a long way from Fort Clatsop, the climax of their two-year journey in the cold winter of 1805–06. Jefferson had just bought the land from the French and wanted to see if he'd bought a pig in a poke. The expedition began in St. Louis, about as far west as anybody from Virginia had been, in the spring of 1804. Forty men trained in all of Jefferson's favorite-ologies paddled up the Missouri to North Dakota, where they built a modest little fort and engaged Sacagawea (and her husband, who no one seems to have noticed) to serve as ombudsman to the Shoshone, who had not yet grasped the significance of the crews measuring off the homeland into rectangular plats. In Montana they switched to horseback for the vertical climb up the Continental Divide, then canoed down the Clearwater to the mouth of the Columbia and Fort Clatsop, named after the Indians it helped eradicate; they knew they were in Oregon because it rained all but 12 days that winter. In addition to the cartography and the zoology, Lewis and Clark proved there was, in fact, no Northwest Passage, the hoped-for lazy river to the Pacific, but that Manifest Destiny was alive and well. The grizzly they brought back for his parlor alone made the effort worthwhile for Jefferson. For all their trouble Lewis was made governor of the Louisiana Territory and Clark, Missouri.

Armstrong, Neil (Alden)

Neil Armstrong, 1969

(Born Aug. 5, 1930, Wapakoneta, Ohio, U.S.) U.S. astronaut. He became a pilot at 16, studied aeronautical engineering, and won three Air Medals in the Korean War. In 1955 he became a civilian research pilot for the forerunner of NASA. He joined the space program in 1962 with the second group of astronauts. In 1966, as command pilot of *Gemini 8*, he and David Scott completed the first manual space docking maneuver, with an unmanned Agena rocket. On July 20, 1969, as part of the *Apollo 11* mission, he became the first person to step onto the moon, announcing "That's one small step for [a] man, one giant leap for mankind."

Babbage, Charles

(Born Dec. 26, 1791, London, Eng.—died Oct. 18, 1871) British mathematician and inventor. Educated at Cambridge University, he devoted himself from about 1812 to devising machines capable of calculating mathematical tables. His first small calculator could perform certain computations to eight decimals. In 1823 he obtained government support for the design of a projected machine with a 20-decimal capacity. In the 1830s he developed plans for the so-called Analytical Engine, capable of performing any arithmetical operation on the basis of instructions from punched cards, a memory unit in which to store numbers, sequential control, and most of the other basic elements of the present-day computer. The forerunner of the modern digital computer, the Analytical Engine was never completed. In 1991 British scientists built Difference Engine No. 2 (accurate to 31 digits) to Babbage's specifications. His other contributions included establishing the modern postal system in England, compiling the first reliable actuarial tables, and inventing the locomotive cowcatcher.

Charles Babbage, detail of an oil painting by Samuel Lawrence, 1845; in the National Portrait Gallery, London

Bell, Alexander Graham

Alexander Graham Bell

(Born March 3, 1847, Edinburgh, Scot.—died Aug. 2, 1922, Beinn Bhreagh, Nova Scotia, Can.) Scottish-born U.S. audiologist and inventor. He moved to the U.S. in 1871 to teach the visible-speech system developed by his father, Alexander Melville Bell (1819–1905). He opened his own school in Boston for training teachers of the deaf (1872) and was influential in disseminating these methods. In 1876 he became the first person to transmit intelligible words through electric wire ("Watson, come here, I want you," spoken to his assistant Thomas Watson). He patented the telephone the same year, and in 1877 he cofounded Bell Telephone Co. With the proceeds from France's Volta Prize, he founded Volta Laboratory in Washington, D.C., in 1880. His experiments there led to the invention of the photophone (which transmitted speech by light rays), the audiometer (which measured acuteness of hearing), the Graphophone (an early practical sound recorder), and working wax recording media, both flat and cylindrical, for the Graphophone. He was chiefly responsible for founding the journal *Science*, he founded the American Association to Promote Teaching of Speech to the Deaf (1890), and he continued his significant research on deafness throughout his life.

Braille, Louis

(Born Jan. 4, 1809, Coupvray, near Paris, France—died Jan. 6, 1852, Paris) French educator who developed the Braille system of printing and writing for the blind. Himself blinded at the age of three in an accident, he went to Paris in 1819 to attend the National Institute for Blind Children, and from 1826 he taught there. Braille adapted a method created by Charles Barbier to develop his own simplified system.

Louis Braille, portrait bust by an unknown artist

Carver, George Washington

(Born 1861?, near Diamond Grove, Mo., U.S.—
died Jan. 5, 1943, Tuskegee, Ala.) U.S. agricultural chemist and agronomist. Born a slave,
Carver lived until age 10 or 12 on his former
owner's plantation, then left and worked at a
variety of menial jobs. He did not obtain a
high school education until his late twenties;
he then obtained bachelor's and master's
degrees from Iowa State Agricultural College.
In 1896 he joined Booker T. Washington at the
Tuskegee Institute (now Tuskegee University)
in Alabama, where he became director of agricultural research. He was soon promoting the

George Washington Carver

planting of peanuts and soybeans, legumes
that he knew would help restore the fertility of soil depleted by cotton
cropping. To make them profitable, he worked intensively with the sweet
potato and the peanut (then not even recognized as a crop), ultimately
developing 118 derivative products from sweet potatoes and 300 from
peanuts. His efforts helped liberate the South from its untenable cotton
dependency; by 1940 the peanut was the South's second largest cash crop.
During World War II he devised 500 dyes to replace those no longer available from Europe. Despite international acclaim and extraordinary job
offers, he remained at Tuskegee throughout his life, donating his life's
savings in 1940 to establish the Carver Research Foundation at Tuskegee.

Cruz, Sor Juana Inés de la

(Born Nov. 12, 1651, San Miguel Nepantla, Viceroyalty of New Spain—
died April 17, 1695, Mexico City) Mexican poet, dramatist, scholar, nun,
and an early feminist. Born out of wedlock to a family of modest means,
she was sent to relatives in Mexico City, where her great intelligence
became known to the viceroy. She soon became a nun, remaining clois-
tered for the rest of her life. Sor Juana had one of the largest private
libraries in the New World. Her most important works are the poem
"Primero sueño" (1692; "Sor Juana's Dream"), which recounts the soul's
quest for knowledge, and the "Respuesta" (1691; "The Answer"), her
defense of women's right to knowledge.

Curie, Marie

Orig. Maria Sklodowska (born Nov. 7, 1867, Warsaw, Pol., Russian Empire—died July 4, 1934, near Sallanches, France) Polish-born French physical chemist. She studied at the Sorbonne (from 1891). Seeking the presence of radioactivity—recently discovered by Henri Becquerel in uranium—in other matter, she found it in thorium. In 1895 she married fellow physicist Pierre Curie (1859–1906). Together they discovered the elements polonium (which Marie named after her native Poland) and radium, and they distinguished alpha, beta, and gamma radiation. For their work on radioactivity (a term she coined), the Curies shared the 1903 Nobel Prize for Physics with Becquerel. Marie thus became the first woman to receive a Nobel Prize. After Pierre's death, Marie was appointed to his professorship and became the first woman to teach at the Sorbonne. In 1911 she won a Nobel Prize for Chemistry for discovering polonium and isolating pure radium, becoming the first person to win two Nobel Prizes. She died of leukemia caused by her long exposure to radioactivity. In 1995 she became the first woman whose own achievements earned her the honor of having her ashes enshrined in the Pantheon in Paris.

Marie Curie

Darwin, Charles (Robert)

(Born Feb. 12, 1809, Shrewsbury, Shropshire, Eng.—died April 19, 1882, Downe, Kent) British naturalist. The grandson of Erasmus Darwin and Josiah Wedgwood, he studied medicine at the University of Edinburgh and biology at Cambridge. He was recommended as a naturalist on HMS *Beagle*, which was bound on a long scientific survey expedition to South America and the South Seas (1831–36). His zoological and geological discoveries on the voyage resulted in numerous important publications and formed the basis of his theories of evolution. Seeing competition between individuals of a single species, he recognized that within a local population the individual bird, for example, with the sharper beak might have a better chance to survive and reproduce and that if such traits were passed on to new generations, they would be predominant in future populations. He saw this natural selection as the mechanism by which advantageous variations were passed on to later generations and less advantageous traits gradually disappeared. He worked on his theory for more than 20 years before publishing it in his famous *On the Origin of Species by Means of Natural Selection* (1859). The book was immediately in great demand, and Darwin's intensely controversial theory was accepted quickly in most scientific circles; most opposition came from religious leaders. Though Darwin's ideas were modified by later developments in genetics and molecular biology, his work remains central to modern evolutionary theory. His many other important works included *Variation in Animals and Plants under Domestication* (1868) and *The Descent of Man...* (1871). He was buried in Westminster Abbey.

Ebadi, Shirin

(Born 1947, Hamadan, Iran) Iranian lawyer, writer, and teacher. After earning a law degree from the University of Tehran (1969), Ebadi became one of the first women judges in Iran but was forced to resign after the 1979 revolution and the establishment of an Islamic republic. She then practiced law, taught at the University of Tehran, and became noted for her efforts to promote democracy and human rights, especially those of women and children in Iran. In 2000 she was briefly jailed after distributing evidence that implicated government officials in the murder of university students in 1999. Found guilty of "disturbing public opinion," she was given a prison term, barred from practicing law for five years, and fined, although her sentence was later suspended. In 2003 Ebadi was awarded the Nobel Prize for Peace, becoming the first Muslim woman and the first Iranian to receive the award.

Edison, Thomas Alva

(Born Feb. 11, 1847, Milan, Ohio, U.S.—died Oct. 18, 1931, West Orange, N.J.) U.S. inventor. He had very little formal schooling. He set up a laboratory in his father's basement at age 10; at 12 he was earning money selling newspapers and candy on trains. He worked as a telegrapher (1862–68) before deciding to pursue invention and entrepreneurship. Throughout much of his career, he was strongly motivated by efforts to overcome his handicap of partial deafness. For Western Union he developed a machine capable of sending four telegraph messages down one wire, only to sell the invention to Western Union's rival, Jay Gould, for more than $100,000. He created the world's first industrial-research laboratory, in Menlo Park, N.J. There he invented the carbon-button transmitter (1877), still used in telephone speakers and microphones today; the phonograph (1877); and the incandescent lightbulb (1879). To develop the lightbulb, he was advanced $30,000 by such financiers as J.P. Morgan and the Vanderbilts. In 1882 he supervised the installation of the world's first permanent commercial central power system, in lower Manhattan. After the death of his first wife (1884), he built a new laboratory in West Orange, N.J. Its first major endeavor was the commercialization of the phonograph, which Alexander Graham Bell had improved on since Edison's initial invention. At the new laboratory Edison and his team also developed an early movie camera and an instrument for viewing moving pictures; they also developed the alkaline storage battery. Although his later projects were not as successful as his earlier ones, Edison continued to work even in his 80s. Singly or jointly, he held a world-record 1,093 patents, nearly 400 of them for electric light and power. He always invented for necessity, with the object of devising something new that he could manufacture. More than any other, he laid the basis for the technological revolution of the modern electric world.

Einstein, Albert

(Born March 14, 1879, Ulm, Württemberg, Ger.—died April 18, 1955, Princeton, N.J., U.S.) German-Swiss-U.S. scientist. Born to a Jewish family in Germany, he grew up in Munich, and his family moved to Switzerland in 1894. He became a junior examiner at the Swiss patent office in 1902 and began producing original theoretical work that laid many of the foundations for 20th-century physics. He received his doctorate from the

University of Zürich in 1905, the same year he won international fame with the publication of three articles: one on Brownian motion, which he explained in terms of molecular kinetic energy; one on the photoelectric effect, in which he demonstrated the particle nature of light; and one on his special theory of relativity, which included his formulation of the equivalence of mass and energy ($E = mc^2$). Einstein held several professorships before becoming director of Berlin's Kaiser Wilhelm Institute in 1914. In 1915 he published his general theory of relativity, which was confirmed experimentally during a solar eclipse in 1919 with observations of the deviation of light passing near the Sun. He received a Nobel Prize in 1921 for his work on the photoelectric effect, his work on relativity still being controversial. He made important contributions to quantum field theory, and for decades he sought to discover the mathematical relationship between electromagnetism and gravitation, which he believed would be a first step toward discovering the common laws governing the behavior of everything in the universe, but such a unified field theory eluded him. His theories of relativity and gravitation represented a profound advance over Newtonian physics and revolutionized scientific and philosophical inquiry. He resigned his position at the Prussian Academy when Adolf Hitler came to power and moved to Princeton, N.J., where he joined the Institute for Advanced Study. Though a longtime pacifist, he was instrumental in persuading Pres. Franklin Roosevelt in 1939 to initiate the Manhattan Project for the production of an atomic bomb, a technology his own theories greatly furthered, though he did not work on the project himself. The most eminent scientist in the world in the postwar years, he declined an offer to become the first prime minister of Israel and became a strong advocate for nuclear disarmament.

farnsworth, Philo T(aylor)

(Born Aug. 19, 1906, Beaver, Utah, U.S.—died March 11, 1971, Salt Lake City) U.S. engineer and pioneer inventor in the development of television. In 1927 he successfully transmitted the first image using electronic means. By 1930 he was perfecting an electronic camera tube, the Image Dissector, which he demonstrated to rival inventor Vladimir Zworykin of Radio Corporation of America (RCA). Through the 1930s Farnsworth engaged in lawsuits against RCA, both sides claiming the invention of electronic television. In 1939 RCA agreed to pay him royalties as part of a patent-licensing agreement; that same year RCA introduced the first successful television system. Farnsworth went on to patent many other inventions, but he never achieved financial success or primary credit for inventing television.

Ford, Henry

(Born July 30, 1863, Wayne County, Mich., U.S.—died April 7, 1947, Dearborn) U.S. industrialist and pioneer automobile manufacturer. Ford worked his way up from a machinist's apprentice (at age 15) to the post of chief engineer at the Edison Company in Detroit. He built his first experimental car in 1896. In 1903, with several partners, he formed the Ford Motor Company. In 1908 he designed the Model T; demand became so great that Ford developed new mass-production methods, including the first moving assembly line in 1913. He developed the Model A in 1928 to replace the Model T, and in 1932 he introduced the V-8 engine. He observed an eight-hour workday and paid his workers far above the average, holding that well-paid laborers become the consumers that industrialists require, but he strenuously opposed labor unions. As the first to make car ownership affordable to large numbers of Americans, he exerted a vast and permanent influence on American life.

Franklin, Benjamin

(Born Jan. 17, 1706, Boston, Mass., U.S.—died April 17, 1790, Philadelphia, Pa.) American statesman, scientist, philosopher, and publisher. He was apprenticed at age 12 to his brother, a local printer. He taught himself to write effectively, and in 1723 he moved to Philadelphia, where he founded the *Pennsylvania Gazette* (1730–48) and wrote *Poor Richard's Almanack* (1732–57), whose proverbs and aphorisms emphasized prudence, industry, and honesty. He became prosperous and promoted public services in Philadelphia, including a library, a fire department, a hospital, an insurance company, and an academy that became the University of Pennsylvania. His inventions included the Franklin stove and bifocal spectacles, and his experiments in electricity led to the invention of the lightning rod. He served as a member of the colonial legislature (1736–51). He was a delegate to the Albany Congress (1754). He represented the colony in England in a dispute over land and taxes (1757–62); he returned there in 1764 as agent for several colonies. The issue of taxation gradually caused him to abandon his initial support for a unified colonial government under British rule. Believing that taxation ought to be the prerogative of the representative legislatures, he opposed the Stamp Act and helped secure its repeal. He served as a delegate to the second Continental Congress and as a member of the committee to draft the Declaration of Independence. In 1776 he went to France to seek aid for the American Revolution. Lionized by the French, he negotiated a treaty that provided loans and military support for the U.S. In 1781 he helped negotiate a preliminary peace treaty with Britain. As a member of the 1787 Constitutional Convention, he was instrumental in achieving adoption of the Constitution of the U.S. He is regarded as one of the most extraordinary and brilliant public servants in U.S. history.

Freud, Sigmund

(Born May 6, 1856, Freiberg, Moravia, Austrian Empire—died Sept. 23, 1939, London, Eng.) Austrian neuropsychologist, founder of psychoanalysis, and one of the major intellectual figures of the 20th century. Trained in Vienna as a neurologist, Freud went to Paris in 1885 to study with Jean-Martin Charcot, whose work on hysteria led Freud to conclude that mental disorders might be caused purely by psychological rather than organic factors. Returning to Vienna (1886), Freud collaborated with the physician Josef Breuer (1842–1925) in further studies on hysteria, resulting in the development of some key psychoanalytic concepts and techniques, including free association, the unconscious, resistance (later defense mechanisms), and neurosis. In 1899 he published *The Interpretation of Dreams*, in which he analyzed the complex symbolic processes underlying dream formation: he proposed that dreams are the disguised expression of unconscious wishes. In his controversial *Three Essays on the Theory of Sexuality* (1905), he delineated the complicated stages of psychosexual development (oral, anal, and phallic) and the formation of the Oedipus complex. During World War I, he wrote papers that clarified his understanding of the relations between the unconscious and conscious portions of the mind and the workings of the id, ego, and superego. Freud eventually applied his psychoanalytic insights to such diverse phenomena as jokes and slips of the tongue, ethnographic data, religion and mythology, and modern civilization. Works of note include *Totem and Taboo* (1913), *Beyond the Pleasure Principle* (1920), *The Future of an Illusion* (1927), and *Civilization and Its Discontents* (1930). Freud fled to

Sigmund Freud would engage his famous patient, Anna O., in what she called "chimney sweeping"—what Freud preferred to call "free association." This previously unarticulated material, Freud believed, was a pipeline to the unconscious, normally kept stuffed in the psyche, and the source of neurosis, née hysteria. Blockage of the pipeline (chimney) is "resistance," which must be overcome through the process of analysis to access hidden conflicts, which just so happen to turn out to be mostly sexual in nature—the fantasies, the repressed desires, the things only wealthier Victorians got to act out. Freud started with female neurotics, but he had some trouble extending the franchise of psychoanalysis to males since, one, they didn't like having their chimneys swept, and two, it was hard to find a benchmark for normality in the male. So, of course, he used himself, despite the fact that everything he said, did, or thought was Freudian de facto. After his father (who had never been much of a father figure to him) died, Freud's self-analysis took a hard turn toward dream analysis, "dreamwork" as he called it, with the libido being the leading character in a drama of lust, denied gratification, and imaginary wish fulfillment similar to what Ibsen was producing for the stage.—M.F.

England when the Nazis annexed Austria in 1938; he died shortly thereafter. Despite the relentless and often compelling challenges mounted against virtually all of his ideas, both in his lifetime and after, Freud has remained one of the most influential figures in contemporary thought.

Gagarin, Yury (Alekseyevich)

(Born March 9, 1934, near Gzhatsk, Russian S.F.S.R.—died March 27, 1968, near Moscow) Soviet cosmonaut. Son of a carpenter on a collective farm, he graduated from the Soviet air force's cadet school in 1957. In April 1961, aboard *Vostok 1*, he became the first human to travel into space. The spacecraft orbited Earth once in 1 hour 29 minutes. Gagarin's flight brought him worldwide fame, and he was much honored in the Soviet Union. He never went into space again, but he trained other cosmonauts. He was killed at age 34 when his jet crashed during a training flight.

Gandhi, Mohandas Karamchand

Known as Mahatma Gandhi (born Oct. 2, 1869, Porbandar, India—died Jan. 30, 1948, Delhi) Preeminent leader of Indian nationalism and prophet of nonviolence in the 20th century. Gandhi grew up in a home steeped in religion, and he took for granted religious tolerance and the doctrine of ahimsa (noninjury to all living beings). He studied law in England but seemed too diffident to become a successful lawyer. He took a job with an Indian firm in South Africa. There he became an effective advocate for Indian rights. In 1906 he first put into action satyagraha, his technique of nonviolent resistance. His success in South Africa gave him an international reputation, and in 1915 he returned to India and within a few years became the leader of a nationwide struggle for Indian home rule. By 1920 Gandhi commanded influence hitherto unattained by any political leader in India. He refashioned the Indian National Congress into an effective political instrument of Indian nationalism and undertook major campaigns of nonviolent resistance in 1920–22, 1930–34 (including his momentous march to the sea to collect salt to protest a government monopoly), and 1940–42. In the 1930s he also campaigned to end discrimination against India's untouchable class—whom he renamed Harijans (literally "children of God")—and concentrated on educating rural India and promoting cottage industry. India achieved dominion status in 1947, but the partition of the subcontinent into India and Pakistan was a great disappointment to Gandhi, who had long worked for Hindu-Muslim unity. In September 1947 he ended rioting in Calcutta (Kolkata) by fasting. Known as the Mahatma ("Great-Souled"), Gandhi had won the affection and loyalty of millions. In January 1948 he was shot and killed by a young Hindu fanatic.

Goddard, Robert Hutchings

(Born Oct. 5, 1882, Worcester, Mass., U.S.—died Aug. 10, 1945, Baltimore, Md.) U.S. inventor, regarded as the father of modern rocketry. He received his doctorate (1911) from Clark University in Worcester, where he taught for much of his career. In laboratory work there, he proved that thrust and consequent propulsion can take place in a vacuum and was the first to develop a rocket engine using liquid propellants (static tested in 1925). In 1926 Goddard successfully launched the world's first liquid-fueled rocket (gasoline and liquid oxygen) from a farm in Massachusetts. In 1935, having relocated his testing site to New Mexico, he was the first to send a liquid-fueled rocket faster than the speed of sound. He patented the first practical automatic steering apparatus for rockets, developed staged rockets designed to gain great altitudes, and developed the first rocket-fuel pumps, self-cooling rocket engines, and other components of a propulsion system designed for space exploration. Much of his work anticipated that of Wernher von Braun in Germany but was ignored by the U.S. government until after his death at the end of World War II.

Goodall, Jane

(Born April 3, 1934, London, Eng.) British ethologist. Soon after finishing high school, she fulfilled her childhood ambition of traveling to Africa, where she assisted Louis Leakey, who suggested she study chimpanzees. She received a Ph.D. from Cambridge University for her work and remained at the research center she founded in Gombe, Tanz., until 1975. In 1977 she cofounded the Jane Goodall Institute for Wildlife Research, Education, and Conservation in the U.S. Her observations established, among other things, that chimpanzees are omnivorous rather than vegetarian, can make and use tools, and have complex and highly developed social behaviors. Noteworthy among her writings are *In the Shadow of Man* (1971) and *The Chimpanzees of Gombe* (1986). She was made a Dame of the British Empire in 2003.

Hillary, Sir Edmund (Percival)

(Born July 20, 1919, Auckland, N.Z.) New Zealand mountain climber and explorer. Hillary was a professional beekeeper but enjoyed climbing in the New Zealand Alps. In 1951 he joined a New Zealand party to the central Himalayas and then went on to help in a reconnaissance of the southern flank of Everest. In 1953, as a member of the British Everest expedition, he and Tenzing Norgay reached the summit of Mt. Everest on May 29, becoming the first known climbers to do so. The achievement brought Hillary worldwide fame, and he was knighted that same year. In

Sir Edmund Hillary, 1956

1958 he participated in the first crossing of Antarctica by vehicle. From the 1960s he has helped build schools and hospitals for the Sherpa people.

Juárez, Benito (Pablo)

(Born March 21, 1806, San Pablo Guelatao, Oaxaca, Mex.—died July 18, 1872, Mexico City) National hero and president (1861–72) of Mexico. A Zapotec Indian, Juárez initially studied for the priesthood but later took a law degree and became a legislator, a judge, and a cabinet minister. He led La Reforma, a liberal political and social revolution in Mexico, and, when liberal forces gained control of the national government in 1855, he was able to implement his ideas. In 1857 he was elected head of the Supreme Court, which, under a new constitution, placed him

Benito Juárez

first in the order of presidential succession. In 1858 a coup by conservative forces sent Mexico's president into exile, but Juárez succeeded him and headed a liberal government that opposed the regime installed by the conservatives. After three years of civil war, the liberals prevailed. Juárez was elected president in 1861 and twice reelected. Early in his first term, the French under Napoleon III invaded and occupied Mexico, putting Maximilian of Austria in power in 1864. When Napoleon later withdrew his troops, Juárez defeated Maximilian's armies and had him executed in 1867. Juárez's final years were marred by a loss of popular support and by personal tragedy. He died in office.

King, Martin Luther, Jr.

Martin Luther King Jr.

(Born Jan. 15, 1929, Atlanta, Ga., U.S.—died April 4, 1968, Memphis, Tenn.) U.S. civil-rights leader. The son and grandson of Baptist preachers, King became an adherent of nonviolence while in college. Ordained a Baptist minister himself in 1954, he became pastor of a church in Montgomery, Ala.; the following year he received a doctorate from Boston University. He was selected to head the Montgomery Improvement Association, whose boycott efforts eventually ended the city's policies of racial segregation on public transportation. In 1957 he formed the Southern Christian Leadership Conference and began lecturing nationwide, urging active nonviolence to achieve civil rights for African Americans. In 1960 he returned to Atlanta to become copastor, with his father, of Ebenezer Baptist Church. He was arrested and jailed for protesting segregation at a lunch counter; the case drew national attention, and presidential candidate John F. Kennedy interceded to obtain his release. In 1963 King helped organize the March on Washington, an assembly of more than 200,000 protestors at which he made his famous "I have a dream" speech. The march influenced the passage of the Civil Rights Act of 1964, and King was awarded the 1964 Nobel Prize for Peace. In 1965 he was criticized from within the civil-rights movement for yielding to state troopers at a march in Selma, Ala., and for failing in the effort to change Chicago's housing segregation policies. Thereafter he broadened his advocacy, addressing the plight of the poor of all races and opposing the Vietnam War. In 1968 he went to Memphis, Tenn., to support a strike by sanitation workers; there on April 4, he was assassinated by James Earl Ray. A U.S. national holiday is celebrated in King's honor on the third Monday in January.

Lewis and Clark Expedition

(1804–06) First overland expedition to the U.S. Pacific coast and back, led by Meriwether Lewis and William Clark. Initiated by Pres. Thomas Jefferson, the expedition set out to find an overland route to the Pacific, documenting its exploration through the new Louisiana Purchase. About 40 men, skilled in various trades, left St. Louis in 1804. They traveled up the Missouri River into present-day North Dakota, where they built Fort Mandan (later Bismarck) and wintered among the Mandan Sioux. They left the next spring, hiring Toussaint Charbonneau and his Indian wife, Sacagawea, who served as guide and interpreter. They traveled through Montana and by horse over the Continental Divide to the headwaters of the Clearwater River. They built canoes to carry them to the Snake River and then to the mouth of the Columbia River, where they built Fort Clatsop (later Astoria, Ore.) and spent the winter. On the journey back the group divided, then reunited to canoe down the Missouri to St. Louis, arriving to great acclaim in September 1806. All but one member of the expedition survived. The journals kept by Lewis and others documented Indian tribes, wildlife, and geography and did much to dispel the myth of an easy water route to the Pacific.

Louis, Joe

In full Joseph Louis Barrow (born May 13, 1914, Lafayette, Ala., U.S.—died April 12, 1981, Las Vegas, Nev.) U.S. boxer. Louis was born into a sharecropper's family and only began boxing after the family moved to Detroit. He won the U.S. Amateur Athletic Union title in 1934 and turned professional that year. During his career he defeated six previous or subsequent heavyweight champions: Primo Carnera, Max Baer, Jack Sharkey, James J. Braddock, Max Schmeling, and Jersey Joe Walcott. Nicknamed "the Brown Bomber," Louis gained the world heavyweight championship by defeating Braddock in 1937 and held the title until 1949. Two of Louis's most famous bouts, those with the German boxer Max Schmeling, were invested with nationalist and racial implications, as Schmeling was seen, unfairly, as the embodiment of Aryanism and the Nazi party. Louis lost to Schmeling in 1936 but defeated him in one round in 1938, causing much jubilation among Americans, and especially African Americans. He successfully defended his title 25 times (21 by knockout) before retiring in 1949. His service in the U.S. Army during World War II no doubt prevented him from defending his title many more times. He made unsuccessful comeback attempts against Ezzard Charles in 1950 and Rocky Marciano in 1951. Louis and Schmeling later became friends, the latter serving as a pallbearer at Louis's funeral.

Maathai, Wangari

(Born April 1, 1940, Nyeri, Kenya) Kenyan politician and environmental activist. Maathai was educated in the U.S. and later earned a Ph.D. (1971) at the University of Nairobi, where she then taught veterinary anatomy. In 1977, as a way of conserving land and empowering women, she founded the Green Belt Movement, which recruited women to plant trees in deforested areas; by the early 21st century, it was responsible for the planting of some 30 million trees. Over time the organization also came to include programs in civic and environmental education, advocacy, and job training. Maathai, an outspoken critic of government corruption and supporter of debt cancellation for poor African countries, was elected to Kenya's National Assembly in 2002 and later served as assistant minister of environment, natural resources, and wildlife (2003–05). In 2004 she received the Nobel Prize for Peace, becoming the first black African woman to win a Nobel Prize.

Macfadden, Bernarr

Orig. Bernard Adolphus McFadden (born Aug. 16, 1868, near Mill Spring, Mo., U.S.—died Oct. 12, 1955, Jersey City, N.J.) U.S. publisher and champion of physical health. A sickly orphan by age 11, he began in his teens to increase his strength as an act of defiance. In 1899 he began publishing *Physical Culture* magazine, and in later decades he built up a publishing empire, bringing out the first confession magazine, *True Story* (1919), followed by *True Romances* (1923), *True Detective Mystery Magazine* (1924), and other periodicals. Macfadden also toured widely to promote his message of vigorous physical exercise and to preach about the dangers of alcohol, drugs, gluttony, corsets, prudishness, tea, coffee, and white bread. Shocking to Victorian sentiments were his advocacy of a diet consisting of carrots, beans, nuts, and raw eggs and his encouragement of sleeping on the floor, nudity, and "physical love." To promote such "love," he encouraged openness about sexual matters and invented a device to enlarge men's penises. To exemplify fitness, he walked five miles daily to his office in Manhattan in bare feet while carrying a 40-pound bag of sand. He also staged the first physique (bodybuilding) contest in America (1903) and fostered the rise of fitness icon Charles Atlas. Macfadden's bids for the presidency, U.S. Senate, and governorship of Florida all failed. Physically fit into old age, he parachuted into Paris on his 84th birthday.

Mandela, Nelson

(Born July 18, 1918, Umtata, Cape of Good Hope, S.Af.) South African black nationalist leader and statesman. The son of a Xhosa chief, Mandela studied law at the University of Witwatersrand and in 1944 joined the African National Congress (ANC). After the Sharpeville massacre (1960), he abandoned his nonviolent stance and helped found the "Spear of the Nation," the ANC's military wing. Arrested in 1962, he was sentenced to life imprisonment. He retained wide support among South Africa's black population and became an international cause célèbre.

Nelson Mandela, 1990

Released by Pres. F.W. de Klerk in 1990, he replaced Oliver Tambo as president of the ANC in 1991. In 1993 Mandela and de Klerk were awarded the Nobel Peace Prize for their efforts to end apartheid and bring about the transition to nonracial democracy. In 1994 he was elected president in the country's first universal suffrage elections; by the time he stepped down in 1999, Mandela was the most universally respected figure of postcolonial Africa.

Marconi, Guglielmo

Guglielmo Marconi, c. 1908

(Born April 25, 1874, Bologna, Italy—died July 20, 1937, Rome) Italian physicist and inventor. He began experimenting with radio waves in 1894. In 1896 he went to England, where he developed a successful system of radio telegraphy. His work on the development of short-wave wireless communication constitutes the basis of nearly all modern radio broadcasting. His improved aerials greatly extended the range of radio signaling. In 1899 he established communication across the English Channel. In 1900 he established the American Marconi Co. In 1901 he sent signals across the Atlantic for the first time. He acquired numerous patents, though probably his most famous one, No. 7777, for an apparatus that enabled several stations to operate on different wavelengths without interference, was later overturned. Marconi shared the 1909 Nobel Prize for Physics with K. Ferdinand Braun (1850–1918). He was made a marquis and was nominated to the Italian Senate (1929), and he was elected president of the Royal Italian Academy (1930).

Mendel, Gregor (Johann)

(Born July 22, 1822, Heinzendorf, Austria—died Jan. 6, 1884, Brünn, Austria-Hungary) Austrian botanist and plant experimenter. He became an Augustinian monk in 1843 and later studied at the University of Vienna. In 1856, working in his monastery's garden, he began the experiments that led to his formulation of the basic principle of heredity. He crossed varieties of the garden pea that had maintained constant differences in such single alternative traits as tallness and dwarfishness, flower color, and pod form. He theorized that the occurrence of the visible alternative traits of the plants, in the constant varieties and in their descendants, was due to the occurrence of paired elementary units of heredity, now known as genes. What was new in Mendel's interpretation of his data was his recognition that genes obey simple statistical laws. His system proved to be of general application and is one of the basic principles of biology. He achieved fame only after his death, through the work of Carl Erich Correns, Erich Tschermak von Seysenegg, and Hugo de Vries, who independently obtained similar results and found that both the experimental data and the general theory had been published 34 years previously.

Newton, Sir Isaac

(Born Jan. 4, 1643, Woolsthorpe, Lincolnshire, Eng.—died March 31, 1727, London) English physicist and mathematician. The son of a yeoman, he was raised by his grandmother. He was educated at Cambridge University (1661–65), where he discovered the work of René Descartes. His experiments passing sunlight through a prism led to the discovery of the heterogeneous, corpuscular nature of white light and laid the foundation of physical optics. He built the first reflecting telescope in 1668 and became a professor of mathematics at Cambridge in 1669. He worked out the fundamentals of calculus, though this work went unpublished for more than 30 years. His most famous publication, *Principia Mathematica* (1687), grew out of correspondence with Edmond Halley. Describing his works on the laws of motion, orbital dynamics, tidal theory, and the theory of universal gravitation, it is regarded as the seminal work of modern science. He was elected president of the Royal Society of London in 1703 and became the first scientist ever to be knighted in 1705. During his career he engaged in heated arguments with several of his colleagues, including Robert Hooke (over authorship of the inverse square relation of gravitation) and G.W. Leibniz (over the authorship of calculus). The battle with Leibniz dominated the last 25 years of his life; it is now well established that Newton developed calculus first, but that Leibniz was the first to publish on the subject. Newton is regarded as one of the greatest scientists of all time.

Nightingale, Florence

(Born May 12, 1820, Florence, Italy—died Aug. 13, 1910, London, Eng.) Italian-born British nurse, founder of trained nursing as a profession. As a volunteer nurse, she was put in charge of nursing the military in Turkey during the Crimean War. Her first concern was sanitation: patients' quarters were infested with rats and fleas, and the water allowance was one pint per head per day for all purposes. She used her own finances to purchase supplies. She also spent many hours in the wards; her night rounds giving personal care to the wounded established her image as the "Lady with the Lamp." Her efforts to improve soldiers' welfare led to the Army Medical School and a Sanitary Department in India. She started the first scientifically based nursing school, was instrumental in setting up training for midwives and nurses in workhouse infirmaries, and helped reform workhouses. She was the first woman awarded the Order of Merit (1907).

Nobel, Alfred (Bernhard)

(Born Oct. 21, 1833, Stockholm, Swed.—died Dec. 10, 1896, San Remo, Italy) Swedish chemist, engineer, and industrialist. His attempts to find a safe way to handle nitroglycerin resulted in the invention of dynamite and the blasting cap. He built a network of factories to manufacture dynamite and corporations to produce and market his explosives. He went on to develop more powerful explosives and to construct and perfect detonators for explosives that did not explode on simple firing (e.g., when lit with a match). Nobel registered more than 350 patents, many unrelated to explosives (e.g., artificial silk and leather). A complex personality, both dynamic and reclusive, he was a pacifist but was labeled the "merchant of death" for inventing explosives used in war. Perhaps to counter this label, he left most of his immense fortune, from worldwide explosives and oil interests, to establish the Nobel Prizes, which would become the most highly regarded of all international awards.

Parks, Rosa

Orig. Rosa Louise McCauley (born Feb. 4, 1913, Tuskegee, Ala., U.S.—died Oct. 24, 2005, Detroit, Mich.) U.S. civil rights activist. She worked as a seamstress in Montgomery, Ala., where she joined the NAACP in 1943. In 1955 she was arrested after refusing to give her seat on a public bus to a white man. The resultant boycott of the city's bus system, organized by Martin Luther King, Jr., and others, brought the civil rights movement to new prominence. In 1957 Parks moved to Detroit, where she was a staff assistant (1965–88) to U.S. Rep. John Conyers. She was awarded the Congressional Gold Medal in 1999.

Robinson, Jackie

In full Jack Roosevelt Robinson (born Jan. 31, 1919, Cairo, Ga., U.S.—died Oct. 24, 1972, Stamford, Conn.) U.S. baseball player, the first black player in the major leagues. Robinson became an outstanding performer in several sports at Pasadena Junior College and UCLA before leaving college to help his mother care for the family. He served as a second lieutenant in the U.S. Army in World War II. He played baseball with the Kansas City Monarchs of the Negro Leagues before being signed by Branch Rickey to a Brooklyn Dodgers farm team (1945–46). On being advanced to the majors in 1947, he endured

Jackie Robinson, 1946

with notable dignity the early opposition to his presence, opposition quickly silenced by Robinson's immediate success as he led the league in stolen bases and was chosen Rookie of the Year. In 1949 he won the batting championship with a .342 average and was voted the league's most valuable player. He retired from the Dodgers team in 1956 with a career batting average of .311. In his later years he strongly supported the cause of civil rights for African Americans.

Ruth, Babe

Orig. George Herman Ruth (born Feb. 6, 1895, Baltimore, Md., U.S.—died Aug. 16, 1948, New York, N.Y.) U.S. baseball player, one of the greatest hitters and most popular figures in the sport's history. Ruth was not an orphan (as popularly believed), but he did grow up poor in a rough

Babe Ruth

neighborhood, living in rooms above his father's saloon and attending a school for orphans and incorrigibles; he had several run-ins with the law. But he excelled at baseball, which offered him a chance to escape poverty and obscurity. He began his career in 1914 as a member of Baltimore's minor league team and joined the Boston Red Sox later that season. He started as a pitcher, compiling an outstanding record (94 wins, 46 losses), but switched to the outfield because of his powerful hitting. Sold to the New York Yankees in 1920, he remained with the team until 1934; he played his last year with the Boston Braves (1935). He coached the Brooklyn Dodgers in 1938, but his reputation for irresponsibility prevented his obtaining a permanent coaching or manager's job. His prodigious slugging earned him the nickname "Sultan of Swat." In 1927 he set the most famous of all baseball records when he hit 60 home runs in a single season, a mark that stood until 1961, when broken by Roger Maris. Ruth hit at least 50 home runs in four separate seasons and at least 40 in each of 11 seasons. His career slugging percentage (.690) remains an all-time record; he ranks second in career home runs (714, behind Hank Aaron), second in runs batted in (2,213, again behind Aaron), third in runs (2,174, behind Rickey Henderson and Ty Cobb and tied with Aaron), and third in extra-base hits (1,356, behind Aaron and Stan Musial). His legendary feats helped to revitalize a sport tainted by scandal in the early 20th century, and he remains a towering figure in American cultural history.

Tesla, Nikola

(Born July 9/10, 1856, Smiljan, Lika, Austria-Hungary—died Jan. 7, 1943, New York, N.Y., U.S.) Serbian U.S. inventor and researcher. He studied in Austria and Bohemia and worked in Paris before coming to the U.S. in 1884. He worked for Thomas Alva Edison and George Westinghouse but preferred independent research. His inventions made possible the production and distribution of alternating-current electric power. He invented an induction coil that is still widely used in radio technology,

Nikola Tesla

the Tesla coil (*c.* 1890); his system was used by Westinghouse to light the 1893 World's Columbian Exposition. Tesla established an electric power station at Niagara Falls in 1893. His research also included work on a carbon button lamp and on the power of electrical resonance. He discovered terrestrial stationary waves (1899–1900), proving that the Earth is a conductor. Due to lack of funds, many of his ideas remained only in his notebooks, which are still examined by engineers for inventive clues.

Thorpe, Jim

In full James Francis Thorpe (born May 28, 1888, near Prague, Indian Territory—died March 28, 1953, Lomita, Calif., U.S.) U.S. athlete. Of predominantly American Indian (Sauk and Fox) descent, he trained as a football halfback under Pop Warner while attending the Indian Industrial School in Carlisle, Pa. (1908–12), where he also excelled at baseball, basketball, boxing, lacrosse, swimming, and hockey. In 1912 he won the Olympic decathlon and pentathlon by wide margins, but he was deprived of his medals in 1913 after it was discovered he had played semiprofessional baseball. He later played professional baseball and football, and in 1920–21 he served as the first president of what would become the National Football League. His Olympic medals were restored posthumously in 1983. Thorpe is generally regarded as the greatest American athlete of the 20th century.

Jim Thorpe demonstrating the drop kick

Nikola Tesla arrived in New York with four cents in his pocket, which, even in 1884, was just shy of a nickel. He also had a notebook with some poems and mathematical calculations for a flying machine. Almost immediately he alienated Thomas Edison (Tesla was AC and Edison DC), who would become his Moriarity over the years in numerous patent disputes, and was befriended by George Westinghouse who bought the rights to Tesla's alternating-current systems—motors, dynamos, and transformers—and the rest is life as we know it today. A showman as well as a scientist, spiritualist, and inventor, Tesla liked to hold a light bulb in his hand and let the power run through his body to light it, something the direct-current people could only try once. He lit the 1893 World's Columbian Exposition, harnessed Niagara Falls, piloted his tele-automatic boat by remote control in Madison Square Garden, invented the Tesla coil crucial to radio and television and omnipresent in electronic devices, and discovered terrestrial stationary waves that allowed him to light 200 light bulbs in Colorado Springs from 25 miles away and create his own lightning for dramatic effect. With financing from J.P. Morgan, Tesla attempted to broadcast worldwide communications and power from a huge tower on Long Island, a project abandoned in the financial panic of 1904.—M.F.

Wright, Wilbur; and Wright, Orville

(Born April 16, 1867, near Millville, Ind., U.S.—died May 30, 1912, Dayton, Ohio) (born Aug. 19, 1871, Dayton, Ohio, U.S.—died Jan. 30, 1948) U.S. inventors who achieved the first powered, sustained, and controlled airplane flight. The brothers first worked in printing-machinery design and later in bicycle manufacturing, which financed their early experiments in airplane design. To test flight control, essential to successful powered flight, they built and flew three biplane gliders (1900–02). Propeller and engine innovations led to their first powered airplane, which Orville flew successfully for 12 seconds and Wilbur later flew for 59 seconds at Kill Devil Hills, N.C. (near the village of Kitty Hawk), on Dec. 17, 1903. Their flyer of 1905 could turn, bank, circle, and remain airborne for more than 35 minutes. They demonstrated their planes in Europe and the U.S.; in 1908 Wilbur gave more than 100 exhibition flights in France, setting a duration record of 2 hours and 20 minutes. They established an aircraft company and produced planes for the U.S. Army. After Wilbur's death from typhoid, Orville sold his interest in the company, which later merged with the company of Glenn H. Curtiss.

Zaharias, Babe Didrikson

Or Babe Didrikson. Orig. Mildred Ella Didrikson (born June 26, 1911, Port Arthur, Texas, U.S.—died Sept. 27, 1956, Galveston) U.S. athlete who excelled in several sports. She became a remarkable performer in basketball and track and field and later a leading golfer. In 1930–32 she was a member of the women's All-America basketball team. During the same period she also won eight events and tied in a ninth in national championship competitions in track and field. In the 1932 Olympics she won gold medals in the 80-m hurdles and javelin throw; she was deprived of the high-jump gold medal for using a then-unorthodox method. As a golfer from 1946, she won numerous championships, including the U.S. and British women's amateur tournaments (1946, 1947) and the U.S. Women's Open (1948, 1950, 1954).

Feldman-ISM

Babe Didrikson was born in Port Arthur and died in Galveston, Texas, but in her 45 brief years she covered a vast territory as yet uncharted by American women athletes. In 1932 alone (at age 21) she played on the Women's All-America basketball team; won eight events and tied one in national track-and-field competitions; competed as a team of one in the Women's AAU, winning six individual events and the team title; and took gold in the 80-m hurdles and javelin at the Olympics in Los Angeles and should have in the high jump. Her spare time was devoted to baseball, softball, football, figure skating, swimming, diving, billiards, handball, and bowling. Famously asked if there was anything that she didn't play, she replied, "Yes—dolls." In 1934 Babe switched exclusively to golf and in one year alone won 17 consecutive women's amateur championships. She turned pro in 1948 just in time to win the U.S. Women's Open, and she repeated in 1950. After cancer surgery for the disease that would claim her life in 1956, she won the Open one last time in 1954. Sportswriter Grantland Rice wrote of Babe Didrikson, "She is beyond all belief until you see her perform. Then you finally understand you are looking at the most flawless section of muscle harmony, of complete mental and physical coordination, the world of sport has ever seen."—M.F.